D0099287

The Fall of First Executive

THE FALL
OF FIRST
EXECUTIVE

The House That Fred Carr Built

Gary Schulte

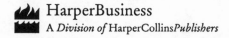

HarperBusiness
A *Division of* HarperCollins*Publishers*

Library of Congress Cataloging-in-publication data

Schulte, Gary, 1946–
    The fall of First Executive / Gary Schulte.
        p.   cm.
    ISBN 0-88730-549-0
    1. First Executive Corporation.   2. Insurance holding companies—United
States. 3. Insurance, Life—United States. 4. Carr, Fred, 1931– . I. Title.
HG8963.F583S38   1991   91-29456
368.3'2'006573—dc20   CIP

International Standard Book Number: 0-88730-549-0

Printed in the United States of America

91 92 93 94 SWD/HC 9 8 7 6 5 4 3 2

To the sales force and employees of
First Executive Corporation. We bought a ticket on the
Fred Carr Express—it was one hell of a ride!

Contents

Foreword

The decade of the 1980s saw a long-overdue transformation of a major American industry, the life insurance industry, from sleeping giant to a key player in the financial services revolution. Although Fred Carr and his First Executive Corporation, which was the holding company for Executive Life, shaped much of the industry's landscape during this period, most of the changes were inevitable. The life insurance industry had existed in virtual isolation for decades. The changes in the financial services industry were coming into focus within the life insurance industry even before Fred Carr appeared on the scene. However, like many of the vanguards of change, he would be credited with much of the good and much of the bad that occurred during this period. It is unfortunate that it will be the bad for which he is chiefly remembered.

The business press tends to look at our leaders in a black or white context. This good/bad mentality of those who chronicle the successes and failures of American business, frequently shaping public opinion, is a simplistic approach in trying to understand who the Fred Carrs of the world really are. Perhaps it is because so many business journalists are products of an educational system that seems to judge business by its worst moments.

Business leaders, like successful athletes or warriors, are bound to turn in some less than great performances from time to time. And yes, as in the case of Fred Carr, they sometimes ultimately fail disastrously in quest of their dreams, yet may still make important contributions along the way. When Lee Iacocca was fired by Henry Ford II, the public attitude at the time was that he probably deserved it. Then, when Iacocca turned around a bankrupt Top 10 corporation and returned it to substantial profitability, he became a hero. In an attempt to preserve his moment of glory, Iacocca wrote an otherwise outstanding autobiography in which he portrayed Henry Ford II in a very unfavorable light. Now that same corporation is again struggling, and people are beginning to look for the chinks in Mr. Iacocca's armor.

Throughout history, famous generals such as Hannibal, Napoleon, and Rommel ultimately met with total defeat. Yet they are remembered as the best of the breed. In the world of sports, Tom Landry, of the Dallas Cowboys, started out a monumental loser and finished the same way. Between his two record-losing seasons, he won two Super Bowls in five appearances and went to the playoffs countless times. Today, he's an American hero. When Whitey Herzog resigned as manager of the St. Louis Cardinals in 1990, he said: ``They were in last place when I got here and in last place when I left, but in between we won a couple of pennants and a World Series.'' In St. Louis, Whitey is held in high esteem. But, for business executives who experience the inevitable ups and downs that accompany long tenures, there is little forgiveness when they leave at the bottom.

First Executive was bankrupt when Fred Carr took it over in 1974, and it was bankrupt when he left seventeen years later. During his stewardship, this fledgling company vaulted from obscurity to become one of the largest financial institutions in America. This was a stunning accomplishment in an industry where companies in their second century of existence rarely nudged past one another among the Top 25. If indeed, instead of a Tom Landry or a Whitey Herzog, Fred Carr is a Pete Rose, or instead of a Ford or an Iacocca, he is a John DeLorean, the current attitudes toward him and his legacy are justified. These are issues that will probably not be resolved in the near future. What has been resolved is that the era he ushered in led to changes in the life insurance industry that were dramatic, sweeping, and in many ways in the best interests of consumers. This era, which we will call the interest-sensitive product revolution, forced companies to compete more openly and to deliver better value to their policyholders. Fred Carr helped consumers to understand life insurance and how it works, as well as whether or not they were being treated fairly by their life insurance company. He also revolutionized distribution through agent owned reinsurance companies, and a host of other innovations that changed the traditionally adversarial agent-company relationship. He built a huge following among the greatest producers in the life insurance industry, and to this day has a level of loyalty enjoyed by few life insurance CEOs in modern times.

Along the way toward reshaping the industry, both First Executive Corporation and the industry itself made a number of big mistakes, notably in reaching too far and promising more than they could deliver to a customer. In an industry not known for producing high-profile executives, Fred Carr is arguably its best-known CEO. As the single biggest purchaser of junk bonds from Drexel Burnham Lambert during the early 1980s, he built what was to become the world's largest junk bond portfolio, which backed the competitive, innovative policies his company sold. Although this is why he became famous in the business world, in the insurance industry his followers' fascination arose from other sources.

Some of the things that occurred while the company was going through its meteoric growth in the early 1980s were clear violations of responsible business judgment. Indeed, the mistakes with regard to his investment strategies will be felt for years and studied by business historians for decades to come. Much can be learned from the explosive growth and collapse of First Executive Corporation, and of the other large segments of the financial services industry that this story touches on in the twelve years between 1979 and 1991.

In this book, we will be reading Fred Carr's story, but in the process we will see how the life insurance industry dealt with changes brought on by the financial services revolution. Many believe that the best perspective from which to view these changes was the Los Angeles headquarters of First Executive Corporation.

I
UP FOR GRABS

1

The Perfect Business

"I ain't nearly so interested in the return on the money as I am in the return of the money."
—Will Rogers

The Executive Life story is the most colorful and far-reaching of the disastrous daisy chain of dramas in the junk bond era. How it occurred during the "go-go 1980s" period of the otherwise staid life insurance industry is a tale in itself. With fully staffed state insurance departments in all fifty states—including New York, where its subsidiary Executive Life of New York operated—Fred Carr's Executive Life companies accomplished the impossible. In one of the most intensely regulated environments in American business, they rose from obscurity in 1978 to a financial service powerhouse which, less than a decade later, was larger than many insurance household names. In the process, Fred Carr incurred the wrath of the life insurance industry for his unconventional practices while building up a growing army of followers among the business's best salespeople and Wall Street's most savvy investors.

Then, in one disastrous year—between the spring of 1990 and

the spring of 1991—he saw his financial monolith evaporate before the bewildered eyes of the legions of agents, investors, and policyholders whose money and careers had been entrusted to him. In all, over half a million policyholders, annuitants, investors, employees, and agents were affected by the collapse of Executive Life and its affiliates.

As we recount the events, which blended together to make the potent brew with which Fred Carr intoxicated some of the business world's most scrupulous people, we will see that this is a story that needs to be told, not just for its topical interest, but for its many lessons. The reason I am the person telling it is because I was one of those closest to it, and one of those to whom the lessons came the hardest. The insurance industry knew me as a spokesman for the Executive Life story, not the one you're about to read, which had a cataclysmic conclusion, but rather the story I and thousands of others believed with all our hearts during the 1980s, the story of a life insurance executive who, through his vision and superior understanding, would rouse the industry from its atrophied state and usher in a new epoch, for which Executive Life would be the archetype and he the patriarch. In fact, Fred Carr came closer to his goal than many people realize. We shall also see that one reason he came so close was because he came to believe in the perception he created of himself just as fervently as his followers did. As a result, he disregarded much of the caution that less enlightened money managers of the era had relied upon. This realization made it all the more difficult for his disenchanted followers when the collapse finally occurred.

Yet it took a great deal more than belief in Fred Carr's vision to turn around Executive Life from the most spectacular rise to the biggest fall in the history of the life insurance business. It took a lot of the timing, luck, and coincidence that usually accompany important events. Things like the birth of the junk bond era, the hot new money period of the early 1980s—and a host of extraordinary personalities who connected with Fred Carr during the incipient days of his seventeen-year tenure as CEO of Executive Life.

The financial deterioration and bankruptcy of First Executive Corporation, which was the holding company for Executive Life and its affiliates, is of interest initially because of its sheer, unprecedented magnitude. In fact, it was bigger than all of the other insurance-related failures in recent history combined. Baldwin United, with assets of $3.9 billion, Integrated Resources, with assets of $6 billion, and First Capital Holding, with assets of $8.6 billion, were the largest insurance-related failures in the 1980s. Together, they still fell slightly short of the $19 billion in assets held by First Executive Corporation in December 1989. This failure was also important because the products of other companies that failed earlier in the decade were sold largely by non-life insurance people. Stockbrokers, mutual fund salesmen, and part-timers were commonly the salespeople involved in noteworthy bankruptcies prior to Executive Life. Executive Life attracted leading stockbrokerage firms like Dean Whitter, Pru-Bache, and E. F. Hutton; it also attracted a core segment of the industry establishment—the upper echelon by any measure. No other big company failure had reached into this generally conservative group of blue-chip salespeople and their sophisticated clientele. Fortunately, the hundreds of thousands of policies these agents brought to the company are in the process of being conserved by the authorities. That is not to say the funds were not in peril at one point, and that many people will not suffer some losses; but they are now in the hands of the insurance regulators, and the rest of the insurance industry is offering support, so that at least most funds have been protected. This, of course, is entirely to the credit of the regulators and the rest of the industry, and has nothing to do with Executive Life—except to the extent that Fred Carr did a good job of matching assets to liabilities, thus keeping the company solvent during its initial liquidation period until an orderly transition could be worked out.

The controversy surrounding Executive Life goes beyond the headlines in the business journals. Much of the fascination and benefit to us all lies in the story of exactly how it happened. Through a series of gaping holes in one of the most regulated industries in the country, certain things were allowed to take place in a number of life insurance companies that jeopardized their solvency during the free-for-all of the 1980s, and ripple effects will be felt until the turn of the century. It is important to the start of this story that we understand the prevailing environment in the life insurance industry when Fred Carr crossed over, after his white hot success as a go-go mutual fund manager in the 1960s. To provide the proper backdrop for the *The Fall of First Executive*, we must first take a look at the industry Fred Carr encountered in the mid-1970s and proceeded to change in ways that made him a dominant influence for the next fifteen years.

The End of an Era

During the thirty-year period from the end of World War II until the mid-1970s, no major business in America could rival life insurance as a place where ordinary people, delivering ordinary performance, could enjoy extraordinary profits. A peculiar contradiction to the basic tenets of free enterprise, the life insurance industry was crowded with a relatively large number of companies while experiencing none of the normal competitive pressures usually present in such an environment. Those of us who studied Samuelson's economics in college will recall the necessary conditions for perfect competition: on one end of the continuum we had *imperfect* competition, in an environment where there was an oligopoly (i.e., very few providers in a market with great demand). At the other end, we had *perfect* competition, where multiple providers competed with one another for the consumer's loyalty. Typically, when you approached the neighborhood of one hundred companies nationwide, you were at or near perfect competition.

The life insurance industry had about 1,500 companies in the decades 1950–70, of which at least 300 were serious players, competing for the consumer's purchase of a life insurance policy. One would think, if Dr. Samuelson is correct, that it was a very competitive business, in which margins were thin, and values to the consumer were at their best. Just the opposite was true. Life insurance enjoyed the benefits of being a product that everyone needed but few understood well enough to distinguish between a good value and a ripoff. By the end of World War II, when the industry was already 150 or so years old, most people had begun to accept the fact that life insurance was a necessary part of their financial plans; yet practically no one outside the industry really understood how the product worked. Indeed, it would become apparent in the 1980s that many of the people who sold it didn't know how it worked. Although I do not believe it was by design, the industry enjoyed an advantage over the consumer that allowed it to be far less efficient in delivering its service than most other industries of the day.

Few consumers really understood how much life insurance should cost. Since the death rate in America is one per person, to the untrained consumer's eye of the 1950s it did not seem illogical that a product would ultimately have to accumulate premiums, which even allowing for the use of the money, would have to come fairly close to the face amount of the policy. Life insurance quite simply was the greatest beneficiary of the financial services industry's most guarded advantage: *the fact that time has an effect on the value of money which usually exceeds its perceived role in the end result.* Stated bluntly, when it comes to investing money, time can camouflage a lot of inefficiencies. As we shall emphasize throughout this story, life insurance is a very long-term purchase. Sales illustrations typically focus on results after twenty, thirty, or more years. That approach can cut a good deal of slack for the high loads and expenses built into the product, and before the 1980s, the industry used this advantage to the fullest. The second great advantage unique to life insurance is that the cash values that build inside the contract, as premiums are paid over the years, accumulate tax-free. This issue of the tax-free accumulation of the "inside build-up"—as it is known to the industry—has been the periodic target of criticism by Congress; despite some restrictions in recent years, it remains the main reason why life insurance can compete as a savings vehicle.

In this benevolent environment, life insurance companies accumulated sizable war chests in their capital and surplus accounts (the industry equivalent of what most corporations call retained earnings). However, there were no wars to be waged. Everyone was making out well, so the money just kept rolling in. Some of it was used to build the typical thirty-story home office skyscraper with the company's name blazoned up top that graces the downtown of practically every significant city in America.

Most of the profits, however, were used to sell more insurance through a costly and ineffective method of distribution called the career agency system. Basically, the way people were brought into the life insurance business involved subsidizing the regular commissions with monies to support the agents while they learned the business, as well as provide income to the managers who trained them. This concept is common in most sales ventures, but the life insurance industry was plagued by terrible results in two key areas. First, the survival ratio was between 10 and 15 percent, with any real measure of success set even lower than that. Second, the productivity of the typical agent was such that for every forty-hour work week he or she turned in, about one new sale emerged. The subject of much criticism within and outside the industry at the time, the career agency system provided the nouveau companies, like Executive Life, with the armies of agents needed to lead the product revolution of the 1980s—which is what this book is about.

Most of the major life insurance companies in America are mutuals, meaning that management is accountable only to the policyholders who own the company, but who rarely exercise any coordinated authority. In most cases, this means they are essentially accountable to no one. The esoteric nature of the business, and the consistency of acceptable results—or at least results perceived to be acceptable—lulled managements into a complacency that left them unprepared for the many traumatic events of the tumultuous 1980s. The life insurance industry in the 1970s was a classic example of the proverbial sleeping giant. Contrary to public perception at the time, paying death benefits to widows and orphans through policies sold by a dedicated and valued sales force was only a fraction of the business. Not that it wasn't important; it just wasn't the bricks and mortar that most people thought it was.

In fact, the life insurance industry was an arcane financial haven, protected from many of the constraints under which the rest of the business world had to operate. It had its own sect of accounting rules, which permitted companies to amortize expenses for the acquisition of new business over ten or more years. There were tax codes designed for the industry that enabled many companies to pay no federal income taxes year in and year out. Most importantly, the product of life insurance itself provided a savings vehicle for the consumer, which allowed the cash-value portion of the contract to accumulate free of income tax prior to withdrawal. In short, *it was a wealth accumulation machine, which even mediocre management couldn't keep from being profitable*. The industry was conservative, low profile, and the product had important social value. There was really no reason why anyone should rock the boat by challenging the efficiency of these venerable institutions. However, not everybody was naive about the industry, and by the late 1970s, consumer groups and Congress were beginning to ask some questions about how the system operated. Further, some of the more liberated agents of the period had concluded that home offices considered agents an entertaining diversion from their primary business of asset management, which enabled the company to call itself a life insurance company and thereby enjoy the benefits unique to the industry. Agents questioned the very career system that spawned them, because industry statistics showed that so few reached any level of real success, despite the huge sums spent to finance them into the business. In fact, by the late 1970s, industry statistics revealed that it cost the typical career agency company over $200,000 to put each agent through his or her fourth year in business. The expense of financing ten agents so that a company could grow one success seemed unreasonable to those who survived. Agents felt that the system exploited them by having their policyholders subsidize the numerous failures endured to get one good agent. As a career agency manager myself at the time, my view was not quite so harsh. I believed that the weak, failing agents subsidized themselves, while the successful agents were pockets of high profitability. During my days as a career agency manager, I called this condition the *ambergris factor*.

In the American whaling industry, which got under way during the eighteenth century, whalers slaughtered the giant Sperm whale for sperm oil, which came from the head and blubber and was important as fuel for lamps. Another type of oil, called spermaceti, extracted from the head, became the chief ingredient in candles. While boiling up the blubber and parts of the Sperm whale, whalers occasionally noticed a very pleasing fragrance. It turned out this was a third oil-like substance, located in the intestines of the whales. Called ambergris, it became the basis for very expensive perfume. The problem was that whalers found ambergris in very few of the whales they killed; nevertheless, the substance brought them a good income because the perfume manufacturers paid extremely high prices for it. So the whalers killed a lot of Sperm whales looking for those chosen few who had the right intestinal stuff.

The way I saw it, the life insurance industry was a lot like those whalers. We could get along okay without the perfume. But finding that occasional guy with the right intestinal stuff sure made things smell a lot better, not to mention the profitability such a catch brought to the enterprise. With a success ratio of less than one in ten, it was hard to believe that the typical career agency company was dependent upon the occasional survivor, or even more rare, the genuinely successful agent, for its survival. Rather, I believed that the occasional successful agent was the ambergris, the perfume, that proved extra profitable. The rest of the blubber in the sales force was still profitable without him.

Rude Awakening

The life insurance industry first began to unravel in late 1978, when the Federal Trade Commission (FTC) conducted its now-famous Task Force Insurance Report. The FTC severely criticized the life insurance industry, stopping just short of an outright recommendation that the public should "buy term and invest the difference." Most damaging was the report's conclusion which estimated that the industrywide rate of return on the savings component of existing cash-value life insurance policies in 1977 was between 1.2 and 1.85 percent, with a best estimate of 1.3 percent. The industry later challenged the methodology used by the FTC, both philosophically and mathematically, and countered with a report which argued, in essence, that the return was more like 5 percent, or perhaps as high as 6 percent. But the damage was done. There were also a host of other criticisms of industry practices that the FTC viewed as misleading and deliberately intended to confuse the consumer.

The FTC report hit the industry like a thunderbolt, not because it wasn't used to some criticism, but because of the tremendous credibility given the report by the press. It was as if everyone had suspected life insurance was a ripoff all along, and now the government had proved it. An unlikely hotbed of controversy, life insurance suddenly became big news.

By the late 1970s, the typical life insurance agent's income was declining steadily. The FTC report had seriously hurt the sale of permanent insurance and, due to the price war, term insurance premiums were plummeting, taking commissions with them. Agents started to do some serious thinking. They looked at how life insurance companies made and spent their money. The survivors reasoned that the capital to fuel the inefficiency they saw came from their own labors and their policyholders' premiums. This, many concluded, was the reason for the unavoidable truths outlined in the FTC report. In reality, successful agents were probably too scarce to fund the tremendous expense of the distribution system. If you believe in the ambergris factor, as I do, it was not so much that the successful agent subsidized the others as that successful agents acted as pockets of exceptional profitability to the company. Either way, it was devastating to companies when they lost their established agents; and that was just what was about to happen. These conditions caused the system of independent agents or PPGAs (Personal Producing General Agents) to flourish. These were agents who dealt directly with companies, and were "non-captive," meaning they were independent contractors rather than employees.

The PPGA company of the 1980s was typically a smaller life insurance company that did not have the resources to engender a career agency force, by financing inexperienced agents in the business as employees. The typical PPGA company was a tenth the size of the Eastern mutual (the household names like Travelers and Prudential) on which it fed. Their pitch was simple: Become an agent who is given the commission at the agency-manager level, and functions as both his own manager and agent. Since theoretically there were no failures to subsidize under the PPGA system, because they recruited only established agents and did no financing, much of the extra profits could go to commissions and policyholder values. In theory, these companies could develop more competitive products because they did not bear the yoke of an expensive distribution system. Although not nearly as cost-effective as they were perceived, at least for the decade of the 1980s, the PPGA concept was somewhat valid. A large number of traditional Eastern mutual career agents fled their environment to become part of the independent producer system. They could seemingly make more money, and pass on the benefits of a more cost-effective distribution system to their policyholders in the form of a more competitive product.

In addition to losing agents they had spent a fortune to develop, the traditional Eastern mutuals now had to deal with the erosion of their premium base in two ways. First, people who were buying new insurance were leaning toward term coverage, which was a lot less profitable than traditional whole life.

Secondly, as the end of the decade of the 1970s approached, interest rates began to increase. By the early 1980s, we were in the environment of an inverted yield curve, with long interest running in the high teens and the prime rate reaching as high as 22 percent. Most of the old traditional whole-life policies that had been sold allowed the policyholder to borrow money out of the contract at 6 or 7 percent. Obviously, when the policyholder could get the kind of rates that were available at the time from banks and government securities, there would inevitably be tremendous movement of policyholder funds out of the company (known technically as "disintermediation") among the bigger firms. The withdrawal of policyholder funds for more competitive rates was a new experience for which the industry was utterly unprepared. Often its money was tied up in low-yielding, long-term mortgages and bonds that were very illiquid at the time. As a result, many companies had to go to the bank to borrow money at a rate of 15 percent or more in order to loan it to our policyholders at 6 or 7 percent.

The environment of the late 1970s and early 1980s was the first meaningful stress experienced by the life insurance industry within memory. New sales were down. Agents' incomes also were down, and they were being recruited by new independent distribution systems that were perceived to be more cost-efficient and more lucrative for the agent. The long investment portfolios of most companies were put under tremendous pressure, due to the shorter and shorter duration of liabilities that they had assumed would never be called early. In many companies there was a genuine liquidity crisis.

The luxury of a career agency force now belonged to those few companies that had parlayed large amounts of capital and surplus in times gone by—times that the industry would never see again. The stage was set for dramatic change. Too often we assume that major change is brought about by the leadership and innovation of extraordinary people. In this case—as I believe is usually true—it was an extraordinary moment, at which prevailing conditions made such change inevitable. A handful of exceptional men recognized the opportunity to capitalize on the long-overdue changes already under way. They could reshape, or rape, the life insurance industry, depending upon the perspective from which one views their approach to the opportunity at hand.

As the 1980s approached, the perfect business was reluctantly pushed into the spotlight of the financial services industry. In the process it would prove to be an anachronism.

2

Fred Carr, Gunslinger

"The dazzling success of Enterprise Fund has earned Fred Carr a reputation as perhaps the best fund manager around."
—"A Fund Wizard Builds an Empire,"
BusinessWeek, May 3, 1969

While the life insurance industry was lumbering through the 1960s, the mutual fund industry was exploding. A handful of characters were at the center of the storm of change in the mutual fund industry. As in life insurance, there were a few key players. In both cases, the most prominent figure would be Fred Carr—a fact that would make him a legend in the financial services industry, but would also be the bane of his professional life. These successive roles made him a controversial figure, whose deeds would be endlessly reported on by the press for over a quarter century. Featured on the cover of *BusinessWeek* in 1969 as a mutual fund "wizard," on the cover of *Forbes* in 1984 as an insurance "empire builder," and on the cover of *Barron's* in 1991 as the "Judas goat" who lured the insurance industry into junk bonds, few money managers have had a longer run in the spotlight than Fred Carr.

Three Freds and a Jerry

David Babson, the founder of a successful investment advisory company that bears his name, once told *Fortune* magazine, "The trouble with the mutual fund business in the late 60's was that there were too many Freds in it."[1] In 1968, Fred Mates was responsible for the best performing equity mutual fund, the Mates Fund. By 1974, he was running a Manhattan singles bar. He died in 1983 relatively unheralded by the investment community. Although somewhat of a celebrity at the time, little was written about Mates.

Fred Alger ran a research company that picked stocks for the Security Equity Fund, the best performer in 1965, and also worked for the ill-fated Bernie Cornfeld family of funds. Later, due to the fact that securities laws allowed fund managers to accumulate their own clients, Alger began selecting certain institutions and individuals to work with. He also bought a couple of mutual funds. By the late 1970s, he had $50 million in assets under management, which grew to over $2 billion by the mid-1980s.

Perhaps better known than the first two Freds was Gerald Tsai, the Shanghai-born investor who managed the Fidelity Capital Fund in the 1950s and 1960s. Tsai's performance ranked among the highest, bringing in returns of up to 50 percent a year. He then started his own fund, the Manhattan Fund, in 1966; its initial offering attracted nearly a quarter billion dollars, which for those days was a record. Although the fund didn't make money for everyone, Tsai came away with $30 million when he sold out to CNA Financial. He then bought controlling interest of Associated Madison Companies, an insurance holding company, which he sold in 1982 to American Can, of which he later became vice chairman. Tsai ran American Can until it became Primerica through yet another merger. He was sidelined when Primerica named Sandy Weill, of American Express

1. *Fortune*, July 25, 1983, p. 88.

fame, as its chairman. Interestingly, Primerica then completed the acquisition which Tsai had started of the A. L. Williams organization, valued at over $1 billion. A. L. Williams was clearly the hands-down winner, from a profitability standpoint, among the new-wave life insurance companies of the 1980s covered in this story. Its founder, Art Williams, also holds the record for the biggest personal gain on his industry involvement in the era.

Best known of the gunslingers, however, was Fred Carr, who back in 1967 and 1968 dazzled Wall Street with his back-to-back number one performances in the Enterprise Fund. His fund delivered industry-leading performances of 117 percent and 44 percent annual growth, respectively, in those two years.

Fred's rise from the streets of Los Angeles to prominence on Wall Street was a genuine rags-to-riches story. In fact, so impressive was his rise from poverty that his story was featured as the opening chapter in a book called *The Young Millionaires*.[2] Born Seymour Fred Cohen in 1931 in the area of Los Angeles now known as Watts, he would change his name later to Fred Carr. He says he did it because of anti-Semitism, which certainly ran strong in Los Angeles during his childhood. Those of us who know him, however, tend to think it was because of his lifelong desire to be disconnected from any affiliation, position, banner, or cause. He certainly wasn't ashamed of being Jewish—he simply didn't want to be obligated to take a position on any issue or expected to have predetermined attitudes because of his origins. Fred is a man who wants his options open on every issue.

Both of his parents had a background in sole proprietorships, which would be a key in the formation of Fred's work ethic and business values. His father, a Romanian immigrant, had pushed a fruit and vegetable wagon through the streets of New York; his mother, one of nine children, worked with her siblings in the family candy store. In the late 1920s, in an effort to escape the

[2] Lawrence A. Armour, *The Young Millionaires* (New York: Playboy Press, 1972).

Depression, the couple moved to Los Angeles. The hope was for a new life, but they had to start from scratch. Fred's father knew only the produce business, so he again opened up a vegetable stand. In time, it evolved into the classic American Mom and Pop grocery and liquor store that could be found on so many East Los Angeles street corners in the 1930s and 1940s.

Early on, Fred showed more interest in part-time jobs hustling his money-making schemes than he did in school. Fred was smitten with stocks and bonds even as a child. He earned money with odd jobs and a paper route, which he somehow funneled into investments in the stock market. At the age of fourteen, he started hanging around the lobby of downtown Los Angeles brokerage firms to pick up bits and pieces of his education in the stock market. After high school, he attended Los Angeles city and state colleges, majoring in Finance. In 1952, he was drafted into the Army; afterwards, instead of returning to college, he continued his interest in entrepreneurship through a series of schemes. Having come from a family where it was not uncommon to work seven days a week, Fred found it easy to make money doing various odd jobs. His objective was to save so he could begin investing. His goal was $5,000, with which he could begin an investment program. He went into several part-time businesses with a Hispanic high school chum, Al Villasenor, who eventually went into the insurance business and became a leading producer for Fred at Executive Life. Al, a gracious and charming man, is but one example of many lifelong acquaintances whose lives were enriched for having known Fred. However, almost all were close acquaintances rather than close friends. This is the style of Fred's enigmatic personality.

With Al, and also on his own, he poured concrete driveways in the mornings, pumped gas at a service station in the afternoons, and sold life insurance at night. By 1957, the twenty-six-year-old Carr had saved $10,000 and was ready to pursue a career in stocks and bonds. He went to work originally as a trainee at Bache & Co. But his interest in securities took a different tack. Rather than focusing on the blue chips and household names, he sought out smaller companies he felt had the potential for growth. So, rather than growth stocks, he looked for what he called "emerging growth stocks." Over time, the term he coined would become a legitimate specialty for future securities analysts.

Fred became fascinated by the due diligence aspect of the business, in that he saw a huge industry in which the stockbrokers did "seat of the pants" selling that often led to disaster. Since most of the companies he was interested in had no market makers, and no one was really tracking them, he had to do his own research. An early choice of his was Winchell's Donuts, which was one of the first franchises that generated terrific returns for investors. This led to a fascination with franchises that later caused Fred to pick some real winners like Kentucky Fried Chicken and McDonald's. Operating from Los Angeles, Fred Carr earned quite a name for himself out on Wall Street. By 1966, he had taken the small savings garnered from his earlier days pumping gas and selling insurance and parlayed it into $1 million. Not bad in those days for a college dropout from Watts.

In 1966, Fred decided to make a significant career change, which necessitated a reduction in his income from $100,000 to $25,000 a year. In addition, he had to invest $200,000 in his new business, which was a substantial part of his newly earned fortune. What he got in return was a 20 percent equity interest and the management of a new company known as Convertible Securities & Growth Stocks. This firm was the forbear of the Enterprise Fund for which Fred Carr would achieve his first great fame. In his new position as owner/manager, he initiated unconventional conditions similar to those he would later use in the life insurance industry. First of all, Fred insisted that he make all decisions with regard to the portfolio, retaining complete authority to make all buy-and-sell decisions by himself. In addition, rather than working with the customary staff of in-house experts, he chose to rely on outside consultants for his information. He ran a very lean shop and lorded over it with unwavering authority.

The key strategy, however, was to focus on his emerging

growth stock concept. Fred likes to remind people that at that juncture, "Wall Street spat upon me." They thought he was crazy to pick up stocks with embarrassing connotations like Kentucky Fried Chicken and put them in his portfolio. Today, of course, most major wirehouses set up their research activities to include a division focusing on the contemporary equivalent of emerging growth stocks. Ironically, a favorite pick of many of them in the 1980s would be First Executive Corporation.

Kentucky Fried Chicken is probably Fred's favorite example of the flak he took for his strategy. "We got an unbelievable amount of ridicule on that one," he likes to remind people, "especially from the East Coast establishments. They wanted to know how we had the nerve to put something with a name like that in our portfolio. The answer was simple. The homework I did in the early sixties on companies like Winchell's Donuts and McDonald's convinced me that the fast food business was embarking on what I could see to be a tremendous growth spurt. Kentucky Fried Chicken had a name the public recognized and trusted, and the company had the kind of management that knew how to exploit the market potential. What more could anyone ask for?" In less than three years, Kentucky Fried Chicken—some 400,000 shares of which were now in the Enterprise Fund portfolio—soared from an adjusted price of 2⅜ to a high of around 50. Fred Carr was on his way to legend as a gunslinger of Wall Street.

The Enterprise portfolio contained a lot of small growing stocks such as Tonka Toys, Kelly Services, Commerce Clearing House, and Jostens. As Fred became known for his lean, mean operation and his characteristic hands-on management, the Fund grew explosively. He did, however, have a group that he consulted with in running the Fund that he referred to as "Carr's dirty dozen." This was a loosely constructed round table of analysts: Fred had confidence in them and shared his insights in exchange for their due diligence.

The Fund began to snowball, with assets reaching almost $1 billion in 1968. The holding company that owned Enterprise Fund was called Shareholders Capital; Fred took it public in late

1968. Shareholders Capital too, did well, with the stock trading at levels giving Fred's 20 percent ownership a value of about $30 million by 1969. Not once during the five-year period between 1964 and 1968 was the Enterprise Fund out of the Top 25 funds in the nation! Fred Carr had the best track record in the industry during this period. He became a celebrity, not unlike Peter Lynch twenty years later, whose every observation and word was noted by the investor community. Amazingly, he attained all of this prominence without ever leaving Los Angeles. Like his later protégé, Michael Milken, Fred shunned Wall Street, preferring the sunny comfort of his native Los Angeles. The Street never accepted either of them as members of the establishment, regardless of their performance.

All Good Things...

Fred Carr's success was not without its critics, however, and the things for which they criticized him have an alarmingly familiar ring today. Some practices used by Fred were perceived to lend themselves to stock manipulation. A shortcut to success practiced by some fund managers is a practice called bootstrapping. This involves buying round-lot shares of obscure companies where the float, or shares available in the trading market, are scarce. Thus the fund manager can "bootstrap" the stock price to a much higher level. Fred admitted to routinely buying shares under these conditions—which, because they were thinly traded, were called "Twiggies" (after the fashion model of the day)—but he maintained that it was simply because he couldn't get as much of a stock as he would like. Whatever his motives when Fred Carr started acquiring shares in a Twiggy, his fans would follow and the price would often run up at an astonishing rate. In fact, many of the top over-the-counter securities in his portfolio in 1968 were trading at price-earning ratios ranging from multiples of 20 all the way up to 80. His response to critics in a *New York Times* article on January 5, 1969, was that "[Our] consistent record was created not only in good markets, but in bad markets, which really tests the quality of downside risks of a funds investments." Another concern expressed in that same article was the perception that too much of the money invested in performance funds was so-called greed money— money which flees at the first sign that a fund is faltering. Of course, the real criticism came when the Enterprise Fund and the market that fueled its meteoric growth collapsed.

In these early days, Fred Carr was a sought-after speaker at such podiums as the New York City Harvard Business School Club and the Metropolitan Club. Some of his ideas showed great insights into the future. For example, in 1968 he told the Harvard Business School Club that his emerging growth stock concept provided an excellent high-return strategy for "whole-sale to pension funds and insurance companies." This, of course, is the exact strategy that was embraced by his associate, Michael Milken, a few years later, with his high-yield bond strategy.[3] He also cautioned Wall Street in a 1973 "Heard on the Street" article against the pending dangers of insider trading: "You've got to get rid of historical abuses, specifically ... continuous use of inside information, manipulative acts of issues hidden in the haze of generally accepted accounting treatments, and poor performance of specialists in failing to provide liquidity."[4] It is interesting that during his entire thirty years of running public companies, Fred Carr never once traded in his own account.

It was at this point that Fred began to make the transition from hands-on portfolio manager, accountable for nothing other than performance for clients, to "securities executive." It was a transition that didn't go well for him and probably affected the Fund's performance in that it began to lose a good deal of its luster. Fred would experience similar problems when he made the same transition at First Executive Corporation. As a risk-taking entrepreneur, Fred Carr has few peers in the financial world. As a corporate executive, he also has few peers, because

3. *New York Times*, ``Market Place,'' April 3, 1968.
4. *Wall Street Journal*, April 18, 1973.

few of his style would ever be chosen to run a big company unless they grew it themselves, which of course he did on two occasions. But the market was changing, and basically the golden days of the go-go mutual funds were coming to an end.

In November 1969, due to a dispute over control issues, Fred Carr resigned from Shareholders Capital and his various posts within the corporation. After that, the Fund more or less collapsed, with values plummeting over a period of a couple of years. Fred would forever be held responsible for the collapse for the Enterprise Fund, even though it occurred some time after his departure from the firm. He also would be saddled with the "gunslinger" image the press tagged on him. Even twenty years after the decline of the Enterprise Fund, *Forbes* characterized him as a gunslinging cowboy in one of their many articles covering his exploits at First Executive Corporation. Whether things would have worked any differently had Fred Carr stayed with Enterprise is really just conjecture. The fact is, he was long gone when things fell apart. However, he was the person who built the firm, and he would have to live with the moniker of "Fred Carr, gunslinger" for the rest of his business career.

The go-go mutual fund era of the 1960s gives us a number of striking parallels to the go-go life insurance era of the 1980s. I believe the most important lesson, which went unlearned, was about the mass psychology of greed. No one had to be dishonest or to misrepresent the situation; they only needed to get the customers' avarice juices flowing so that their emotions surpassed their common sense.

In 1970, Fred decided to set up Carr Management & Research Corporation, a consulting company designed to work with and manage money for institutional and individual clients, and to provide financial counseling services for a broad list of client companies, ranging from those on the New York Stock Exchange to small, privately held corporations. His scratch firm quickly amassed $100 million in funds under management.

Although not known for his philanthropy, Fred did personally fund the UCLA-Pennsylvania Center for the Study of

Financial Institutions with half a million dollars of his own money in 1969. I'm sure it was also gratifying for Fred, a junior college dropout, to be invited to teach a postgraduate course entitled "Changing Markets of the 70's" at UCLA Graduate School of Business. Although he was rumored to be fabulously wealthy already, the comfortable life of consulting and teaching were sidelines far from the fray of the financial services industry in which Fred believed he should continue to be a player. A person of almost unlimited patience, Fred Carr would move along his sideline career—consulting and dabbling here and there in various investments for half a dozen years—before the right situation presented itself. The situation came in the unlikely form of a fledgling, virtually bankrupt life insurance company. At the time it ranked 355th in the United States, with little prospect of going anywhere other than South.

3

Fred Carr, Lightning Rod

" ... Milken was convinced that one of the many benefits of his moving [back] to L.A. would be his ability to cultivate a relationship with Carr and First Executive."
—Connie Bruck, *The Predator's Ball* (1988)

In 1974, the life insurance industry was embarking upon the series of woes described in Chapter 1. At that point, as if fate wanted to give Fred Carr a couple of years internship that would tune him up for his role as the key player in the explosive events from 1978 through 1990, he was approached by Albert Handschumacher about assuming a position on the board of struggling First Executive Corporation, the nearly bankrupt parent of Executive Life.

Executive Life of California was founded by Otto Forst in 1961. Like most stock life insurance companies, it was owned by a holding company, First Executive Corporation, which was publicly traded on the over-the-counter (OTC) market. Executive Life of California, in turn, had a subsidiary called Executive Life of New York. Due to the more restrictive insurance codes in New York state, many companies wishing to do business there do so through subsidiaries that limit most of their activities to that state. Throughout this story, when we refer to Executive Life we are talking about the California company, which did about 80 percent of the corporation's business. However, for the most part, the New York company was the mirror image of Executive Life of California, and can therefore be considered as part of our story.

The initial capital to form the company was raised personally by Mr. Forst, an Austrian immigrant who had made some money as a successful agent in the business. As was done for so many other entrepreneurial adventures in the affluent West Los Angeles area that required venture capital, Forst went to the Hillcrest Country Club to peddle the founders stock for his company. There, like many other entrepreneurs before him, he found the seed money to fund his enterprise. For the record, despite Forst's spotty performance as CEO and Fred Carr's pursuant victories and difficulties, those who bought their stock from Mr. Forst initially and sold it in 1986 would have experienced a 1,000 percent return on their initial investment. Of course, it's a lot easier to identify these dates than it is to identify someone who bought and sold on them. Before too long, Forst encountered the financial difficulties that always plague young life insurance companies, namely, capital shortages. In growing a life insurance company, the inevitable pitfall is too much success. Life insurance is a long-term investment: profits to the company on a given policy seldom emerge before it has been on the books for several years. It costs more than a dollar to put a dollar of premium on the books, which means the writing company must dip into its capital base if it expects to grow. When capital is gone, management must go to the traditional sources such as the equity markets, banks, and a source unique to the life insurance industry known as surplus relief, which we will discuss in later chapters.

Forst's company was selling a brand-new form of insurance called Split Life^{SM}, which was a forbear of the revolutionary interest-sensitive products. This was one of the first products that attempted to unbundle the mystique of life insurance by separating the term, or death, portion from the cash accumulation portion. Clients were asked to purchase a term policy, which they could get only if they made a lump-sum deposit into an annuity on which interest accrued at a competitive rate. The product was heavily loaded with surrender charges, and therefore generated good commissions for the agent while locking up the policyholders' funds more tightly than a conventional product would and sticking them with an uncompetitive term policy. The lack of competitive rates on the term policy was offset by interest rates credited on the deposit portion that were more competitive than traditional whole-life policies. Although not much of an improvement, in actuality the product was at least conceptually a step in the right direction.

Otto Forst's problems began when he borrowed $14 million from First National City Bank (now Citibank) in part to purchase a New York subsidiary, Executive Life of New York—a unit that would be a sore spot not only then, but also later on. To gain admission to the state of New York is almost impossible for a life insurance company unless it is accomplished by an acquisition. Yet, for companies wishing to be truly nationwide in scope, such admission is essential. So, New York-domiciled companies were hard to come by. Forst knew this and jumped on an opportunity, but he paid too much money. Also, just because you own a New York company doesn't mean the New York State Insurance Department will approve your policies to be sold there, especially if they think you're not superstrong financially. With no significant profits flowing out of the new company to help service the debt, the burden fell on its parent, the California company.

Interestingly, Otto Forst's downfall came because of problems similar to those encountered by Fred Carr seventeen years later. Both grew their companies rapidly and then ran out of sources for capital. Both were in technical default on their bank notes. When the board removed Forst, it had to look for a new CEO, which seemed a difficult task for a company on the brink of declaring bankruptcy.

The situation they had to offer a candidate in 1974 was bleak. First Executive Corporation held only about $77 million in assets, making it an obscure 355th in size among U.S. life insurance companies. Of the $77 million, $22 million was in the form of policy loans, on which there was little likelihood of repayment. The investment portfolio was $20 million under water, and the company was in default on its $14.6 million loan to Citicorp, on which they were threatening to foreclose. In addition, the Internal Revenue Service was conducting an audit of the previous four years' returns, and the New York Insurance Department was investigating practices at the company's New York unit. Executive Life of New York had no rating from A. M. Best, and its accountants, Touche Ross, were unwilling to express any opinion on the financial statements. It is eerie to note that seventeen years later, almost identical conditions existed at the company, except that the defaulting bank debt was ten times greater and the amount by which the bond portfolio was under water was one thousand times greater! The situation with the rating agencies, the New York Insurance Department, and Touche Ross was also parallel. For Fred Carr, 1990 must have been, in the immortal words of Yogi Berra, "déjà vu all over again." It is also interesting to note that when the company was again in near-disastrous shape in 1990 and the board thought about replacing Fred Carr, they concluded that he was the one that got them there and he deserved a shot, for a year or so anyway, at getting them out. Otto Forst had no such luck. Tragically, his luck became much worse when, not long after his ouster, he and his wife were brutally murdered in their Beverly Hills home. The crime was never solved.

One wise move by Forst was in putting Al Handschumacher on the board of directors. Handschumacher is a 24-carat Beverly Hills character. A brilliant engineer, he was the skillful day-to-day management talent behind the late Bill Lear, legendary founder of the Lear Siegler Corporation and inventor of the plane that bears his name. As president of Lear Siegler, Al had a long history of dealing with an eccentric, deep genius in the form of Lear, his boss and lifelong friend. Like the more famous Lear, Al is a bit of a rapscallion and enjoys the status of life in Beverly Hills, much in the style of the rich and famous. He loved to attend our Executive Life sales conventions, usually bringing his latest fiancé or wife, or if not, dancing with everyone else's wife. Though in his seventies when I met him, no one liked to party better than Al, except perhaps his late partner Bill Lear, who Al told me made him look like a monk.

Al was the first American ever appointed as syndicator by Lloyds of London. As most insurance people know, the way Lloyds works is very different from other insurance companies. Rather than having the corporation assume risk, individuals as syndicators (the British equivalent of underwriters) pledge their entire net worth as assurance that a claim presented to Lloyds will be paid. This honorable approach of putting your money where your mouth is when asked to assume a risk is one that only the Brits would think of. For obvious reasons, most American insurers would find this level of commitment by company owners to be unacceptable. To this day, the headquarters of Lloyds is replete with pomp and ceremony, including the tradition that all of the syndicators don a top hat and tails. To have been admitted to this elite fraternity as an American, I assume Al made a few bucks and some friends in high places in his long association with Bill Lear. Al kept a post-retirement office at Executive Life; although he spent time at his apartment in London, or on other globe-trotting activities. Occasionally I would spot his Corniche convertible parked next to Fred's car and ask him to have lunch. It was during these visits with Al, who was a really sincere and open man, that I learned more about what was going on at Executive Life than I ever did in any management meetings. Al was also a great source of history about the business world in general. He is one of those people who, at seventy-something, made it look like more fun than being thirty-something. Al was fascinated with the study of Fred Carr, who he said was the most brilliant man he knew—next to Bill Lear.

Handschumacher recruited Fred Carr to the company's board in early 1974, and on July 11, 1974, he was elected president of First Executive Corporation while Forst was simultaneously removed. In addition to spending his first year in constant negotiations with First National City Bank trying to restructure the debt, Fred had to unwind two ill-fated foreign acquisition attempts that Forst had botched. In these early days, there was little time to think about marketing or sales; avoiding bankruptcy court was the only issue. Then, through a long series of complex transactions, Fred got the debt whittled down to just under $6 million in 1975 and things began to turn around. From that point, he retired the debt altogether through a series of restructurings and a private placement of $1 million of equity. To build confidence among investors, Fred invested $1 million of his own money in some of the securities used for the restructuring; the rest came from various long-time clients from his days as a portfolio manager. During the four years that Fred took the corporation's bank debt from $14.6 million in 1973 to $1.6 million in 1977 and subsequently $0, he developed his well-publicized aversion to debt. For a dozen years, until 1988, Fred would lecture in his annual reports and in other forums on the evils of debt. He would shout, "We have no debt at First Executive Corporation. No long-term debt. No short-term debt. None." "No debt" was a central theme in his corporate philosophy. With hindsight, in 1988 when he agreed to a $235 million bank loan, those who knew him should have seen a very big red flag. Indeed, it was the bank debt that again became Fred's nemesis in 1988. He prides himself on not repeating mistakes. He, too, likes to quote Yogi Berra, when he told John Dingell's House Subcommittee in June 1990, "We can't afford to make the wrong mistakes." Fred's first experience with debt was the result of another person's mistake. His second experience turned out to be his own "wrong mistake."

By 1975, Fred tried to focus on the marketing aspects of his company. A tireless promoter, who loves to create a lasting impression on prospective producers who visit him, Fred did benefit in one way from the legacy of Otto Forst. Forst had somehow negotiated a lease for the office space that housed his little company (thirty-five employees) in a new building (circa 1966) on the corner of Wilshire Boulevard and Santa Monica Boulevard, the gateway to Beverly Hills. In exchange for a thirty-year lease on one and a half floors of the twelve-story landmark building, he got his company's name on both sides of the building's top. The gigantic "Executive Life" sign was the first thing one saw driving into Beverly Hills on either Wilshire Boulevard or Santa Monica Boulevard. The advertising value of that sign over the thirty years was greater than that of the whole company when Fred took over!

Otto Forst's luxurious quarters within the building were appointed with kitchen, bath, bedroom, and bar, and looked more like what one would expect to see housing the chairman at the Prudential than struggling little Executive Life. When Fred moved in, he promptly trashed the place by filling it with memorabilia, such as a life-size dummy of a sailor (from the movie *Sleuth*, given to him by a show-biz friend), dozens of drawings by his small children, a couple dozen Pinocchio dolls and Einstein likenesses (which he collected), and a host of other garage-sale items, piled literally to the ceiling. The beautiful walnut block paneling was peppered with nails to support every picture or note his kids ever sent him. In those early days, Fred was known as the "Beverly Hills' Sneakered CEO," because more often than not he wore his favorite outfit—jeans, sneakers, and a sweatshirt—to the office. The contrast between the Beverly Hills setting, the impressive sign, and the Fred Carr trappings made for a lasting impression on prospective agents who were frequently invited to Los Angeles for recruiting interviews.

When I joined the company, Fred moved to the new twelve-story headquarters he had constructed on Olympic Boulevard, and turned over his enclave of eccentric contradictions to me. (We had to maintain offices there to keep our sign on the building.) I promptly brought in decorators and carefully restored it to the resplendent beauty that Mr. Forst had originally intended. I figured Otto would have wanted it that way. By that time, Fred had gotten over some of his eccentricities and made the transition to a sort of rumpled Brooks Brothers look, so his new offices were more what one might expect for an insurance company president. However, out of sentiment for his preference for a California casual working environment, he declared

Friday "T-shirt day." Every employee was issued an Executive Life knit shirt and was encouraged to follow Fred's lead by wearing it, along with jeans and tennis shoes, on Fridays.

In getting sales off the ground, it was only natural that Fred would gravitate toward his strong background in the securities industry. He developed a series of annuity products to be marketed through stockbrokers in the large wirehouses. In 1975, they produced a modest $1 million of annuity premium, then went to $11 million in 1976, and to $56 million in 1977. First Executive Corporation had done well in its union with Fred Carr. In less than four years, he had taken it from bankruptcy to profitability with one hand, while personally building a distribution system in the lucrative securities industry market with the other. For his labors, in 1977 the board rewarded Fred with a combined salary and bonus, which for the first time exceeded $100,000 (although only slightly).

By himself, without knowing the insurance business, Fred Carr had worked a minor miracle in turning around First Executive Corporation—mostly by using his instincts, which are brilliant, and his considerable promotional talents. While doing so, however, he began to notice and learn things that were very different about his new business. As he studied the life insurance industry with his customary diligence, and as he got the lay of the land, he became increasingly enticed. He saw an industry that was insulated from much of the pressure of the rest of the financial services industry. It sold a product with the advantage of a tax-free build-up for those who invested premiums in the contract. This was especially exciting to Fred, who was used to investing after-tax dollars that normally required paying regular income tax on the returns generated for his clients. On top of that, he saw an industry that was mired in inefficiency and bureaucracy. The distribution systems costs were out of sight. The salespeople averaged an incredibly unproductive one sale per week. Less obvious, and really exciting, was that many investment aspects of the business were completely untapped. Both the asset and liability sides of the balance sheet were stuffed to the gills with opportunity for a portfolio manager like

Fred Carr. He knew he was onto something big—although even he could never have imagined how big.

The Team Takes Form

Fred had enjoyed some quick success, but he sensed that the main event of his career in life insurance was yet to come. After all, the opportunities of the moment were enormous, but to cash in on them, some important hurdles had to be overcome. The magic that was about to occur required the convergence of four crucial components: investment performance that was markedly superior to the rest of the industry; innovative products that were both profitable and competitive; a nationwide distribution system; and a source of unlimited capital to fund the growth. The likelihood of all four of these dynamics converging on the doorstep of obscure and frail Executive Life would seem to be infinitesimal. Perhaps the gods of the financial services industry were smiling on Fred Carr for a second time, because that's exactly what happened. One by one the players appeared who would give Fred his second shot at immortality in the financial services industry and a chance to redeem his sullied reputation on Wall Street.

Sometime in those early days, Fred had the now well-publicized luncheon with Mike Milken where, over tuna salad at Cafe Beverly Hills, they decided to change the course of the financial services industry. Along the way, Milken would make himself a billionaire and be crowned "the most influential man in American finance since J. P. Morgan" in 1986, and then be thrown into jail for ten years for securities fraud in 1991. What a lot of people don't realize is that none of it could have happened without Fred Carr. Anyone close to the situation would agree that it was Fred whose huge blanket purchases of Drexel's junk issues in the early 1980s made Milken the junk bond king and paved the way for the stampede of business that would deluge Drexel Burnham Lambert.

Milken's kingdom was based on the absolute certainty that if you did a deal with him, you would get the capital you came for. No exceptions. The Milken empire was built on confidence in the ability of Drexel to get it sold—every time. Fred Carr played the role of underwriter to the underwriters. In the early years, if it was offered, he bought it. If it all didn't sell, he sometimes bought the rest. In the early 1980s, this was a key source of Milken's credibility and, therefore, unwavering loyalty among his customers. There has been a lot of ink spent on the Milken-Carr partnership over the ten years or so of their association. We will take a more detailed look at what went on between the two men later. Our point here is that it is not an overstatement to say that the bond between the two financiers, formed in 1977, not only was key to Fred's need for superior investment performance for First Executive Corporation, but also gave rise to the entire Mike Milken–Drexel Burnham Lambert–junk bond machine, which was to dominate the financial world in the United States for the next ten years.

We have already touched on the fact that a successful life insurance company is in constant need of capital to fund its growth. This is because of first-year expenses and requirements by the regulators for reserves that will exceed first-year premiums, leaving the company temporarily in the red on newly written business. In the late 1970s, the interest-sensitive revolution, as it became known, introduced a new series of products that passed on the yields earned by the company to the consumer in the form of credited interest rates applied to the policy cash values, which therefore reflected the investment results of the company. In the high-yield environment of the 1980s, this concept dramatically altered the attractiveness of life insurance as a cash accumulation vehicle. In 1978, the new interest-sensitive products and the enormous potential they held were mostly the purview of the stock life insurance companies rather than the mutuals. This was chiefly due to a quirk in the tax code that favored stock companies, which were taxed on their operating income, while mutuals were taxed on their investment income. The stock companies credited interest to policyholders with before-tax dollars, while the mutuals had to do it with after-tax dollars. The other consideration was that if these products were truly the wave of the future, and a lot were sold, it would require a good deal of capital infusion into the companies selling them. Mutual companies could not go to the capital markets to sell stock or other equities, so they were much more restricted in getting large amounts of money for sudden expansion. Stock companies were definitely in the cat bird seat.

When Fred Carr and Mike Milken saw the synergy that existed between their two businesses, it must have seemed magical. Carr saw an industry of sleeping giants whose policyholders and agents were up for grabs. In addition, his already significant success at selling annuities through stockbrokers told him he could literally have all of that business he wanted, and he wanted a lot. In addition to an investment strategy that would allow him to earn a good spread so his products would be competitive, he needed a story to tell Wall Street that would excite investors enough to give him the capital to fund it all. After hearing Fred's side, Milken must have exclaimed, "Boy, do I have a deal for you!" Milken's side was the mirror image of Fred's. He had corporations that wanted to raise capital and would pay a premium for it to someone willing to back them. Corporate bonds were the traditionally accepted investment for a life insurance company. The new breed of high-yield corporate bonds gave the kinds of spreads that would allow Fred to give the policyholder an interest rate unlike anything ever to come out of a life insurance company, and still keep a handsome profit. Junk bonds gave Fred all he needed to dominate the single premium deferred annuity (SPDA) market with stockbrokers, and later the interest-sensitive whole-life market with insurance agents.

As to the issue of raising capital, that was a matter both men knew a thing or two about. Fred would prime the pump for Milken by gobbling up at least some of every issue Drexel came out with and creating a "can't-miss" image among his customers. Then, when the success of Fred's marketing strategy created the need for more capital, Drexel's loyal and grateful customers would jump on the offerings. As Fred's gamble on lower-quality securities paid off, he was able to develop his own following on Wall Street. Eventually, some of the savviest investors of the time would wager heavily on First Executive Corporation: Martin Sosnoff of Sosnoff Capital, 7.8 percent; John Templeton of the Templeton Galbraith Funds, 7.3 percent; Peter Lynch of Fidelity Investments, 11.4 percent; and oil heiress Caroline Hunt of Rosewood Financial, 10 percent. All bought in big on the First Executive bandwagon. Underpinning the whole thing was the Milken strategy of reciprocity that made it all go round. In fact, in 1984, *Forbes* did a cover story on this strategy, with a cartoon depicting a merry-go-round carrying caricatures of Fred and other Milken cronies, with Milken at the controls.

In Mike Milken, Fred found a person whose views and personal values were startlingly similar to his own. Natives and lovers of Los Angeles, both men are somewhat soft-spoken and bashful. Both are fiercely secretive about their business dealings, sharing only bits and pieces as necessary with their closest associates. Both lived very modestly for men of their means, and both had capacities for work that were insatiable. Perhaps most interestingly, both men built their fortunes on identifying undervalued assets. For Fred, it had been his emerging growth stock strategies that Wall Street held in disdain in the 1960s, then embraced as its own in the 1970s. For Milken, it would be the non-investment grade bonds of smaller operations and "fallen angels" of the larger ones, for which no serious market had existed. Here again, Wall Street criticized the strategy, then embraced it in the mid-1980s when all major wirehouses established emerging growth stock and junk bond departments. Although the two rarely met publicly, especially after they had attained celebrity status, they talked on the phone several times a day as they developed their strategy for building their complementary empires. It was Milken who was first attracted to Carr, and indeed considered the move for Drexel from New York to Los Angeles partly to be closer to his best customer, yet Carr was soon caught up by the Milken aura. On those rare occasions when the two met publicly, it was clear to those of us present that Fred had come to hold Michael Milken in awe.

The next key event occurred in 1977, when Fred was intro- duced to Albert Jacob, an actuarial consultant known for his creativity in product design. Although Al's products were inno- vative and responsive to marketing needs, some of the actuarial community questioned their aggressive pricing and long-term profitability. Fred's strategy of getting most of the profit from the investment spreads was a perfect fit for Jacob's aggressive product designs. As is the case early on with almost all of us who know Al Jacob, Fred and he did not click right off. Iraqi by origins, Jewish by faith, raised in India, and educated in Eng- land, Al is a unique mix of the best and the least charming char- acteristics of all four cultures of which he is a product. And what a product! Undoubtedly one of the all-time great charac- ters the insurance industry has produced, Al is legendary in actuarial and worldwide reinsurance circles for his wheeling and dealing. Sometimes making multi-million-dollar reinsur- ance treaties on a handshake rather than by signed contract, he is viewed with both admiration and disdain, depending upon which side someone was on in one of his deals. When it soon became evident that even with Carr's and Milken's talents it was not practical to fund First Executive Corporation's incredi- ble growth by the sale of equities alone, Al introduced Fred to surplus relief. Surplus relief is an alternative to raising new cap- ital that allows a company, in effect, to borrow the excess capital of another carrier for purposes of meeting its reserving require- ments. As we shall see later, this would turn out to be a double- edged sword. Suffice it to say here that Al's tactics for slapping together surplus relief contracts created a great flap in the industry and ultimately led to the promulgation of new rules by the New York Insurance Department.

The lore of Executive Life is rich with Al Jacob stories. Read- ing the testimony from the New York Insurance Department hearings over his reinsurance treaties that were disallowed in 1986, it is almost laughable. He spent several minutes going back and forth with the depositioner about the correct pronun- ciation of his name. He was frustrating to the point of rage and managed to be confusing on many issues. This behavior was not contrived for the Insurance Department, it's simply the way Al conducts himself in most discussions.

Mastery of the salvo is but one of Al's many talents. His greatest gift lies in the insurance products he designs for specific markets. Agents love coming to Al with a marketing opportunity that requires a customized product. Al's marketing and sales insights, his instincts about what will sell, are highly unusual for an actuary. These were the type of skills that Fred Carr, who knew so little about the product side of the life insurance industry, desperately needed.

Most of the industry responded to the Federal Trade Commission report on the poor yields offered by life insurance, and to the accusations by consumer groups about the value of traditional whole life, by stampeding to universal life. But Al Jacob chose to go in a different direction. Universal life was the first generation of products that passed through competitive interest rates to consumers, thus giving birth to the industry's "interest sensitive revolution." As it turned out, universal life has since proven to be a less than perfect choice for many companies that have struggled to make profits from a product that offered more flexibility than the consumer needed, and created an inconsistency of premium flow that has raised havoc with asset and liability matching. Al invented a product called Irreplaceable Life^{SM} that represented simple efficiency and guaranteed profitability. It is arguably the best product of the day in that it does an excellent job for the consumer, the agent, and the company alike. One important characteristic is that it is most successfully sold by strong agents. This is because there is less flexibility with regard to premium payments than with universal life. Al did not believe the consumer would have the discipline to make premium payments that were optional, as they are with universal life. He wanted the premium flow for the company to be consistent, so they could invest the funds in higher-yielding, longer-term vehicles and the policyholder could enjoy the benefits of the high returns Fred could deliver. If the insured didn't pay a premium, the policy would lapse, just as it did in the old days of traditional whole life. Time has proved Al correct in that the happiest companies and policyholders are those who had policies with ongoing premiums that accumulated substantially more cash than those with lower or optional premiums.

Al Jacob's initial offering, Irreplaceable Life I℠, was test-marketed in 1978 and introduced in 1979. It was the industry's first rear-end-loaded, current interest, whole-life product. Basically, the company would calculate a premium pro-actively, based upon interest mortality, expense, and persistency assumptions. It would then pause at the end of five years, and every five years thereafter, and recalculate the premium based upon experience. The premium could go up or down, depending on certain contractually guaranteed maximums. Irreplaceable Life I℠ was an excellent product to get Fred's marketing effort off the ground. It was not, however, a cash accumulation vehicle, giving what Fred really wanted—assets to manage. This would come later, with Irreplaceable Life II℠, the hottest insurance product of the decade, and Al Jacob's crowning achievement.

Fred now needed agents strong enough to sell a product that was expensive, but if maintained by the policyholder, would deliver better value than anything on the market, at greater profitability to the company. This problem was solved more by good fortune than design when Fred was approached separately by two Los Angeles supersalesmen, each of whom had a scheme they were sure couldn't miss. Both were correct, even beyond their own blue-sky expectations.

Two Harbingers

The most recognized professional organization for those who manage life insurance agencies is the General Agents and Managers Association (GAMA), a suborganization of the National Association of Life Underwriters. This important organization has recognized many a great agency manager over the years. Periodically it publishes a coffee table book called *Essence of Excellence*, which profiles the inductees to the GAMA Hall of Fame. These are the all-time greatest agency heads. If that book were updated today, it would surely *exclude* Jerome "Jerry" Schwartz, which would be a good example of what's wrong with the industry. Of course, Jerry is not a member of GAMA; but if he were, he still wouldn't make their nominee list. That is their loss, because he is among the industry's most successful sales managers.

In 1977, Jerry Schwartz was coming out of his second bankrupt company and looking for the third time that would be a charm. Jerry had been an agency manager in the Equity Funding disaster of the late 1960s, a well-publicized fraud that gave the life insurance industry its first black eye in modern times. Jerry left a couple of years before the collapse at Equity Funding because of his sense that something was wrong. Although a relentless risk taker, Jerry is a person of the highest ethical values, and when he saw smoke around the executive suites, he didn't wait for the flames. Jerry's role in this fiasco, like that of most of the field people, was innocent; but still a lot of people that he worked with got hurt. After he left Equity Funding in 1967, Jerry spent a couple more years at a broker dealer network which, because of the market in the early 1970s and poor management, also went broke.

Twice bitten and a bit gun-shy, Jerry became manager, and eventually executive vice president, of Piedmont Capital, a mutual fund and insurance operation owned by the fabulously wealthy Richardson family of Vicks Vaporub fame. A medium-sized broker dealer with thirty branch offices, it was a good fit for Jerry's marketing and administrative skills. He chose Piedmont because it was known to be a conservative firm that attached its name to only the best endeavors. Jerry did not want to build another organization, only to get surprised by things over which he had no control. Piedmont was probably an over-reaction by Jerry to his two previous bad experiences. Fiercely independent and entrepreneurial by nature, he didn't fit into the culture of the Richardson family. Aided by the sagging results of the mutual fund industry in the mid-1970s, Jerry made the decision to strike out on his own again.

This time, at forty-three years old and with a broad base of securities and insurance experience, he had an idea whose time he was certain had come. Jerry believed the turnover and policy lapse problems in the industry were caused by the fact that the agent's incentive was mostly up front, in the form of first-year commissions, while the company's reward was on the back end when profits emerged from policies several years after they were sold. His solution: make the agents partners with the company in their book of business. His idea was to form a third-party entity, owned by the agents, into which part (preferably half) of their business would be placed (reinsured) by the insurance company. The agents and company would then be partners and have the same long-term interests at heart. Because he would be concerned about the profits on the policies he put with the company, the agent would be more selective about the type of risk he insured and, once sold, would work harder at keeping the policyholder with the company over the long pull. All of this, Jerry reasoned, would lead to much greater profits. An additional benefit would be that if both the claims experience and the lapse ratios were better, the policies could be made more competitive, which would increase their sales and attract more good agents to the concept. Everybody wins—the company, the agent, and the policyholder. He called his idea an agent owned reinsurance company (AORC).

Jerry wanted to sell his idea to a company that was hungry, hopefully non-Eastern so it would be more tolerant of his creative, independent style, and that had the capital to deal with rapid growth. It also had to be a company that didn't have a large existing sales force, which would have to be cut in on the deal. After all, the idea was for the company to give up half its profits, and half a loaf of bread only looks good to someone who has none. He narrowed his search down to a handful of candidates, one of which was right in Los Angeles, so he went there first. He had known of Fred Carr from Fred's days in the securities industry, where both he and Jerry operated, though they had never met. The chemistry between the two men was instantaneous. Both are very diligent, yet they have great instincts, which, when they sense big opportunity, they sometimes allow to override their need to know all the facts ahead of time. Jerry and Fred knew they had the makings of something exciting. In those days, Fred was much more adventuresome than he became later. Until about 1987, if something smelled right, he would take a chance on it. Later, he took no meaningful risks, no matter how tempting or even appropriate. Rather, he spent his time managing the outcome of those he had taken earlier. With Jerry Schwartz, in 1977, the timing was perfect, and Fred went with his instincts.

They struck a deal for Jerry to take his concept and develop a business plan, doing the necessary legal and Securities and Exchange Commission research so that Fred could feel comfortable. Jerry's idea was simple, and a natural for the environment of the emerging independent agent of the late 1970s.. Getting regulatory approval for so innovative an idea was another matter. Legal counsel from Executive Life, as well as the outside counsel of Fulbright & Jawarski, agonized and worried with regulators for months. Finally it was decided that the nation's first agent owned reinsurance company would be domiciled in Arizona (the state most receptive to the idea). In 1979, Executive Life of Arizona (ELAR) was born.

Jerry Schwartz's idea would become the Executive Life model around which other marketing corporations were built. Eventually, they would be allowed to have their own agent owned reinsurance companies and become the industry model. At the time, Executive Life was selling term insurance and annuities. Although the annuity business was really starting to take off, Fred understood he needed to balance his liabilities with some more stable traditional life products. He also understood that whole-life products are six or seven times more profitable than annuities. Jerry pointed out that although Fred had done well through his existing distribution system of independent brokers and registered representatives at securities firms, he still did not have the professional life underwriters who sell the really good stuff. Jerry's idea was a group of marketing general agencies that would represent Executive Life exclusively, devoting all of their time to recruiting quality agents for the company. Unlike other companies starting a new distribution system of captive agents, Fred would not have to subsidize it or put up front money. Instead, he would share the profits on the back end through the AORC. Jerry's deal was right up Fred's alley: reward only those who do the job, and reward them on the back end, but promise to reward them big!

Not long after Jerry Schwartz walked into Fred's life, a nationally known, young super agent in the Los Angeles area, who had seen the sign on the building but had also never met Fred, walked in with *his* blockbuster idea. His name was Erik Watts, and his idea was for a company to create a relationship with a group of "exceptional producers" that would give each of them general agent status and fully vested contracts. Previously, most top agents, regardless of their stature, had to work through some type of distributor, an agency manager or marketing general agency (MGA). These individuals received an override or commission on the agent's business. When the relationship turned sour or the producer decided to leave, the agent lost some or all of his (or her) commissions due to vesting schedules.

Agents receive renewal commissions on most of the policies they sell each year that the insured pays a renewal premium. Traditionally, when an agent left a company, he left part or all of his renewal commissions behind. Erik Watts convinced Fred Carr that he could attract the top producers in the industry if he would give them the first fully vested, no-holds-barred contract, and give them the opportunity to deal directly with the company, waiving the middleman relationship and the compensation attached to it. The attraction was that if there were individuals out there who, by themselves, could produce as much as a typical agency, why not treat them accordingly and give them an agency contract that eliminated the middleman? To qualify as an exceptional producer, an agent had to document annual personal first-year commissions of $200,000, and commit to producing at least $100,000 with Executive Life. Again, Fred liked what he heard, and bought in. Exceptional Producers Group became a mega-million-dollar money machine for Executive Life that made millions for Erik and his partners. In short order, Executive Life, between Jerry Schwartz and Erik Watts, had built two distribution systems that would rival those of many a hundred-year-old traditional company.

As an aside, a third harbinger in the insurance industry was charting his course just down the street. In the mid-1970s while Fred Carr was at the Beverly Hills end of Wilshire Boulevard taking charge of an ailing Executive Life, down the street on mid-Wilshire was a general agent for the Connecticut Mutual (the blue-chip company) by the name of S. Caesar "Sy" Raboy. Raboy was an outstanding general agent for Connecticut Mutual, an up and coming member of the Eastern blue-chip society. Sy's burning ambition was to work his way up through the ranks of the venerable Connecticut Mutual and become the first Jewish CEO of a Top 20 life insurance company.

Sy Raboy came about as close to his objective as one could get and still miss. He had every reason to believe he would be the next CEO of the great Connecticut Mutual. He had paid his dues not only by outstanding performance as chief marketing officer of Connecticut Mutual but also as a major industry figure, active in LIMRA (Life Insurance Marketing and Research Association) and GAMA (General Agents and Managers Association). Then, in 1985, he became president of Connecticut Mutual, which left the last step of eventually replacing the chairman, Dennis Mullane. In 1989, the industry was stunned when, at the climax of a supposed power play, the details of which are still unknown to most, Mullane and his board summarily fired Raboy. So bitter was whatever brought it on that the Connecticut Mutual's boardroom chambers, which enshrined the portrait of every Connecticut Mutual president, removed Raboy's picture. (The party line was that Raboy took early retirement, but he told me it was "Retire or get fired.") If it's any consolation, his dream would not have been realized anyway, because someone else beat him to the punch. Fred Carr, the upstart just down Wilshire, would become the first Jewish CEO of a Top 20 life insurance company.

It happened in 1986, when the company Fred Carr built, virtually from scratch, passed the Connecticut Mutual to become the fifteenth-largest life insurance company in the United States. Fred had joined this elite club the way most Jews gain entrance to the exclusive fraternities created by American culture—he performed his way into it. He didn't get invited, he simply arrived one day as CEO of the number 15 company, whether they wanted him or not. For a lot of reasons which I choose to believe had nothing to do with Fred's ethnic background, the establishment definitely didn't want Fred Carr among the Top 20.

Fred had achieved, as an outsider, what Sy Raboy had coveted as an insider. However, the admiration or even acceptance of the establishment was never Fred's goal. Many thought his attitude toward the rest of the industry was arrogant, but that was really not the case. It's just that Fred is a man of broad horizons who has little interest in his immediate surroundings. He had a goal just as Sy Raboy did. He wanted to be number 1, not number 15. He wanted to change the future of the industry, not to assimilate into its past. He aimed for the stars and hit the moon. Like Raboy, Carr's lifelong ambition would never be realized. One man's self-actualization can be another man's stepping stone. Their critics might brand them both as failures, and they might even view each other that way, yet I believe that these two men of very differing business philosophies both accomplished much that is worth studying.

The Birth of a Movement

While Fred Carr's team was taking form in the late 1970s, a revolutionary new product concept was also taking form, right there in Southern California. This concept became the vehicle for Executive Life's eventual success, as well as that of a number of other nouveau companies that would lead the industry into the next decade. The interest-sensitive product revolution in the life insurance industry was started in 1975 by a prominent actuary named Jim Anderson, when at the 7th Pacific

Insurance Conference in Santa Barbara, California, he called the industry's attention to a little-known concept. Called universal life, the product Jim suggested would unbundle the life insurance contract in a way that broke out the mortality (cost of providing the death benefit) interest credited on policy values, and the expense charges allocated to the policy (loads), which are its key components.

The key to the concept lay in how companies calculated the cash values within the contract. In the past, cash values had always been calculated on a prospective basis. This meant the company had to look one year ahead and guarantee an assumed interest rate to reach the cash value the company wanted to provide for the policyholder. Of course, when you're guaranteeing anything, you fall under the constraints of the insurance regulators, who have a very guarded view about anything that is guaranteed. The structural difference in universal life had to do with the way non-forfeiture values (those guaranteed cash values available upon surrender) of the contract are calculated. By working only within the realm of guarantees, the life insurance company was restricted from passing on periodic superior performance to the consumer. By declaring an interest rate at the end of the year rather than guaranteeing it in advance, the company was encouraged to reach for better yields, knowing that if it fell short, it would not be stuck with obligations it could not fulfil on current performance.

The universal life concept that Jim presented permitted retrospective interest rates—later to be called declared rates—based upon the actual experience of the company. Also, the company under this proposal could annually declare a mortality charge, pro-actively in this case, based upon *actual* experience rather than the conservative 1958 CSO (Commissioners' Standard Ordinary Mortality Table) rates, which were put into the policy as guarantees. The CSO mortality table, as the name implies, was based upon the rate at which people died in a given year. This meant that although the contract required a guaranteed maximum mortality charge based upon the 1958 CSO, they could declare annual charges based upon experience. Each year the policy would have a guaranteed maximum premium, based on the maximum (1958 CSO) mortality and the minimum guaranteed cash values, which in turn were based on the conservative minimum contractual interest rates. It would also have a "target" premium, based on the mortality charge resulting from current experience, as well as on the interest rate declared on last year's cash values and projected by the company as the interest rate it feels it can pay on into the future. This resulted in two schedules of values in the contract. The first, and by far lowest, would be the guaranteed cash values, based upon guaranteed mortality and interest. The second would be the illustrated or projected values, based upon company expectations for interest and mortality.

The earliest successful attempt at turning Anderson's concept into a product came in 1979, from Life of California (later to become E. F. Hutton and owned by the brokerage firm of the same name and eventually to become First Capital Life which collapsed shortly after First Executive). It piloted a product called Complete Life™. At about the same time, another California company, TransAmerica-Occidental Life, introduced its offering in the form of a universal life product whose interest rates were indexed to U.S. Treasury Bills. At Executive Life, Al Jacob liked the concept of an interest-sensitive product—that is, one that passed company investment performance on to the consumer. However, as we have already seen, he felt that the flexibility it offered the consumer by the universal life approach would hurt profitability and eventually affect the quality of product the company could afford to offer the public. So, in 1979, he introduced his own offering, which Executive Life called Irreplaceable Life I℠. The old cliché that says California is the birthplace of innovation in America was certainly operating when the life insurance industry started to look at interest-sensitive products.

Just why so much of the innovation and leadership in the life insurance industry during the 1980s came out of California is hard to figure. One thing is certain: those of us who hail from the Midwest and have a predisposed attitude about what goes on out there are usually surprised by what we find when we move to California. At least I was. The first thing I learned, which should have been obvious, is that most of the people are from somewhere else, which makes it a melting pot of cultures from around the country and the world. A hundred years earlier, the East Coast was the same way, and it became the source of new ideas and new leaders. In the financial services industry, the world's money is moving to the Pacific rim and, of course, California is the gateway to this region. Although this was not true of the insurance industry, which, when Fred Carr took over at First Executive Corporation, was centered in the Northeast, I believe this too may change in years to come. Today, the world's largest life insurance company is in the same country as the world's largest bank: Japan. Just as the banking and real estate industries on the West Coast have been the first to feel the influx of the Pacific rim interest in their businesses, so the life insurance industry may experience it in the future.

4

The Management of Risk in a Product-Driven World

"The company [FEXC] has been at the forefront of the sweeping product changes that have transformed life insurance from a staid, mortality-oriented industry to one where success depends largely on a polished investment strategy and new product development. ... First Executive also has a rock-solid balance sheet, one of the strongest in the industry."
— Udayan D. Ghose, Donaldson, Lufkin & Jenrette Securities Corporation

Armed with a source of capital, an investment strategy that assured profitability, and a potential for nationwide distribution, Fred Carr needed only to turn loose the artistic Al Jacob to design the innovative products that would bring it all together for Executive Life. To understand today's life insurance products, we must first look at three things: the actuarial risk management factors a company considers when developing a product line; the actual assumptions that go into designing the policy; and the sales environment and practices used to get it on

49

the books. Then we can look at the actual construction of the interest-sensitive whole-life product and see why it and its universal life counterpart had the impact they did. A simple review of these aspects of life insurance can once and for all take the mystery out of the product so many spend so much of their money on *and yet so few really understand.*

Risk management is central to the casualty business, where you have to insure against claims that can vary dramatically from one state to the other, from one courtroom to the next, as well as common disasters, which are totally unpredictable. Life insurance mortality is easier to manage, in that people die over a long period of time, usually in a quite predictable fashion. The thing that you are insuring against, death, can be thoroughly assessed as to probability by a good actuary, backed by a good underwriter. There is only one claim per policy, and you know what the exact amount of that claim will be. On the other hand, one cannot examine a physical property to determine the incidence of earthquake, hurricane, fire, tornado, and other types of natural disaster. The closest you can come is to determine which properties, by way of their location, are more susceptible to this type of event. Nor can one determine very easily upon becoming ill, what the severity of the illness and the various medical costs and physicians' fees will be. Again, you can look at the propensity of the risk toward illness, but cannot determine the expected claims with too much accuracy. In fact, the health-care industry has practically given up on calculating rates. Instead, it offers ASO (Administration Only) Plans and nets the cost of coverage to the insured. On the other hand, the death rate is one per person, and the cost involved when you're selling life insurance is predetermined, agreed to, and prepaid.

Fred Carr quickly figured out that the life insurance industry was no longer in the mortality business. It was in the asset management business. During the twenty years since the introduction of the Commissioners' 1958 mortality table, the risk rates charged on life insurance policies had dropped 90 percent or more, and with them went the profit on the mortality aspect of the life insurance contract. True, there were certain companies, primarily health carriers like Washington National or term insurance companies like Federal Kemper, that were more in the risk management end of the business. But Fred felt strongly that in the middle and upper markets, where the big boys played, life insurance was fast becoming an investment product, and asset management would be the name of the game. He was also fairly confident that most of the companies he planned to compete with didn't know asset management as a discipline of daily vigilance. In an industry where investment committees typically met quarterly to give their rubber stamp of approval to the stodgy choices of the investment officer, a portfolio manager like Fred would seemingly run circles around his competitors. Still, as we shall see, there are other risk factors in managing an insurance company, none of which should be taken lightly.

Rather than worrying about the mortality risks on the liability side of the balance sheet, Fred reasoned that the industry should have been worrying about the more uncertain risks with regard to the assets backing the liability. He called these risks the *persistency* of the liability. This approach is broken down into the *duration* of the liability, the ability of the liability to be *called upon demand*, and the *probability* that the liability *will be called*. The concept of liability persistency was introduced by Fred, and although the term "asset/liability matching" had been tossed around in the industry for some time, he was the first one actually to build his entire balance sheet around it. As we shall see later, his commitment to this concept enabled the company to withstand pressures in the disastrous meltdown environment of 1990 that would have buried almost any other financial institution in America. Despite the ultimate outcome for his company, this discipline of asset/liability matching is probably Fred's most enduring contribution to the industry.

On the asset side of the balance sheet, the issues were *liquidity, duration,* and *interest-rate exposure.* Fred constructed a balance sheet in his company whereby the average duration of the asset was less than the expected duration of the liability. In other words, the invested assets matured and became cash more quickly than the liabilities came due in the form of benefits or surrenders. Because of this, Executive Life was consistently by far the most liquid company among the Top 25 insurers in the United States throughout the 1980s. Fred paid a big price to stay liquid and focused on interest-rate exposure, which was one reason the company was viewed by the experts as almost unsinkable.

The Management of Risk

In insurance underwriting, there are basically four risk characteristics:

1. Catastrophic events that may never happen, such as an earthquake.
2. Non-catastrophic, but also non-manageable, events, such as an automobile accident.
3. Fluctuation events that are likely to happen, but where the timing and frequency vary, such as sickness.
4. Events that will happen, but the timing is uncertain, such as death.

When we narrow risk management down to the life insurance business, we see that it tends to become more *financially* focused than *event*-focused. In the life insurance industry, recent performance emphasis has been placed on return on equity or return on invested surplus. Because of the shortages of capital in the industry, companies must plan for surplus needs created not only by the natural course of writing business, but also by certain risks inherent in the nature of the business. Today, these risks are essential in the inherent considerations of products and markets a company chooses to pursue. Actuaries separate such risks into various components, defined as C-1, C-2, C-3, and C-4 for purposes of quick reference and use in their actuarial equations.[1] Today, these considerations are at the very center

1. Source: Michael L. Smith, FSA, ``Financial Disciplines Seminar and Quantifying Surplus,'' *Actuarial Digest* (December 1985), with the Life Insurance Marketing and Research Association (LIMRA).

of the financial services industry crisis. A simple understanding of the components can help in grasping many of the problems facing not only the life insurance industry, but also the banking and the late savings and loan industries.

Asset default/yield impact (C-1). The key issue here is the drive for yield. Those companies whose investment strategies reach for yield must pay the appropriate risk charge for access to a higher yield. In the junk bond market, a life insurance company does that through a special reserve required by the National Association of Insurance Commissioners (NAIC). This special reserve is known as the Mandatory Securities Valuation Reserve (MSVR). MSVR is required to be set aside in addition to normal reserves specifically to prepare for possible fluctuation in values due to the riskier nature of certain investments.

As we know from the experience at Executive Life, even the extra cushion of MSVR can be inadequate to meet the risks inherent in certain types of investments. However, when a life insurance company invests in what the NAIC calls a "no bond," meaning it is rated below BBB with Standard & Poor's or Baa with Moody's, it must put up this special reserve. Depending upon how poorly the bond is rated, the reserve may range from an additional 5% to an additional 20%. Thus, in the event of a default, when you reach for yield, you must price the expected default rate into your expected net yield. This, in actuarial terms, is simply a need to pay a risk charge for access to higher yields.

Premium inadequacy (C-2). Premium inadequacy is simply the validity of experience assumptions. The assumptions used by actuaries to determine how much premium is needed to meet morbidity or mortality charges in an insurance company are based on fairly predictable events so far as disability and death are concerned. However, one must take into account such factors as the business environment at the initial pricing of the product, and monitor results to consider repricing the existing books of business.

One of the powerful tools used by life insurance companies of which the consumer is generally unaware is the fact that a company can adjust for premium adequacy, even thoughthe actual premium on a whole-life policy does not change. They do so in a mutual company by increasing or reducing the dividend they pay, based on mortality and/or persistency and expense experiences. In a stock company, they do it by adjusting the credited interest rate and/or the mortality charge levied on the contract. In either case, the company can, in the current regulatory environment, use sales materials that illustrate results beyond current experience. Then, once the policy is on the books, if they fail to achieve projected results, they can adjust the mortality or risk-rate charges up or down based upon actual experience. They also can adjust the credited interest rates up or down based on experience. This is all well and good, but in reality there are no effective regulatory restrictions in most states that require increases to be based upon experience. In other words, the old bait and switch is alive and well in the life insurance business, and is indeed practiced by many companies.

Interest-rate change—product design impact (C-3). This is the underwater risk that occurs when, due to an environment of higher interest rates, certain assets in the portfolio are discounted on a mark to market basis, due to perceived decline in value. For example, in a 12% interest-rate environment, a 9% bond in the company's portfolio would trade at a discount from its carrying value, should it have to be liquidated to meet an obligation of the company. If assets and liabilities in the company are properly matched, then the underwater issue is not as damaging because, in theory, the company can hold the asset to maturity and receive its full carrying value before it becomes necessary to meet the obligation. However, as recent times have shown, assumptions about the duration of liabilities can often be incorrect.

Business risks (C-4). These risks are not actuarial or financial by design, but simply have to do with the choices and decisions executives make in running the company. Sometimes these can just be matters of bad judgment, such as going into markets for which the company is ill-prepared. Poor expense management would probably be the most common of C-4 risks; in addition, we should mention lawsuits whereby the management behaves in an inappropriate manner, causing shareholders, investors, or policyholders to sue, or any other unexpected event caused by management performance. Historically, some of these risks seemed remote. Today, the suits piling up against those who set the investment strategies of a number of Top 25 companies are a painful reminder of the fiduciary responsibility companies have for the policyholder funds entrusted to them.

Obviously, in addition to the C-1 through C-4 risks, there are other factors that affect the profitability of a life insurance company. Some of these items include experience fluctuations, inflation, regulation, tax laws, competition, production projections, sales processes, and assumption mismatches. All these factors affect the strategy of how a life insurance company develops its book of business and manages its assets and liabilities.

The Psychomedia Risk

To all of these considerations, I would suggest to the industry's actuaries and investment officers that in 1990, First Executive Corporation demonstrated that there is yet another risk—one none of them factored into their strategies. Fred Carr was responsible about the C-2, C-3, and C-4 risks. As to the C-1 risk, which is the asset default risk, he was covered by requirements laid down by the NAIC because of the heavy mandatory reserve requirements (Executive Life had almost $1 billion in this MSVR cushion fund by 1989). What neither he nor the actuaries had counted on was a fifth risk, which we will coin as the

C-5 risk, or *psychomedia risk*. C-5 is the risk that even though you do everything right, something unexpected will happen, which creates the perception of failure although the facts don't support it. When this occurs, the actual facts become subordinate to the perception. The result is a crisis in confidence, which leads to a run at the bank, or in this case, an avalanche of policy surrenders. It was this psychomedia risk created by the media that everyone, especially Fred Carr, so greatly underestimated.

The psychomedia risk has its origins in the media, which promulgates notions and perceptions that move like electricity through our computerized financial services industry and can create a crisis in confidence overnight. This modern technological phenomenon of the instantaneous communications environment has advanced dramatically over the past decade. I believe the C-5 psychomedia risk may be the most difficult to manage in the future.

Policy Design

As we have seen, the life insurance industry was able to disguise a host of inefficiencies because of the complexity of the product, the tax advantage of all inside build-up, and the fact that time has an effect on the value of money that usually exceeds its perceived role in the end result. Fred Carr and other leaders in the interest-sensitive movement eliminated much of the mystery when, in 1979, they introduced the new, unbundled, interest-sensitive products. The dominant product of the movement was universal life, which also made its debut in 1979. Then, in 1980, Executive Life introduced Irreplaceable Life II℠, the product that would scoop universal life in the big case market and be the backbone of the company's portfolio. A look at this product is helpful in showing not only how simple life insurance can be, but also what a genuinely excellent place it has in almost everyone's financial plans. The unbundling approach to whole life promoted by Jim Anderson of the actuarial firm of Tillinghast, Nelson & Warren (now Towers Perrin) in

1975 was perfected by Al Jacob with Irreplaceable Life II^{SM}. Interestingly, the way he perfected it was by *not* abandoning some of the more fundamental aspects of traditional whole life. There are four, and only four, basic assumptions that go into the design of a life insurance contract. Everything else is a derivation or embellishment on these four points:

- **Mortality.** The amount of the premium annually allocated to the cost of providing death benefit for a given year. This component has been dramatically reduced, due to improved experience and aggressive assumptions.

- **Expenses.** The cost of putting the policy on the books and keeping it there. This includes agent commissions, underwriting expenses, and maintenance costs, the largest of which is data processing.

- **Persistency.** The assumption of how many of those policies sold will renew each year after the first. This is important because the longer a policy is kept by the holder, the more profitable it is to the company.

- **Investment spread.** This consists of the assumed spread between what the company predicts it can earn on funds invested and what it projects it will credit to policyholders. For example, if the company feels it can earn a net of 10%, and wishes to retain 150 basis points for its profit margins, it may design a product on which it assumes that 8.5% interest will be credited to the policyholder.

The Irreplaceable Life II^{SM} product is an excellent example of unbundling. It was the industry's first no-load product, in that instead of applying expenses across the board to the early cash values of all policies, there were no direct expense charges to the policy. Instead, it allocated expenses in the form of a heavy surrender charge, applied only to those policies that lapsed during the first twenty years. This created a dual schedule of values in the contract, one known as an *accumulation account*, which was what you got if you kept the policy over the long haul, and the other known as *cash surrender value*, which was what you got if you quit before the surrender charges expired (*Accumula-*

tion account = Premium – Mortality Charges + Interest). Each year the insured was given an annual statement that explained exactly what was going on with his or her policy. It showed the accumulation account (what you got if you kept it), the cash surrender value (what you got if you quit early), the mortality charged for the cost of the death benefit, the interest rate credited, and the premium due. That was all there was to it. At last, a policyholder could understand where his money was going and what he was getting for it.

Irreplaceable Life II^SM offered guaranteed-level premiums, a guaranteed face amount, and a vanishing premium that became available when, at a given point (usually after six to eight years), the accumulation account, based on current credited interest rates, projected results that carried the policy without any further premium payments.

Through the management of assumptions about mortality, expenses, persistency, and investments, the company was able to design very competitive products because Executive Life had good reason to be more aggressive then most. After all, its net investment yield was by far the highest among the Top 25 peer companies. As we shall see, experience taught Executive Life and the rest of the industry that extrapolating the performance of a few good years over the life of a policy can prove disastrous to one's credibility.

Each of these four assumptions can dramatically impact profitability to the company and performance to the policyholder. In the environment of the new-wave products, companies became more and more aggressive in their assumptions about these four variables. Expenses for the data-processing systems to service the new products far exceeded expectations, and had to be amortized over unrealistically long periods, considering the short shelf life of today's insurance products. Mortality assumptions led to a literal price war that went so far as to project continued reductions into the future for which there was essentially no factual support. Persistency assumptions in most universal life products were often more optimistic than experienced. For example, according to a 1984 LIMRA study, many companies assumed that people would pay the second year's premium 90 percent of the time on a universal life product. When the experience was measured a few years later, it was learned that only about 60 percent were doing so.

Mortality and persistency assumptions were just that—assumptions. You really cannot, as a company, affect these variables too much one way or the other. One company underwrites a risk about as well as another, and persistency is a function of the caliber of agent the marketing general agency (MGA) recruits, which is something over which the company has little direct control. Expenses and investment spreads *are* directly the responsibility of the company. Fred Carr built his company to have some of the lowest expense ratios in the industry, year in year out.

The biggest disparity between promises and performance, however, was in the area of investment spreads. This was the portion of the contract from which most companies derived their greatest profits, and it was also the key assumption that drove the competitiveness of the product. It was in the area of investment spreads that Executive Life went into overdrive and blew away the competition.

From Need to Greed

In the context of the 1980s, there was a great opportunity for the individual agent to revisit everybody he or she had ever sold life insurance to and convince them to move to the new interest-sensitive products. And that's exactly what they did. This raised havoc for many establishment companies in that much of their book of business was being rolled. They had a simple choice: develop their own competitive products, or have their book of business fed upon by their own agents and replaced by Executive Life and its peers. They chose to develop competitive interest-sensitive products; but, understandably, there was a period of time during which they were reluctant about commissioning agents to resell existing policies and update them into a product that was less profitable for the company. This was certainly logical since the company was going from a very attractive position to a much less attractive position. On top of that, the agent wanted them to commission him for the transaction. Unfortunately, the agent had the company over a barrel. In most cases, the companies acquiesced, going ahead and paying full commissions or near-full commissions to agents for rewriting their own policies within the company. Even this, however, had only limited success in that the products developed by the Eastern mutuals—given the restraints of their investment strategies and their substantial assets already locked up in various less attractive investments—were not as competitive as those of the new breed.

To the agent of the 1980s, it was a windfall. No longer did he or she have to try to convince people to buy life insurance out of need, because they loved someone else whose financial security they wanted to provide for. Instead, he could talk about greed, competitive interest rates, internal rates of return! He could now sell cash accumulation vehicles that simply beat everything in the conservative arena, including treasuries, CDs, corporate bonds, and similar types of fixed-asset investments. Meanwhile, the best part of all was that the agent never had to ask the client for a check: "Just give me your old Prudential policy, and I'll give you a new policy for a larger face amount and the same premium that will accumulate much more value, or a smaller premium that will accumulate the same value as your old contract." Either way, the agent had it so good he could hardly believe it. No need to sell the need, no need to ask the person to write a check payable to his company. "Just give me your old policy, I'll give you a better one, and I'll make a dandy commission."

This, of course, raised havoc with the balance sheets for a number of life insurance companies. Naturally, one might expect that Executive Life, having been the purveyor of many of these changing products, would receive its share of criticism. Historically, life insurance had always been perceived to be somewhere between a safe but mediocre investment and a safe but terrible investment. Now, safety was the sizzle. If one can use that conflict in terms, that's what made it a viable product. Great interest rates on what everyone knows is one of the safest things you can buy! Life insurance became all the rage as a cash accumulation vehicle. Life insurance agents had always done needs selling—emphasizing the importance of providing family security in the event of premature death or disability. Now, they could go to an individual and talk about accumulating fat amounts of money for retirement on a tax-free basis. Much more exciting.

In 1983, Executive Life introduced a concept that really crossed the line so far as the rest of the industry was concerned. In that year, they introduced Irreplaceable Life VI^{SM}, a truly revolutionary product. It was designed solely to move the cash values out of other companies and stuff them into their own coffers, even if it meant some serious mortality risks with agents stampeding to their old clients to convince them to upgrade to the new interest-sensitive products. Time was of the essence. The idea behind Irreplaceable Life VI^{SM} was to go to any individual who owned a traditional whole-life policy and offer to exchange it for a new Irreplaceable Life VI^{SM} policy, *without any evidence of insurability whatsoever*. "Give me your policy and I'll give you a new one, which pays a competitive interest rate and requires absolutely no evidence of insurability!"

The agents had a field day with this one. Many of them took advantage of the guaranteed insurability aspect of Irreplaceable Life VI^{SM} with regard to the types of risks they brought in. However, Al Jacob priced the product accordingly, and permitted for mortality charges that could accommodate any shortfall in the profit projections created by higher-than-expected claims. Furthermore, he arranged a pool of ten reinsurers who shared the mortality risk with them from the first dollar, so the risk the company retained on any one life was minimal. The product was designed to grab the assets that had accumulated in older policies sold by the traditional companies. To this end, it was enormously successful. Within just a few years, Executive Life accumulated several hundred million dollars of assets on this one product line alone.

With all this newfound success, Fred was confronted by the

ever-present problem that it costs money to grow a life insurance company. As we have seen, when you write a dollar of premium, it costs more than a dollar to put it on the books. The difference comes from the capital and surplus of the company or, in the vernacular of most corporations, retained earnings. But Fred Carr had a place to go for the money. Wall Street. He still had quite a reputation there; although somewhat tarnished by the collapse of the Enterprise Fund, he was still known as a brilliant and creative fund manager, who was more diligent than most of his peers in the industry. People believed that Fred, with his reputation for thoroughness and due diligence, would surely have gleaned the *créme de la créme* from the junk bond market. For no knowledgeable money manager would deny that the majority of the earlier issuers of junk bonds were solid, mainstream corporations, which wanted the money to fund their growth through the sale of such securities to the public, just as Fred did when he went to the Street. Given his acumen, many believed that his company was a surefire winner in an otherwise lethargic industry. Every time Fred went to Wall Street, he had no problem raising capital—whether he was selling more common stock or various Preferreds, including certain convertible types. When Wall Street wasn't receptive, there was always surplus relief, the arcane method whereby life insurance companies solved the problem created by surplus strain by borrowing surplus from other carriers. In effect, they rented the surplus of other companies and paid a fee for it, which was tantamount to interest. For these complicated transactions Fred relied upon Al Jacob, which may have been his first big mistake.

So, Fred had solved the problem of Executive Life founder Otto Forst and dozens like him, who had grown life insurance companies only to have them collapse due to the shortage of capital. He could go to the Street for capital, or he could go to his friend, Al Jacob, for surplus relief. Al had also given him Irreplaceable Life II^{SM}, the flagship of the industry's most innovative product portfolio. There was no stopping him now. Executive Life was on a roll as no life insurance company before it.

II
ON A ROLL

5

The Hottest Franchise in the Life Insurance Business

"First Executive Corporation is one of the strongest life insurers in the United States, with shareholders' equity of more than $1.5 billion at year end 1986, no debt, and total assets of $14.4 billion ... the company's strong financial position is a counter to potential criticisms of investment policy."
—Johnson, Lane Equity Research Report,
February 23, 1987

There is a small village in Germany, nestled on the banks of the Rhine. It is called Bingen, and the only thing they do there is make wine. Very tasty wine. After World War I, American soldiers stationed in the region used to take their furlough in Bingen. Because that was all there was to do there, they would drink the wine. Lots of it. When they returned to camp, very hungover, they would tell friends that they had been to Bingen, which they pronounced with a soft "g," which made it sound like they had been "bingeing." Hence the slang term, "going on a binge," was born. Webster defines a binge as a drunken celebration or spree. Binge is the only word to describe the decade-long spree much of the life insurance industry was on in the 1980s. We had been as sober as a judge for our entire history, but we made up for lost time during this extraordinary period. Companies and agents alike binged, and many are now paying the price.

The Promise Binge

The companies went on an illustration binge. As Hay Group consultant Philip Dutter put it in a 1987 paper in the *Journal of American Society of CLU & ChFc*, "with few exceptions, life insurance companies continue to set premium rates using expense assumptions that are *substantially better than anything they have achieved to date* and crediting rates that chew up expected investment margins. Yet, this reckless price competition continues unabated."[1]

The life insurance industry is one of the most heavily regulated with regard to protecting existing policyholders, but one of the least regulated so far as what an agent can do to convince a person to become a policyholder in the first place. We have looked at risk management, the assumptions that go into the design of a policy, and the way a good interest-sensitive policy works. Now we will look at the biggest risk that life insurance companies took in the 1980s: the risk of illustrating policies in a way that could eventually cause a complete collapse of their credibility with the consumer.

It wasn't so apparent at the time, but when the interest-sensitive products hit the streets, the impact was not just the product itself. Equally important was the personal computer explosion, which took place simultaneously. For the first time, with the aid of his pc, the agent could create company-sponsored, cus-

1. Philip Dutter, ``Now for the Really Tough Times," *Journal of American Society of CLU & ChFC* (May 1987).

tomized proposals. He could now show a real investment proposal to a prospective customer, instead of a corny, pre-fabricated brochure, with pictures of widows and old people looking forlorn, and blank spaces in which to pencil in the numbers that would save them from a life of abject poverty. The agent finally had something competitive to sell and the credibility of a computerized illustration with which to sell it. The impact of these two innovations at the same time was intoxicating to companies and agents alike. In fact, many believe the interest-sensitive product revolution would not have had nearly the impact it did, had it not been for the complementary pc revolution. It was an extraordinary example of the role timing can play in innovation.

Many thought the agent would never buy into computerized illustrations in place of the personalized illustration he or she was used to working with. They were dead wrong. No other single industry embraced the pc and the many support functions it offered the way life insurance did. In fact, a number of observers view this as the single most important development in the sale of life insurance in recent times, including the introduction of interest-sensitive products.

What computer-generated illustration gave the agent was the thing he needed most with the customer: credibility. Prospective buyers tended to believe computer illustrations. People assumed that the numbers were, if not a guarantee, at least a promise of the company, even if there were disclaimers at the bottom of the page. If the computerized print-out projected it, people expected it. For example, a key development of the period was vanishing premium life. The main feature of these policies was that they would project a point at which, given the continuation of current company experience, the policy would require no further premium payments and, in effect, become paid up. The problem arose in later years when, due to poor mortality experience or lower investment returns, a policy whose premiums had vanished suddenly reappeared, requiring additional premium payments. However, to the typical buyer, *a projected vanish is an expected vanish*. Failures to vanish on schedule, or "unvanishes," are viewed as broken promises not just by the policyholder, but also by most agents. Companies became indignant when agents reacted angrily in the early 1990s to the fact that practically nothing they sold in the mid-1980s was vanishing as projected in the sales illustration.

Although many in the home office wouldn't admit it, the agents had a right to be upset. These were the same salespeople who had been trained by the same companies for decades to sell dividend projections, which were presented as promises the insured could expect would be kept. They were trained to tell the policyholder that "although these dividends aren't guaranteed, the XYZ Mutual has either met or exceeded its dividend projections for each of the 100+ years it has been in existence." That may not have been a factual guarantee, but when you deliver your projections for as long as the life insurance industry has, one can certainly argue that it is a de facto guarantee. And I fear that, with the guidance of some eager lawyers, many policyholders will. The big mistake the established companies made was that they let the newcomers, like Executive Life, who had no track record, pull them into the prevailing mentality of the hot money of the 1980s. Newer companies had no history, so they could only talk prospectively. It so happened that the current high-yield environment of the time projected into the future better than the long-term results of the past.

The illustration game was off and running by 1982. Some companies even allowed agents to plug their own interest-rate assumptions into their computers, until things got out of hand. Then they put caps on the rates that the systems showing their products would accept.

Agents became numbers salespeople instead of needs salespeople. There were obvious benefits, not the least of which was the fact that the products were easier to sell, so the agents' commissions soared. One positive development was that new agents coming into the business found the entry barriers lower because they could sell living benefits that competed with other investments.

The real problems started when companies realized that their product could be as good as they were willing to say it was! Unbelievable as it seems, this is a true statement. All you had to do was build assumptions into your policy projections that were more optimistic than the next guy's. Experience needn't have anything to do with projections unless you wanted it to. We weren't selling insurance anymore. We were selling configurations of numbers designed to leapfrog those of the last agent on the premises, or the one we were competing with for the sale. Many industry watchers called it the shift from a need sale to a greed sale. The real product of most life insurance companies of the 1980s *was* their illustration system. The ability of an agent to reconfigure the numbers until he got the deal was the name of the game. In the end, the credibility that the computerized illustration gave to the agent worked against him. Those illustrations were required by law to be delivered with the policy. Now, when a policyholder gets a notice that his projected vanished premium of seven years will be twelve years instead, he pulls his illustration and calls his agent. Exactly what he calls his agent, I will leave to the reader's imagination.

As we have seen, only four basic assumptions go into a life insurance policy: mortality, expenses, persistency, and investment spread. To be more competitive, all a company had to do was be more aggressive in how it predicted its performance in one or more of these variables. So, companies began to outreach one another's illustrated projections. As Philip Dutter stated, most projected interest and expense assumptions were beyond anything they had experienced. If that wasn't enough, some companies actually projected that after ten or fifteen years, they would experience reductions in mortality and increases in interest spreads earned. Usually there was no logical basis for this, let alone one that was factual. One might say that the life insurance industry went from ineptness to irresponsibility in its attempt to compete. First we delivered less than we were capable of, then we promised more than we were capable of.

To his credit, Fred Carr was never willing to project credited interest rates in a given year beyond the company's current net investment yield. Of course, he reached for yield and he got it, for a while. Still, Executive Life never did project beyond what it currently experienced. It was an honest product, based on credited rates that were tied to the actual company performance. The thing Fred forgot, however, is that life insurance is a long-term purchase. This fact really demonstrated for Executive Life, as for the rest of the industry, the difference between an honest product and a product with genuine integrity. The second takes into consideration in its illustrations more than just what is expected of a company trying to make a sale *today*. It considers the long term and the many unknowns the future holds, with the focus on performance rather than promises for the policyholder. Many observers feel that much of the life insurance industry went too far in its effort to give more competitive value to its policyholders during the 1980s. In the process, the product lost a good deal of its integrity.

The rest of the industry, which followed the lead of Executive Life and a few others, was forced into credit rates that were unrealistically high in order to compete. This created a real credibility gap that agents and companies are going to have to live with for a long time to come. The consequence of this ill-thought-out behavior probably is likely to result in a number of lawsuits, and errors and omission insurance will probably go through the roof. As was the case with Executive Life's perceived weaknesses, the issues are more complex than they appear at first blush.

The debate about illustration credibility is an interesting one. On the one hand, there were the large, established companies, which had built up their investment portfolios in a different era. They bought the most conservative corporate bonds and invested heavily in long-term commercial mortgages in the lower-interest-rate environment of the 1960s and 1970s. Most of these credits were still on the books when the new-wave products hit. At the time, few people took note that the high interest rates prevailing simultaneously with the introduction of these new products were the basic reason they looked so great. Obviously, the new money rates for older companies were much higher than their reported net investment yield, which was spread over their entire portfolio. To compete in the new environment, companies had to distinguish between old policies and the old investments backing them, and new policies and the new money backing them. Critics, notably Executive Life, argued that this was a bait and switch, and that some day the new policyholders would become old policyholders and could look forward to the same double standard. It was a good argument. On the other hand, if high rates prevailed for a decade or so, then plummeted for a long while, could old policyholders look forward to better treatment than new policyholders? I don't think so.

Meanwhile, the new-generation companies like Executive Life didn't have old portfolios or old policyholders to look after. They had new money rates at a time when new money was hot and, therefore, so were their products. They didn't have to project rates beyond those they were getting. In fact, for ten years, Executive Life consistently projected interest rates that were not only below their net investment yield as a company, but were also below those rates they were currently crediting on existing policies. Some critics argued that long-term projections on credited rates should be based upon long-term historical averages, rather than on one period of extraordinarily high rates that had not withstood the test of time. That, too, was a good argument. However, the industry didn't buy it. Everyone got on the bandwagon of long-term double-digit projections, which turned out to be a big mistake.

What many in the life insurance public and many life insurance agents don't really seem to understand is that we don't just *buy* life insurance. Rather we *are buying* it, year in, year out, as we pay the premiums. The performance of the company on invested premiums will fluctuate, based upon investment performance, expenses, persistency, and other factors affecting the book of business. They will adjust the credited rates on your contract based on the dividend schedule they elect if a mutual company, or the interest rates and mortality charges they choose to apply if they are a stock company. Companies can only project what they think their experience will be in these areas; but it is inappropriate, in my opinion, when they project performance beyond that they have previously experienced. Although at Executive Life they never did this, given the way things turned out, I believe companies should go a step further and consider both the average duration of the projected interest period and the average duration of the liability. For example, if the company's average universal life policy is on the books for ten years and its average asset has a duration of seven years, adjustments should be made in projecting the rate beyond their net investment yield on average over the previous seven years. The matching of yields, based on duration of assets and liabilities, would be a breakthrough in product integrity.

The Replacement Binge

The illustration binge set the stage for the second binge, that of the agent. Armed with the new credibility of computerized illustrations and a product almost too good to be true, agents were ready to redefine life insurance selling.

At first, agents just went out and sold as they always had, only with a new, dedicated zeal. Everybody was a winner. It quickly became apparent, however, that the real economic opportunity for salespeople was not as a missionary looking for new converts to the more competitive interest-sensitive policies. One could make more money and serve the public interest just as well by saving the old flock from the errors of their ways, the chief error being their misfortune in owning a traditional life insurance policy. Up to this point, the replacement of another company's insurance policies was considered unprofessional by the established voices of the industry. Referred to as "twisting" in earlier uniform state insurance codes, replacement usually required extensive paperwork justifying the agent's action in most states. As it became obvious to all that the new products could supply superior value to almost any holder of an old policy (unless their health had deteriorated), the rules for twisting changed. The industry term went from "twisting" to "replacement." Then finally to "updating." *What had been considered a questionable business practice at best became an industry-within-an-industry.*

The agents of the life insurance industry went on a binge the likes of which it had never seen and hopefully will not see again. Established agents went after the old policies of everyone they called on. Soon, agents realized that their own policyholders were being called on by competitors and asked to update their coverage. In an effort to update their own book of business, they presented their companies with a difficult choice: Either the existing carrier paid the agent a new first-year commission for rewriting a policy that was already on the books; or the agent would take the client to a competitor where he or she could get paid. The company, on the other hand, lost a very profitable piece of old business on which all the acquisition costs had been paid, in exchange for a new policy with narrower profit margins and on which it had to use its surplus to pay first-year commissions all over again. The agent had the company against the wall. In most cases, the companies paid all or at least most of the new commission in order to keep the policyholder. This was devastating to the financial strength of many older companies with large blocks of very profitable old policies.

To their credit, some of the biggest companies stood their ground and proposed non-commissionable or minimally commissionable update programs for their policyholders. Most noteworthy was the noble Northwestern Mutual, always the conscience of the industry, which went through the interest-sensitive revolution almost without missing a beat. Management there launched a massive campaign, offering policyholders more competitive yields in exchange for forfeiting the low policy loan rates of yesterday. In exchange for a direct recognition rate (a narrower spread between credited and loan rates, whereby borrowed values receive a lower yield than those left in the policy), the insured would begin experiencing the pass through of more competitive investment rates.

Other giants, such as the mighty Prudential and Metropolitan

Life, had mostly captive agents, who were told that if they wanted to remain with the company, they would update policy-holders according to the company program. But most companies did not have this kind of hold over their agents. More often, agents with a large book of business that was vested in renewals and pension plans simply left. This happened to a number of big Eastern mutuals. When the agents left, they would systematically roll over their entire book of business to their new company, except for those in poor health who were left behind to die at the expense of the old carrier. These situations hit a lot of companies pretty hard. To the agent, they were a bonanza. And of course, to the newer companies which facilitated these changes, they were the foundation for their growth.

The binge for the life insurance agent of the early 1980s meant an uncontrollable frenzy of replacement that doubled and tripled the incomes of many agents. No longer need they painstakingly uncover needs and cultivate the values of prudence, foresight, and responsibility that make people decide to buy life insurance. They didn't even have to close the sale by asking the prospect to part with his or her money. They just showed a computerized illustration of the prospect's old kind of insurance and compared it to the new kind. Did he want a lot more coverage and cash values for the same premium? Or the same coverage and cash values for a lot less premium? Whichever the answer, the agent filled out a surrender form for the old policy and used the surrender values to fund the new sale. No cash exchanged hands, just paperwork. It was too good to be true.

During the replacement binge, new agents came into the life insurance business and earned six-figure incomes without ever really asking someone to buy life insurance. In the process, many life insurance agents *forgot what it was that made them necessary in the first place.* An order taker could have done much of the same updating that occurred during this period. Life insurance salespeople were supposed to be those rare men and women with the right intestinal stuff—the ambergris factor we discussed in Chapter 1. Instead, they were setting new sales records while forgetting their trade, or in the case of many new-comers, without ever really learning it in the first place. It wasn't that the agent was doing anything unethical, it was just that he was losing sight of his mission.

Nowhere were the excesses of these two binges more evident than at Executive Life in the mid-1980s. They had the best product illustrations, and none of the inhibitions about replacement that encumbered most of their competitors. Although replacement was a significant part of their annual premium business, they were much more than just a company rolling policies out of the Eastern giants and into Executive Life. They were redefining the life insurance product, from one of conservative protection to among the strongest investments a person could make. They were attracting new money in much greater volume than almost any other company. It was against this exciting backdrop of an industrywide binge, with one company that appeared to be the pace car in the race to lead the industry to change, that my career at Executive Life began.

L.A. L.A. Land

When I arrived at Executive Life in the spring of 1986, the company was at the apex of its power. To those of us present, it seemed like just another milestone, another plateau in an unstoppable ascent to the top of the industry. For me, the learning curve at Executive Life was almost too steep. Sophisticated products, unlike anything else I was familiar with in the industry, were just the tip of the iceberg. As chief marketing officer, I was made chairman of their agent owned reinsurance companies (AORCs), the mechanics of which were unknown to me. The stockbrokerage division, also new to me, had produced $1.5 billion in annuities the previous year and was on schedule to do far more that year, yet I had no one reporting to me who was responsible for this important production resource—they all just talked to Fred or one of his assistants if they had a question. The company's largest marketing organization, Exceptional

Producers Group, had formed a subsidiary called First Annuity of California, which marketed a product Al Jacob had invented for pension funds wishing to fund benefits for retired employees. Their products were called QRA and CQRA—and they sold over $300 million in premiums in 1986 alone. Meanwhile, Fred was in a state of ecstasy because he was on schedule to sell $2 billion worth of municipal GICs that year—another product I didn't understand, which we will discuss later. I was getting calls from litigation houses that specialized in structured settlements about which I knew nothing, but of which we sold $200 million in premiums for the year.

Aside from all these areas new to me, I was charged with directly overseeing the PPGA (personal producing general agent) division, which was the industry's largest, and the brokerage division, also the industry's largest. And to be sure I stayed busy, Fred made me CEO of First Delaware Life, a subsidiary they were trying to get off the ground which had no president. Perhaps most overwhelming was the fact that every person I met or heard from within the sales force was absolutely livid over the terrible service they were getting from Executive Life. It was literally the only thing they wanted to talk to me about or, in most cases, shout at me about.

Of course, Fred Carr just dropped me into the job and left me to sink or swim. He only did an announcement of my arrival after I requested it three times. At Executive Life, all authority and power were earned; none was bestowed. If I wanted the respect of my constituency, I would have to earn it on my own. Fred had no intention of smoothing the way for me. He met with me only twice before he offered me the job, after I apparently passed a handwriting analysis, in which he reportedly had unwavering confidence. So, I assumed I was going through some type of post-selection process. If I survived for a few months, I figured he would then take the time to show an interest in me. Friends in the industry had told me the company was impossible to work for and that in a week or two I would throw in the towel and head back East. They were right about it being difficult. The place was an absolute madhouse. I had never been more excited or challenged in my life. For me, leaving the mainstream of the industry and joining Executive Life was like stepping out of a World War II bomber and onto the *Starship Enterprise*. I didn't understand much of what I saw, but I knew I'd soon be exploring new frontiers and traveling at the speed of light. I knew I had made the right decision. Today, even after the unbelievable disaster it turned into, I still regard these as the richest years of my career.

When I looked around for staff, I was introduced to Tina Begley, my administrative assistant, who had been with the company longer than almost anyone except for Fred. That was essentially it. No vice presidents of sales or marketing, no regional "steak-and-whiskey guys" to travel around and do the glad-slapping with the field force. I had technical assistance from some solid product managers, which was what Fred felt you needed in a product-driven company, but no line management. My counterparts in similar-sized companies would have had a staff of at least a half dozen vice presidents or equivalent-level people. I had none. As it turned out, because of the way Fred had constructed the company as a manufacturer in a product-driven environment, this approach was more correct than not. I only added two vice presidents, one for brokerage sales, Steve Christopher, and one to head up single premium sales, DeVaux McLean, to balance out the team. Surprisingly, with this still smallish staff, we got by very well.

Even for the environment of the 1980s, Executive Life was product-driven like no other company. The life insurance product is constructed in basically the same way at every company. Although the ground rules for designing a life insurance policy are the same, the variable is how well you meet your assumptions. If you want to be product-driven, then you must excel in those areas where exceptional performance will make a difference. The problem in the life insurance business is that since it is a long-term purchase, *the company can assume performance long before it has to actually deliver it.* This is what many companies did in the 1980s: they made unrealistic assumptions about mortality, expenses, persistency, and investment performance. It was kind of like the old joke about the guy who couldn't afford the surgery his doctor recommended, so he just had them touch up the X-rays.

At Executive Life in 1986, no one was touching up the X-rays. They had the best product in the industry. Not by a little bit either, it was Irreplaceable! More importantly, they were able to build very favorable assumptions into their products while still being conservative based upon the available facts, when compared to the rest of the industry. Walt Duemer, the stalwart president of Exceptional Producers Group, the company's largest field-marketing arm, educated me about the products of Al Jacob when I joined the company. He used to give new agents (and new chief marketing officers) a presentation on the four variables going into a life insurance contract and, all other factors being equal, explain why, "when you try to compete with Executive Life, you lose every time." "My actuary can beat your actuary every time," he'd crow, "and that's why we've got the best product in all the life insurance industry. Not the second best, but the best!"

His argument was a compelling one. They had the highest average premium in the industry, paid by high net worth individuals. The average annual life insurance premium paid by their policyholder was about $6,000, which is ten times greater than the industry average. Typically their policyholders were men, in their mid-fifties, who usually paid annually, so the persistency was outstanding. They had the lowest unit costs in the industry because of the average-size policy. Also true, with 850 employees, they had at best 20 percent of the number of people of other companies their size. Mortality was a push because it was just a matter of how stringently they wanted to underwrite applicants. Furthermore, even though they were a California company, their problems with AIDS claims were less than most other companies' because of the older, more affluent clientele (although they did have exceptions, such as Liberace, who was a policyholder).

That left investments, which by 1986, everyone had figured out, or should have, were as important as the other three combined. A key statistic on investment performance for a life insurance company is its Net Investment Yield ratio, which reflects net investment income divided by mean invested assets. Company results in this area are filed with the NAIC and reported to key rating agencies such as A. M. Best. As the table below shows, Executive Life led the majors (Top 25 life insurers in the U.S.) during the five-year period 1984–1988. It should be noted that the higher yields reflected the high level of funds as a percentage of total assets received by the company during the early 1980s, when yields were at record levels. Further, companies with substantial policy loans or surrender activity were often precluded from achieving higher yields. Still, with a net investment yield that was 25–30 percent greater than companies like Northwestern Mutual, Connecticut Mutual, and Manu-

Net Investment Yield (%)

Rank	Company	1988	1987	1986	1985	1984
1	Executive Life	11.64	11.52	11.77	12.75	12.18
2	Connecticut General Life	11.04	10.21	10.51	10.55	10.29
3	Teachers Insurance & Annuity	10.70	10.84	11.54	11.66	11.50
4	IDS LIfe Insurance Company	10.38	10.51	11.33	12.36	11.92
5	AETNA Life & Annuity	10.18	10.30	10.91	11.38	11.04
6	Principal Mutual	10.10	10.49	10.82	11.03	10.60
7	Variable Annuity Life	9.97	10.46	11.17	12.01	12.06
8	New York Life & Annuity	9.93	10.06	11.27	12.92	13.38
9	Allstate Life	9.89	9.31	9.68	9.25	9.38
10	State Farm Life	9.81	9.97	10.08	10.20	9.78
11	AETNA Life	9.77	9.98	10.46	10.80	10.67
12	Nationwide Life	9.68	9.80	10.55	10.78	10.24
13	Mutual Benefit Life	9.49	9.69	10.04	10.02	9.50
14	John Hancock Life	9.36	10.53	8.30	8.42	8.43
15	Massachusetts Mutual Life	9.22	9.27	9.41	10.16	9.73
16	Equitable Life Assurance	9.13	8.09	8.32	8.72	8.90
17	New England Mutual	9.05	9.47	10.15	10.08	10.05
18	New York Life	8.98	8.71	9.04	9.03	8.73
19	Metropolitan Life	8.94	9.04	9.42	9.79	9.49
20	Prudential Insurance	8.81	8.66	8.87	9.07	8.82
21	Mutual Life of New York	8.79	8.06	8.41	8.32	8.44
22	Travelers Insurance	8.77	9.76	10.88	11.58	10.85
23	Manufacturer's Life	8.73	7.48	8.85	9.43	8.72
24	Connecticut Mutual Life	8.64	8.47	8.84	8.85	8.95
25	Northwestern Mutual	8.62	8.17	8.44	8.66	8.47

facturers Life, it was easy to see why even without the other advantages, Executive Life's actuary *could* beat the other company's actuary, every time.

The years between 1980 and 1985 had been a blur of explosive growth of truly staggering proportions. They were topped only by 1986, which was a year it is unlikely any life insurance company will again experience. During the explosive years, Executive Life established its position with the field force as a manufacturer of life insurance products, leaving the wholesale and retail functions to others. This is important because like so many of the trends of the times, such as asset/liability matching and agent owned reinsurance companies, everyone was paying lip service to the idea, but Executive Life was the only major company practicing it.

Executive Life distributed all of its products through independent, self-employed wholesalers, which, in industry vernacular, are called managing general agencies (MGAs) and brokerage general agencies (BGAs). MGAs represented the company exclusively, and looked for agents willing to give Executive Life most of their business. BGAs represented several companies, and they brought a menu of choices to agents, from which the agent chose as needed from one sale to the next with no ongoing production commitment. (For purposes here, we will refer to both groups as MGAs). In addition to MGAs, Executive Life used other wholesalers to reach stockbrokers, pension fund managers, and litigation houses specializing in structured settlements (Structured settlements are annuities awarded by the courts to plaintiffs in personal injury suits). Unlike other companies which employ an in-house staff to work with the wholesalers, Executive Life had no one other than a single contact person for each market. That person might have a secretary, but by and large, that was it. In fact, in some cases, the person was the secretary! In the case of certain relationships with large firms, such as Pru-Bache, Fred was the contact person and the one they dealt with on their day-to-day problems. If they couldn't get Fred, there was no one else available to help them.

The life brokerage market is dominated by about one hundred MGAs nationwide, which historically built their businesses by offering specialty products such as cheap term insurance and coverage for substandard risks to the agents of other companies. When the interest-sensitive revolution hit, many companies were slow to react to the opportunity, so the life brokerage industry lined up carriers to accommodate the needs of agents whose primary companies did not have the new products. This was a great opportunity for Executive Life to obtain an instant distribution system. Its greatest good fortune in this market came in 1978, when Marty Greenberg and his wife Lisa hooked up with Executive Life in Los Angeles and started a brokerage agency that was to become the company's largest and one of the industry's top five. Marty cast a long shadow in life brokerage, and his uncontained enthusiasm for Executive Life's products caught on like wildfire. Along with the help of a couple of other bell cows, Executive Life soon became the hottest company in life brokerage. Its products were in such demand that the company had to limit the outlets in a given territory, or virtually every conceivable candidate would have snatched up a franchise and dissipated the effectiveness of the distribution system. As chief marketing officer, I had to select from those beating down the door for a chance to represent Executive Life. For me, it was a bizarre experience in an industry where getting shelf space with distributors was usually a tough selling job for marketing officers like myself.

On the PPGA (personal producing general agent) side of the house, they were looking for MGAs willing to start scratch agencies representing Executive Life exclusively. These organizations would look for personal producing general agents who were willing to make a long-term commitment to Executive Life as their lead company. The carrot for this group was that the MGA would, upon proving himself, be given his own AORC (agent owned reinsurance company) into which he could recruit shareholder/agents. Nobody in the industry could touch the appeal of the deal Executive Life MGAs and PPGAs had when one considered the product, the compensation, and the AORCs.

Indeed, it was so strong that their MGAs financed their enterprise by themselves, with no help from the company. It is quite unusual for a life insurance company to build a nationwide network of outlets, representing it exclusively, without a dime of capital investment. Instead, the MGAs went to the bank and borrowed the money to start their enterprise much the way one might do with a McDonald's franchise. This was an example of the drawing power of Fred Carr. He could get people to put their entire net worth on the line for an opportunity to share in the profits that would come from his vision. Many of us did, both in the field and in the home office.

The Executive Life rocket was fueled by products—innovative, flexible, and above all, competitive products. The original product introduced at Executive Life, Irreplaceable Life I^{SM}, was a low-ball-premium, whole-life product, with a periodic adjustment to the premium (every five years). It competed favorably with a number of products in the market, but was missing certain key ingredients for the type of product around which Fred Carr wanted to build his company. The market Executive Life wanted to tap was the high net worth individual and business insurance market. These were people with cash flow. They were more interested in paying off the obligation early, accumulating cash through the tax-free build-up aspect of a life insurance contract, and finding ways to roll dollars out of their businesses on a tax-free basis. Such prospects appealed to Fred because he wanted to accumulate assets to be managed in his company. They appealed to his agents, too, because products accommodating this market develop bigger premiums, which means bigger commissions.

The most important product developed during this period was Irreplaceable Life II^{SM}, which became, as we have already discussed, the flagship of the fleet, and along with its successor, Irreplaceable Life XII^{SM}, composed the bulk of the company's individual sales. The two concepts around which all of the products were built were simple yet innovative. One product was projected, the other guaranteed. The projected product assumed an interest rate and mortality charges, and projected the necessary minimum premiums to carry the policy over the lifetime of the insured. Each five years, the rates would be recalculated based upon company experience, and a new five-year rate would be set. If experience was favorable (which it was on the first five-year calculations in 1984), premiums would be reduced. If experience was less favorable (as it was on the second calculation in 1989), premiums would go up.

The second product guaranteed that the premium never would go up. The variable here was that based upon experience, the company would calculate a point at which no further premiums were necessary to carry the policy, at which time premiums were projected to vanish based upon current performance. One product had low premiums that were paid for life and adjusted periodically; the other had high premiums that were payable for a few years (six to eight), until the accumulation account created a policy that on a projected basis was paid up. From these two product concepts, Al Jacob developed a portfolio of Irreplaceable Life℠ products that covered the gamut of every market need an agent might encounter. Although the appearances varied significantly, the fundamental components and assumptions were all projected or guaranteed, and varied little beyond that.

One of the assumptions that Executive Life was very aggressive on was mortality, which meant if they were serious about the pricing assumptions, they had to have tight underwriting, meaning the evaluation of the risk being insured. And they did. Their products had no tables built into them to "shave" for good agents or a big sale. They thoroughly underwrote each applicant, and if the applicant wasn't squeaky clean, he or she did not get a Preferred rating, which was the lowest premium available for the healthiest applicants. Because their average insured person was fifty-four years old (old by industry standards), they had a lot of rated risks, which meant the expected premiums (those used to make the sale) were often higher when the policy came back due to the risk being substandard.

After a number of complaints from the field, Al Jacob came up with another ingenious idea called Irreplaceable Life 88℠.

The concept was so simple, one wonders how it could have been overlooked. When a person gets rated up for health reasons on their life insurance, they don't want to pay the extra premium because they always believe the company is wrong and that they will live as long as the next guy. Irreplaceable Life 88SM gives the insured a chance to prove he or she is right. It charges the same premium anyone else would pay, but requires one or more additional premiums on the back end before the premiums vanish. For example, if the premiums were projected to vanish in seven years for a Preferred risk, a person who is an impaired risk may have to pay nine or more premiums, depending upon the degree of their health impairment. Then, if the insured is correct and they live, the company returns those extra premiums in years 16–20 by increasing the regular cash value of the contract by the amount of the extra premiums charged. The impaired-risk person pays the same premium as the person in perfect health, but pays a few more years. If they live, the company makes them whole by restoring the extra premiums in the form of cash value. Once again, everyone wins.

Perhaps Executive Life's most daring product was the guaranteed exchange product, Irreplaceable Life VISM, which we have already touched on. At the time, we were earning spreads of 300–400 basis points over the rates they were crediting, so one can quickly see that there wasn't a lot of risk involved in this product from an investment standpoint. Furthermore, one must remember that in a life insurance contract, it's not the gross amount at risk, but the net amount at risk that counts. If you give a company an older policy, in which the $100,000 death benefit is offset by cash values that are already up to $40,000, then the net risk is only $60,000. That is to say, if you die, the company only has to come up with $60,000 above the asset (cash value of the policy) that it has taken on in the exchange. With this single product Executive Life took in over $400 million in cash values in less than four years. As the industry goes, $400 million in assets would make for a nice little company, let alone the short run take on one single innovative product.

Irreplaceable Life VISM was just the first in a series of radical and innovative products that set the industry on its ear. Executive Life did things that simply seemed undo-able to the rest of the industry. Everyone decided that they must be doing it with mirrors and that in fact Fred was building a house of cards. Although they can now say that they were right, it would be a serious mistake for the industry to ignore what really happened. The fact is the people at Executive Life had a number of advantages, in addition to junk bonds, that made it easy for them to compete. First of all, they had a company which did not bear the burden of an existing book of business. They didn't have to worry about updating old policyholders and liquidating assets that they had locked into long durations at low yields. They were starting fresh in an environment where terrific yields on new money were as much as double the yields the typical life insurance company got on its overall portfolio. In addition, they focused on the high net worth prospect, allowing them to cherry-pick among the industry's agents and their upscale clientele. This in turn led to larger dollar amounts per transaction and lower distribution costs. These larger premiums were usually paid annually, and this type of policyholder tended to stay on the books much longer.

In the individual life market, Executive Life was the hottest franchise available. Traditionally, the marketing departments of life insurance companies devote considerable resources and energy to combing the country for MGAs and agents they can recruit to sell their products. This is the primary responsibility of most marketing departments. In my previous environment, I and my staff spent a large percentage of our time riding airplanes and courting the local MGA in every town we visited, trying to convince him or her to give us a try.

At Executive Life, in 1986, recruiting was done through a screening process whereby we qualified prospects over the phone, all of whom called *us* rather than we calling them! If they sounded good, we would invite them to Los Angeles for a visit, but *always* at their expense. This was very new and very bizarre to me. Even stranger was a new activity that I used to call my "border patrol." The products were so hot that many agents who were not authorized to recruit other agents would become bootleg outlets. They would solicit business from local agents, which they would then submit in their own name, passing the commission on to the writing agent under the table. This added to the perception of our poor service since the bootlegger had little interest in servicing his subagent after he got his share of the commission or, for that matter, forgot to pay him the commission altogether. I spent a lot of time tracking down alleged offenders who were bootlegging business in the territory of an authorized outlet. With hindsight, it's crazy to think that I, who regarded myself as a field-oriented marketing officer, spent considerable energy turning away business because it came from an unauthorized source! Much of the rest of my time was spent dealing with the abysmal service problems that plagued the company, the biggest cause of which was that we had more business than we could handle. It was a problem most companies would welcome and probably work a lot harder to solve than we did, due to Fred's aversion to adding personnel.

Although these were all very real problems, there was an underlying sense of jubilance. We were experiencing the most exciting environment in the history of the life insurance business, inventing new products, new markets, and new concepts such as the agent owned reinsurance companies. Much of the rest of the industry was paralyzed by Executive Life's performance, envious of its position, and downright stymied as to how it did what it did. When asked at agent seminars why it was we were so disliked by the rest of the industry, I used to reply: "If you had been in the life insurance business say, twenty years, and the guy next door went into it, say, two years ago and in that time sold more than you had in your twenty years, how would you feel? What would you tell your wife when she asked you how he had so outperformed you? You'd probably say he was doing it with mirrors, wouldn't you?" Then I'd tell them that after being the chief marketing officer of Executive Life I had a feel for what it must have been like for Joe DiMaggio to be married to Marilyn Monroe, and why he never married again: she was unbelievably good, and she was unbelievably bad, but above all she was Irreplaceable! I know all of this sounds arrogant, but that was the situation at the time. Later, you'll hear about the humble pie we eventually had to eat.

In 1986, Executive Life was the cause for a lot of explaining that companies had to do with their agents, their boards, and their stockholders. Five years later, in 1991, the House of Carr had collapsed and the establishment could breathe easy again. But for a while, Fred Carr gave them a lot to think about, and many of the positive actions they took as a result of those concerns were good for the industry.

6

Single Pay Products— The Tail That Wagged the Dog

"In 1980 the life insurance industry was 150 years old. In 1990, the life insurance industry was ten years old. That's how long we've been selling the interest-sensitive products that will make or break our future as an industry."
— Gary Schulte to the San Fernando Valley CLU Chapter, March 1990

On a clear day in 1986, Fred Carr could see the Prudential in his sights. I'm sure that the people at the Pru weren't concerned, but for just that one year they might have given his designs a second thought. Fred had a lot going for him in 1986—more than he had ever had before or ever would again. Of the many things about which he was feeling his oats, none was more important than his freshly won AAA claims-paying rating from Standard & Poor's. What most of us didn't realize was that his euphoria did not come from the importance the AAA gave to existing markets. The real issue was something brand new and more exciting than any opportunity to date, for in 1986, Fred Carr had discovered muni-GIC—a concept he and Drexel perfected from ground zero into a multi-billion-dollar bonanza in the summer and fall of that year. A simple investment vehicle for the proceeds raised by municipal bond offerings, the muni-GIC became a leading Drexel/Executive Life innovation.

Of the $16 billion of policyholder liabilities on the balance sheet of First Executive Corporation by the year 1989, about $13 billion came from the sale of single pay products. Single pay products, as the name implies, are those contracts where the benefits promised are provided by a single payment from the insured. When the payment is made, the provisions of the contract are locked in and no additional premiums will ever be required.

The single pay products at First Executive Corporation essentially consisted of single premium deferred annuities (SPDA), single premium whole life (SPWL), Guaranteed Investment Contracts (GICs), Qualified Retirement Annuities (QRA), Customized Qualified Retirement Annuities (CQRA), and structured settlements, which they called immediate annuities. These products all have three things in common: the purchaser of the contract pays only one premium, with no further requirements; the pricing is essentially a function of assumed interest rates; and, because of the long-term nature of the commitment they make to the policyholder, they develop a lot of surplus strain.

Deferred annuities and SPWL vary in terms of accumulation and payout provision, but the basic characteristics are the same. The appeal is tax-free accumulation of a lump-sum deposit at an interest rate that is guaranteed for a period, usually one to five years, and declared annually thereafter. There are surrender charges during the first five to ten years, ranging from 5 to 10 percent of the account value. Since the interest-rate guarantee was never for as long a period as the surrender charge, contracts typically had bail-out provisions that waived the surrender charge if the annually declared interest fell below a certain level. These products were designed so that the insured could stuff as much cash into them as the law would permit to accumulate tax-free. They were mostly sold by stockbrokers.

The first big move by Fred into the single pay business came through his vast knowledge and experience in the securities industry. Selling annuities through stockbrokers was a natural for Fred. In the mid-1970s, he designed a series of innovative annuities and went to Wall Street, where he was well known as a person who could create excitement and make big things happen. One of the problems for many insurance companies wanting to do business with the big securities firms is that the latter are all headquartered in New York. Unless an insurance company is licensed to do business in New York, it can't tap the New York offices of the brokerage firms, which tend to be some of the most successful. The Eastern mutuals, which are based in New York and New England, tended not to be players in the stockbrokerage system since it created problems with their career agents, who strenuously objected to the competition at the time. The players were mostly non-New York companies, like Baldwin United, Monarch Life (both of which eventually went under), and a host of small annuity specialty companies. Interestingly, none of the household names in the life insurance industry has ever been a long-term player in this huge, multi-billion-dollar market. Given the number of smaller companies that have targeted this market and then gone under, it would seem logical that a move to the majors whose financial strength is more evident would have occurred by now.

Thanks to its founder, Otto Forst, Executive Life had a New York subsidiary, Executive Life of New York (ELNY). Getting a New York subsidiary up and running when Forst did it in the 1960s was not easy, but it was a virtual impossibility later on. So, when Fred went to Wall Street to market his annuities, he was one of the few knowledgeable players who could include New York in his marketing plan. He also had an able and savvy president of that company in Ron Kehrli, a tough-minded, native New Yorker who marched to the beat of his own drummer. It was a good thing, too, because Fred paid little attention to the New York unit. In fact, Ron Kehrli told me that during his eight-year tenure as president, despite his frequent visits to New York, Fred never once set foot on the premises of Executive Life of New York.

At the large wirehouses, non-proprietary products (those not developed internally at the firm) are sold through outside vendors called wholesalers. In 1977, Fred contracted a wholesaler by the name of Vince McGuiness to represent the Executive Life companies exclusively. The products were an instant success. SPDAs are interest-rate-driven, and because of Fred's high-yield strategy, he had the best products in the industry. Also, Fred and Al Jacob created some innovative products that left the competition scratching their heads. Just one example was the Ten-Strike℠ annuity, which guaranteed that the credited interest rate would increase by 10 basis points each year over the previous year, for ten years. Largely due to this strategy, the company's asset base grew from less than $100 million in 1974 to nearly $800 million by 1980.

Then, in 1980, Fred hired a second wholesaler, MSM Corporation. At the same time, individual sales were beginning to take off at the company. Between the two, the company's asset base doubled each of the next two years, reaching $3.45 billion at the end of 1982. During this period, First Executive's largest producing group was E. F. Hutton. Somewhat the innovators themselves in the life insurance business with their E. F. Hutton life subsidiary, they saw the opportunity to develop proprietary products in the annuity market. In 1984, E. F. Hutton abruptly announced that they were pulling Executive Life products from their line because they felt they had too much of their total annuity sales with one company. Shortly thereafter, Merrill Lynch followed suit. With the Baldwin United collapse and more notice being taken of Fred's high-yield investment strategy, the company was about to get its first dose of serious anti-First Executive Corporation propaganda.

Stockbrokers can only make money if they make a new sale. They generally get no renewal or equity compensation for leaving a client in a given investment, whether it's a good one or not. The Baldwin United failure gave the stockbrokers the leverage they needed to convince jittery Executive Life annuitants to take a hit on the surrender charge and move to another annuity product. E. F. Hutton alone had put $2 billion of annuities on the books with Executive Life, most of which Hutton rolled out after it dropped their product line. Despite this and the later barrages of bad press that caused heavy turnover of this book of business throughout the 1980s, it remained profitable because the capital investment in the form of surplus needed to contribute to put this business on the books was heavily leveraged. Still, with hindsight, the life insurance industry went into the securities industry with products designed for relationship-oriented insurance agents, instead of transaction-oriented stockbrokers. They were like lambs to the slaughter. As soon as there was an excuse to churn the business, it was gone. This result had nothing to do with the professionalism of stockbrokers; rather, it was the result of the lack of professionalism with which the life insurance industry went into the business of selling through stockbrokers. In the future, the stockbroker needs to be given products designed so that his best interests are in line with those of the company. I believe we will see this happening as the retail stockbrokers emerge from the disastrous consequences of their own actions during the go-go 1980s.

Product Inventions

Guaranteed Investment Contracts are simple products designed to relieve some of the anxiety for the manager of a pension fund, a profit-sharing plan, or a 401(k) plan. The insurance company agrees to take a chunk of cash and guarantees a return for a period of time, usually five to ten years. The funds are then used by the plan sponsor to fund future benefits. However, it was the muni-GIC that really got Fred thinking about how to "beat the Pru" by mid-1986.

Guaranteed Investment Contracts (GICs), as the name implies, guarantee interest rates for a specified time on deposits received. Municipal GICs are used by municipal bond issuers as a vehicle for parking funds raised from a bond offering until they are turned over for the purposes intended, such as roads, low-income housing, and industrial development. In 1986, while interest rates were down and junk bond yields were still very high, Mike Milken and Fred Carr developed the idea of a muni-GIC. At the time, many bond issuers worried that rising interest rates, like those earlier in the decade, might make it difficult to raise funds for the various projects they had on the drawing board. Additionally, the loss of tax-free status for municipal bonds with the Tax Reform Act of 1986 had now made it necessary to pay higher yields to attract funds.

The muni-GIC provided an opportunity to raise the money now in the lower-interest-rate environment, and put it into a higher-yielding GIC with Executive Life. Because of its junk bond portfolio, Executive Life could pass on a higher yield, which would enable the municipality not only to pay an interest rate high enough to attract funds, but also to keep a handsome profit for itself. It was a very clever concept. However, municipal bonds are perceived to be very safe, and such issuers as the cities of Memphis, New Orleans, and Houston had a responsibility for due diligence. This is where the importance of a AAA claims-paying ability rating from Standard & Poor's came in. It was Fred Carr's ticket to take this new market by storm.

The concept was so exciting to municipalities that many of them floated bond issues whose proceeds never found their way off the drawing board. The muni-GIC had almost unlimited potential for Executive Life and conceivably could have been the major contributor in Fred's quest to "beat the Prudential." However, as the Ivan Boesky scandal broke in late 1986 and junk bond prices began to fall, analysts noted that the municipalities were not responsible for the performance of the GIC-backed bonds, and that investors had unwittingly purchased the equivalent of a junk bond rather than a municipal bond. Since these bonds are thinly traded anyway, this revelation eventually caused their prices to fall by as much as 80 percent. The muni-GIC market for Executive Life dried up almost as quickly as it arrived. Still, during this brief window of a few months, Fred put an incredible $1.85 billion of these products on the books. The man knew how to jump on a window of opportunity!

The Customized Qualified Retirement Annuity (CQRA) was a good example of how Executive Life listened to agents and came up with innovative products to serve emerging markets. A pension specialist by the name of Jack Scott proposed a way of turning lemons into lemonade. Due to the many cumbersome restraints imposed by Congress on qualified pension plans through a series of anti-pension laws, many employers chose to terminate their plan rather than live with the new, complex, and limiting government restraints and the expense of administering them. Agents like Scott were losing their client base as employers terminated their qualified pension plans. When this happened, they were stuck with providing the accrued benefits to employees who had become vested. They needed to purchase a product into which they could transfer this liability.

Walt Duemer and Erik Watts took Jack's idea to Fred, who immediately saw this as a sales opportunity. It was ideal for him in the high-interest-rate environment of the period. Pension plan benefits are based upon assumptions that are a simple function of time, money, and interest. The higher the interest-rate assumption, the less the required deposit needed to meet the future obligation. In an extremely high-interest-rate environment like the early 1980s, if a pension plan could lock in a benefit using a higher rate with a long-term guarantee, the funding requirements would be dramatically reduced. Here again, the high-yield strategy enabled Executive Life always to be the most competitive bidder for pension fund managers seeking to buy benefits. If someone questioned the junk bond issue, Fred pointed to his Standard & Poor's AAA claims-paying ability rating, which was once again his ticket into a huge market. Fred turned the product design over to Al Jacob, who quickly put together the capability for Executive Life to become the leader in this emerging market. Executive Life sold annuity products that were so good that the companies' pension plans became overfunded and they were allowed to pull the extra money back out. This became an additional incentive for employers to terminate their pension plans. They could blame the cumbersome restraints of Congress for terminating the plan, but upon doing so, they could have a windfall from overfunding, due to the low rates Executive Life gave them for purchasing the vested benefits. Fred Carr and Al Jacob had created yet another new market for the company that left much of the rest of the industry scratching their heads.

Another reason for terminating a pension plan was as a source of cash to pay for leveraged buy-outs (LBOs). Those wishing to take a company private might have their eye on an overfunded pension fund or a fat one, which, if terminated, would free up cash to fund the LBO. All they needed was some way of guaranteeing those employee benefits that were vested. Enter Executive Life, with its CQRA.

The CQRA became so popular that Al Jacob began to develop similar products to lock in the vested benefits of pension plans that had no intention of terminating. For this market, he created a product called the Qualified Retirement Annuity (QRA). Like the muni-GIC market, the pension annuity market would eventually fall victim to the junk bond issue. This occurred as the press began to realize that retired employees in companies that had bought LBOs and terminated their pensions were dependent upon Fred's junk bond portfolio for their retirement income. However, it took longer for this market to dry up for Executive Life because it was not as visible to the public nor as controversial as the muni-GICs. In a brief three years, Executive Life sold $500 million in QRA and CQRA business. On his sales alone, Jack Scott earned about $5 million in commissions. Not bad tasting lemonade!

The final single pay product that balanced out the portfolio was the immediate annuity, which was used primarily for structured settlements. Structured settlements are guaranteed incomes, usually for life, provided to plaintiffs by insurance companies against whom they have won some type of settlement. Typically, they would be injuries from auto accidents or workmen's compensation. The courts learned the hard way that lump-sum awards often wound up gone before the plaintiff was, thus leaving them without income. Many of the plaintiffs in these actions are simply working people who, upon receiving a large cash settlement for an injury, have trouble handling the money, or are taken advantage of by those offering to help. A lifetime guarantee is a much better solution. When the insurance company people agree to such a settlement, they usually want to turn it over to a third party to guarantee the benefit, so they can put a cost on it and be done with it. Although not yet adequately tested by the courts, the obligation to provide such a court-ordered benefit to the plaintiff may remain with the insurer against whom the judgment is awarded. If the company guaranteeing the benefit is unable to perform, the obligation could revert back to the original insurance company. This meant that insurance companies which, in effect, reinsured this obligation to another carrier, again wanted assurances such as the AAA Standard & Poor's claims-paying ability rating to feel certain the obligation would not come back to them.

Except for the deferred annuities, all of these single pay products were essentially non-surrenderable. Once purchased, there was no provision for surrender. The customer purchased a benefit, and once finalized, there was no facility for accelerating any payments. These were simple spread products with no risk of the duration of the liability being shortened by adverse events. They were perfect vehicles for the business of asset/liability matching, usually sold on a lowest-bid basis. Given Fred's capacity to earn a spread, he won all the business he wanted.

Some $8 billion of the $19 billion in assets held by First Executive Corporation on January 1, 1990, was in contracts that were essentially unsurrenderable. The only way the holders could get out was to sell their GIC to a third party at a deep discount or to negotiate an out with Executive Life, which basically meant giving the company its profit up front in exchange for a refund—in effect, a surrender charge big enough to make it worthwhile to let them out.

One could say that Executive Life's incredible book of single pay product business was all sold directly or indirectly by Fred Carr. The pension GICs, muni-GICs, QRA, CQRA, and immediate annuities were all markets Fred led the company into or at least jumped on when they were presented to him. They were spread products made in heaven for his investment strategy and the times we were in. With the creative genius of Al Jacob and the marketing talent of Walt Duemer and Erik Watts of Exceptional Producers, who ran the QRA and CQRA projects, the company literally owned these markets in the 1985–86 period.

However, to make things really work, Fred had to make one of the biggest sales of his life. The sponsors of pension plans, the municipal bonds issuers, and the structure settlement specialists all had to have a company for their clients that was of unimpeachable integrity. Especially if Executive Life was one of the bidders, the committees and boards choosing a carrier needed to lean heavily on the rating agencies as justification for choosing a controversial company and a bargain price for the benefits their employees depended upon. An A+ from A. M. Best was good, but they wanted more than that—especially from a parvenu like Fred Carr. They wanted the assurances of the newest status symbol in insurance rating: the Standard & Poor's AAA claims-paying ability. Fred worked long and hard on this one. He cultivated a relationship with Standard & Poor's Mark Puccia, who was the person assigned to head the Executive Life evaluation team. Standard & Poor's was very thorough. After sending "an army of ants to pour over us" on several occasions, they finally came through with the AAA rating in the summer of 1986.

At the time, fewer than thirty life insurance companies in the industry held the coveted AAA. The other recipients were, of course, all part of the Eastern giant establishment, a club from which Executive Life had been and always would be excluded. When Standard & Poor's awarded the company its AAA, I don't think they had given much thought to what the reaction would be in the industry. From their point of view, this was a big mistake. The decision outraged many of those with AAAs but it really infuriated those with lower ratings. More important, from the standpoint of new revenues, others who had yet to apply to Standard & Poor's for a rating told them not to bother. Instead, they went to Moody's, who had followed

Standard & Poor's into the business. The Moody's rating was not as prestigious because it was assigned unilaterally, without the detailed interviewing and meetings Standard & Poor's went through before assigning a rating. Still, Moody's attracted a lot of industry support when they assigned Executive Life an A₃, their fourth-highest rating. They never even called the company to get any information. Although I'm sure their decision had its basis in sound facts, a lower rating for Executive Life than that of Standard & Poor's probably made for a better reception for them among the Eastern establishment.

I don't recall ever seeing Fred more excited than he was about the Standard & Poor's AAA. He ran a number of full-page ads in the *Wall Street Journal* proclaiming, "We asked Standard & Poor's what they thought of us and here's what they said: AAA." The AAA was phenomenal for the entire single pay market, and had great carryover into the individual and business insurance markets where due diligence was becoming more and more important. In all, the assets of First Executive Corporation ballooned from $8.7 billion at the end of 1985 to $16.4 billion at the end of 1987. This was probably the biggest growth for any company in the history of the life insurance industry. The biggest single reason was the Standard & Poor's AAA. No wonder Fred was excited. All in all, it was worth more to First Executive Corporation than any of us (except Fred) had dreamt possible. It vaulted the company into the big leagues in the financial services industry. It was also a great help to the field force and Marketing Department of the company, who relied on this rating and the A. M. Best A+ as our authority for countering more subjective criticisms of the company.

Until they took the rating away three years later, Standard & Poor's spent much time defending their position on Executive Life, including a lot of reviews to reaffirm their position. Had they known how much business it would cost them, even if they had been correct, I'm convinced they never would have given Executive Life an AAA. It turned out to be a decision that would take years to live down.

The Spigot of Growth

For First Executive Corporation, the single premium market was a spigot which Fred Carr could open or close at will, depending on what interest rate he wanted to pay. Although interest rates determined *how many* single pay products the company could sell, they were not the determining factor of its ability to *deliver* the merchandise. Single pay products usually offer the long-term guarantee of benefits to policyholders. Because of these guarantees, the regulators want to be sure the money will be there when promised, so they require the insurance companies to calculate the statutory reserve put aside to meet these obligations at very conservative interest rates. These lower rates then require the putting aside of a larger asset (greater than the premium collected) to meet the regulatory requirements. The shortfall is put up by the company, thus creating a drain on its surplus account. Such a characteristic of growth in an insurance company is known as "surplus strain." We will discuss this in greater detail later, but for our purposes here, one may assume that Executive Life needed a lot of capital to build its book of single pay business. It was the availability of capital, not the ability to offer competitive products, that determined how easily Fred could open the spigot on single pay product lines.

In addition to the high-yield strategy, which gave Executive Life the best interest rates on its annuities, the company also had fairly low surrender charges. Surrender charges are largely there to protect against losses caused by early surrenders, when the company has exposure from the commission loads that have been paid to the securities firms. Fred believed the annuity marketplace was totally product-driven and, accordingly, he paid among the lowest commissions in the industry. This, along with the comfort that he could always credit a very competitive rate, enabled Executive Life to offer low surrender charges. Since the company sold $1.5 billion of deferred annuities in 1985 and $1.7 billion in 1986, it would seem he was correct in his strategies. Still, there was constant pressure on him from the company's biggest producers to increase commissions; but Fred held his ground.

What he did do to enhance relationships with his sales force was invite the stockbrokers who qualified to the company sales conventions, which were the runaway hits of the sales incentive industry. If a stockbroker produced a mere $1.25 million in SPDA (deferred annuities) business, he was invited on a trip that cost Executive Life about $8,000–$10,000 for the producer and their guest. The gross commissions on this amount of production were $50,000, less than half of what a life insurance sales person had to sell in Irreplaceable Life℠ business to go on the same trip. The stockbrokers who went on Executive Life trips returned to their firms with stories of the adventure that made for the best recruiting tool the company could offer. One reason for the easy qualification requirement was that stockbrokers aren't called stockbrokers because they sell annuities. A lot of the brokers attending company meetings became promoters of First Executive Corporation stock. Fred always had a separate business session at the sales conventions with the stockbrokers, which was more like a security analysts' breakfast meeting than a sales session. This way, he had a dual sales force that was invaluable to the company. They sold their clients the annuities *and* stock, and the common and Preferred issues in the company. For a long while, it was a win/win strategy.

The company's explosive success at distributing SPDA and single premium whole life (SPWL) products through stockbrokers began to come undone toward the end of 1986, when it had produced a record $1.7 billion in new premiums. In October of that year, the Boesky scandal broke, beginning a four-year front-page ordeal that would culminate with the sentencing of Mike Milken in the fall of 1990. The Boesky–Drexel–Milken–junk bond issue, as Fred called it, was already sloping over into his rose garden by the start of 1987. The Boesky scandal was only the first of a long series of events that over the next four years would not bode well for the future of First Executive Corporation.

The Tax Reform Act of 1986 further restricted the flexibility of withdrawals from annuities and single premium whole life. Then, in 1988, Congress decided that SPWL was what it called a modified endowment, which essentially killed the product as a tax-free cash accumulation vehicle. Other adverse events which we will cover later included the disallowance of several reinsurance treaties in Executive Life of New York (which led to a record-setting fine by the New York State Insurance Department), a shortage of the necessary capital to continue writing this type of business, and, of course, the ever-growing controversy over the junk bonds. After 1986, Executive Life's single premium sales declined from $1.7 billion to $1 billion in 1987, $425 million in 1988, and $375 million in 1989. Still not chopped liver, but not the direction Fred Carr needed to be going in if he was to catch the Pru. Part of these declines was incurred by design, in that the lack of available capital and regulatory restraints on the use of surplus relief were making it necessary dramatically to slow the company's growth rate for the first time. Fred put the brakes on the interest rates credited for the annuity products; with the uncompetitive commissions it paid, Executive Life started to move out of the business almost as rapidly as it had moved into it.

It is difficult to paint an accurate picture of First Executive Corporation because so much of the culture, color, and innovation revolved around the life insurance division and the Irreplaceable Life℠ products it sold. It was in this arena that First Executive was best known. Yet, at the end of the first quarter of 1990, even after considerable surrender activity in its single premium deferred annuities (SPDA) block, Executive Life still had $4.1 billion of annuity business on the books and over $1 billion of single premium whole life. Add to this $7 billion of GICs, pension annuities, and compare it to $2.9 billion in annual premium whole-life products, and one can easily see that single pay was the tail that wagged the dog. In addition, the New York company's book of business included $3.5 billion of various single pay products. To the objective eye, First Executive Corporation was still a single premium product company.

Historically, it has been believed that because the annual premium business renews each year, it is several times more profitable than single pay—at least in theory. The actual experience with the new interest-sensitive products has not supported this idea. The administrative and data-processing expenses for maintaining a book of interest-sensitive whole-life or universal life products so often exceeds the pricing that I believe the profits are far less than many think or claim them to be. Single pay products, on the other hand, can practically be administered out of a shoe box. They are pure spread products, and in the 1980s, Executive Life had the spreads! From a balance sheet perspective, which isn't a bad way of looking at things, First Executive Corporation was predominantly a single pay company, and most of the business had been put there through the efforts of one man, Fred Carr. He invested the money, found the markets, designed the products, and sold his ideas, at least at the institutional level. He also single-handedly courted and bagged the AAA claims-paying ability rating from Standard & Poor's that was the catalyst for the company's explosive growth in 1986.

The results directly attributable to Fred Carr in building the individual life insurance sales force, which pound for pound was arguably the strongest in the industry, are covered throughout this story. The single pay segment of the company grew from nothing to about $13 billion corporatewide, most of which was due to Fred's ideas, guidance, and salesmanship. The night I agreed to go to work for Fred Carr, I told him he was one of the most insightful and visionary people I had ever met. His typical, understated response was: "I'm just a salesman who knows how to read a balance sheet." He is much more than that; regardless of how things turned out for him, much can be learned by examining the things he did right while he was on a roll.

7

The Fortune 500 Sole Proprietorship

"Executive Life's capital structure and, hence, operating leverage are substantially more conservative than virtually all its `AAA' rated counterparts."
—Standard & Poor's *CreditWeek*, November 3, 1986

When I was a teenager, I packed groceries for a large supermarket chain. They paid me $1.50 per hour, from which were deducted federal, state, and city income taxes, Social Security, and dues for a union I was forced to join. They told me what hours to work. If I wanted to drink a coke or eat a candy bar, I paid for it like anyone else. I was a specialist and was only allowed to sack groceries. Others were stock boys or cashiers, or worked on the loading platform. The jobs were monotonous to say the least.

I left the large grocery chain after a year or so to work for a small, independent grocery store owned by a Chaldean family. (The Chaldeans are Christian Iraqis from the northern region of that country. In my native Detroit, they dominate the independent grocery business.) They paid me 75¢ an hour, or one-half the gross of my previous employer. I loved the job and stayed with them through my first year in college, even though they never gave me a raise in spite of repeated requests. Why? They paid me in cash—no deductions. They let me do a number of jobs, not just sweep and pack groceries, but also stock the shelves, run the cash register, and most importantly, drive the store panel truck to make home deliveries. Since I was the only non-family member, they more or less treated me as one of their own. If I wanted something to eat or drink, I took it without having to pay for it. I was able to gorge myself on candy, potato chips, and other junk food. On Saturday night, on my way out after a twelve-hour day, one of the four brothers who owned the store would usually toss me a cold six-pack of beer.

The brothers squeezed more out of me than the supermarket chain ever did. At the large chain, I always got two breaks and a lunch hour. There were no breaks; if I wanted lunch, I just grabbed a sandwich on the way to a delivery. When I became restless, they would tantalize me by telling me that if I really worked hard and hung in there with them, when they opened up a second store, they might permit me to be the manager. Of course, even at eighteen, I knew this was a lot of bunk, but still it was very flattering to feel that the family would consider inviting me into the business. I worked hard and gave the Chaldeans more than their money's worth. They taught me a lot about hard work and how to squeeze a buck.

I suppose it's true that this small independent store broke many of the rules and practices of the major chains. Yet anyone who knows that business knows there was no way they could survive if they accommodated the cumbersome restraints under which the large chains operated. The entry barriers for a family of immigrants into the world of the major chains were seemingly insurmountable. Yet the four brothers somehow overcame them. They beat the giants at their own game; but to do so, they had to circumvent those rules of the game that favored the establishment.

I hadn't worked for Fred Carr for very long before I figured out that he had probably been raised in an independently owned family store. Most of his personnel practices had the Chaldean brothers' thumbprint all over them. Nobody, however, not even my Chaldean employers, could stretch employee relationships to get more bang for their buck than Fred Carr did at Executive Life.

In the mid-1980s, Executive Life was known industrywide for three things, and two of them were bad: competitive, innovative products; junk bonds; and the poorest service to agents and policyholders in the industry. Executive Life was known in the Los Angeles area as something of a sweatshop mostly because of the low wages and long hours. This was true throughout the company, including the senior officer level where the overall package was very uncompetitive, except for the stock options on which all of us hung our hopes. It was particularly true in the systems area where the Data Processing Department was buried with so many projects that, had they tripled its size, it still would have been behind schedule. It was not uncommon for the turnover in the Data Processing Department to run 30 percent a year. Today, it is difficult for a life insurance company not to become a slave to its Systems Department.

Life insurance is a business that is totally dependent upon the computer and its ancillary hardware and software. All we really sell in the life insurance business are pieces of paper with configurations of numbers produced by a computer-generated print-out. We then process the application electronically and take it through the underwriting, paperless all the way to the point of issue, using pcs and other data-processing equipment to build our file. When we issue the policy, we print the face pages with a laser printer and assemble the pages electronically through a process called Documerge. Most important, all the values within a policy that are tracked from year to year—annual statements, premium payment notices, and automatic bank drafts—are computer-generated. Add to this reinsurance, valuation and accounting, and the dozens of other number-crunching jobs you do to manage $19 billion in assets, and you can easily see that a life insurance company's activities are virtually centered around its Data Processing Department. Yet

Executive Life was notoriously low in compensation and high in work demands for that department. They had good leadership, but without the resources in so labor-intensive a department, they were always hopelessly behind.

There were other problems, too. The life insurance industry had developed its interest-sensitive products without much regard for the data-processing systems modifications necessary to administer these lines of business. Then, years later, the software industry still had not come up with satisfactory support and administrative systems for the most popular products being sold. The type of interest-sensitive products that Executive Life sold were offered only by a handful of other companies and were never a priority of the software vendors when they finally did get around to producing support packages for the new-wave products. The system that supported the Irreplaceable Life℠ portfolio of products in 1990 was called Life 70™. Its name tells you when it was first introduced.

Other areas such as Policy Holder Service, New Business, and many operations departments of the company were even worse off than Systems, although it was the lack of systems that was at the bottom of most service problems. In a continual deluge of new sales between 1978 and 1988, the New Business Department was literally buried with work. They had seemingly mountainous stacks of applications waiting to be processed in the annuity and life departments through most of the early 1980s. It would take three and four times as long to issue a policy at Executive Life as it might at another company. In addition, because of the low pay scale and the high turnover, a lot of paperwork was mishandled or lost. I spent my first few months at Executive Life fielding angry complaints from our top producers about the outrageous service the agents received. Agents even organized into groups and stormed the home office, demanding meetings with Fred, me, and others to address the service issues.

Unbelievably, in 1986, the turnover in the operations area of the company was 106 percent! Employee morale at Executive Life always seemed to be low. Although the company did a number of special things to try to make it as enjoyable as possible to work under burdensome circumstances, most employees eventually gave up out of frustration and left for a more sane working environment. Fred was apparently convinced that this environment was acceptable in the overall scheme of things and that he was getting the best value for his money.

One of Fred's great skills was to do things for employees that were charming and personable in lieu of something substantive and costly. Employees were given a beautiful cake each year on their Executive Life anniversaries. Often they were remembered personally by Fred with a phone call; it was not uncommon for somebody at the managerial level or below to get a call from Fred congratulating them on their fourth or fifth Executive Life anniversary. During the holiday season, he did a great job of what he called "year-end" parties in which everyone went to the company annex building and had a lot of good food and entertainment. Typically, Fred would auction off something valuable such as an automobile or $10,000 in cash. Fred loved the hoopla of such occasions and took enormous pride in handing out the grand prizes and recognition.

Fred subscribed to the old adage of General Patton that morale in an army consists of "pride in the outfit and confidence in the leadership." He loved to be earthy and affable around his employees. He would pick an occasion such as the end of summer, Halloween, or once his fifteenth anniversary with the company, and throw a companywide bash. There would be a lot of advance promotion, with special little gifts arriving on each employee's desk before the party. It might be a jar of candy or a memento of the occasion. There would also be the trademark Fred Carr promotional T-shirt, commemorating the event with a picture and catchy saying. Then the party would begin at four or five in the afternoon with lots of refreshments and goodies. We never served alcohol at any Executive Life function, other than our sales conventions with our agents, where Fred had little choice. But he loved treats, particularly cookies and ice cream. Usually he would walk around passing out balloons or serving piles of chocolate chip cookies to employees as if he were part of the hired help. Fred's lack of formality made it impossible for any of the officers to pull rank or act pretentious. When you worked at Executive Life, the only respect you got was the respect you earned; your station in the company gave no particular assurance that anyone would pay much attention to you.

Fred was the classic avuncular company patriarch. He clearly understood that a little warmth, humor, and some chocolate chip cookies could go a long way to soothing an employee's ruffled feelings about the poor compensation and benefits he or she received at Executive Life when compared to the other insurance companies around town. I called this his "balloons instead of bucks" strategy. I must emphasize that he took genuine pleasure in these activities and that his motives were not just economic. Contrary to the images conjured up by the press, Fred Carr is a very sweet guy.

People Who Need People

Executive Life was the only life insurance company, of any size, that had no pension plan or profit-sharing plan. In fact, the only significant fringe benefit it had was the group health insurance plan, which was excellent. Fred reasoned that the type of employee he attracted didn't plan on being there long enough to accrue any long-term benefits. Typically they were young, single, sometimes itinerant, and tending to be focused more on short-term needs such as health care. When it came to equal opportunity employment, be it race, creed, or sexual preference, Executive Life was a model even the federal government would admire. Knowing his customer, Fred also provided two relatively inexpensive benefits that got a lot of appreciation. The first was a first-class health club, located in the lobby of the building and available to employees for a nominal fee of $5 per month. The second was an excellent lunch in the company cafeteria called the Garden Cafe, for which they only charged a dollar. Fred believed that a fringe benefit the employee could feel, smell, taste, and see had far more value than something as abstract as a pension plan or disability insurance, which always costs the company more than employees realize. I must say, after observing the situation, that the company health club and inexpensive lunches are two of the few benefits I have seen an employer provide where they got their money's worth.

Led by the Personnel Department in 1985, Executive Life came close to putting in a 401(k) Plan. However, Fred killed the whole deal at the last minute when he realized that it was customary for employers to make matching contributions to these types of qualified plans. Fred gave no reason for killing the plan other than to say that it was "a throwaway." This was his favorite term for things that cost money which he did not want to do or felt were not a good investment of his funds. After the 401(k) Plan died, employees pushed for an ESOP (Employee Stock Ownership Plan). Fred killed that idea when he realized that there were considerable expenses associated with it and that we could only set aside a maximum of $50,000 per year per employee. This didn't get the kind of private stock ownership he was looking for.

They did have a 125 Plan for a short while. This is the benefit plan whereby an employee voluntarily takes a pay cut, which is then earmarked for such things as medical reimbursement, day care, and dental expenses, allowing these expenditures to be made with before-tax dollars. At the time they instituted the plan, Executive Life, like many life insurance companies, was paying no federal income taxes. Then, with the Tax Reform Act of 1986, it eventually became a taxpayer like most other corporations. This meant that it would lose the income tax deduction it could otherwise have had on those monies employees took out of their compensation and put into the 125 Plan. When it was paying no taxes, the company had no need for deductions; but now the loss of a deduction such as employee compensation triggered taxation. The cost was about $500,000. In 1989, Fred ordered the elimination of the company's 125 Plan. For many, that was the final straw. They lost some good people.

The one benefit, other than health insurance, they did have

was a Stock Option Plan. It was not a particularly attractive plan in that, unlike most such plans, which vest over a period of five years and then allow the employee to have an additional five years to exercise the options, Executive Life's plan vested over five years, but required all options to be exercised within those five years or be lost. However, for a time, it was an exciting idea for a company whose stock had increased approximately 1,000 percent in value between 1974 and 1986. It certainly was the main economic reason for my joining the company. Unfortunately, as things played out, very few people made any money on the Stock Option Plan. Most of these options were awarded during our rapid growth period, 1980–86. Since they all vested and had to be exercised by the late 1980s, when our stock price started sliding, very few people had options that were in the black. Even those who held older options that did have value got killed because they borrowed money to buy the stock at the reduced strike price, only to have it come crashing through shortly afterward, leaving them permanently under water. These poor folks then wound up owing the bank the money they had borrowed to buy the stock in the first place.

The stock reached its all-time high in June 1986, at $23 a share. That was when I joined the company and received stock options, well into the seven-figure range, which I felt were a considerable offset to an otherwise low-paying job for someone at my level in the life insurance industry. Others joined the company on the same premise. All of us wound up with bushel baskets full of options that were worthless. In my case, I negotiated options in lieu of compensation for a period of about two years, during which I amassed more options than any officer in the company other than Fred. Of course, this was part of the risk we assumed, and for his part, Fred did a fine job of giving us upside potential. I think it was the rank-and-file employee who depended upon stock options as a type of deferred compensation who got hurt the most. Fred used to grow angry when we pointed this out because he felt that stock options, by their definition, carried no assurances of any value. Stock options were right up Fred's alley. They didn't require any immediate cash outlay. They appealed to one's sense of greed. And since our company didn't pay dividends, it cost nothing to have employees added to the role of shareholders other than that existing shareholders were slightly diluted by the additional stock that was authorized for the option plan.

So many of the employees were poorly qualified, young, single, and immigrants that the sales force called Executive Life the "Ellis Island of the West." It also became a comfortable employment environment for a number of people who needed a source of income while they pursued careers in show business. Executive Life attracted a lot of the people who moved out to L.A. in hopes of breaking into show business, but needed a job to sustain them in the meantime. I think the unofficial choice among the masses of show-biz hopefuls upon landing in L.A. was to be a singing waiter in a restaurant or work at Executive Life.

When management tried to convince Fred that he needed to do more for his employees, his answer usually was to give a party complete with balloons, cakes, and treats. Even though he was very accessible and unpretentious, he never really had personal relationships with the people who worked for him. To him, one was pretty much as good as another. It wasn't that he had any contemptuous feelings toward his employees, and he certainly didn't look down on them, for Fred Carr never looked down on his fellow human beings. He just dealt with his people as best he could and tried to get as much work out of them for his money as possible. Then, when they wanted a raise or promotion, or felt they were being mistreated, he would sincerely tell them that he would like to have done better for them and wished them well in their future endeavors. For a long time, Fred somehow got by with his "balloons instead of bucks" approach. Eventually, however, as things turned sour for the company and the stock options that had once been so important became worthless, people began to realize that a pension plan or a 401(k) Plan would have meant a lot to their financial security.

When things got ugly in the spring of 1990 and thousands of

annuity surrenders indicated a run at the bank, people pulled together and tried hard to process the burgeoning demands for surrenders. The company surrendered nearly $2 billion in annuities alone during the first half of 1990. This meant an awful lot of people had to work evenings and weekends to get the business processed and the checks out to the public. It was very important to Fred that it be perceived the company had no problem paying—and paying in cash. He made sure it had more than enough cash on hand ($2.9 billion in the First Executive Corporation on March 31, 1990). The last thing he wanted was for people to say the company was slow to process surrenders because it didn't have the money. I remember being asked by a reporter if there was any truth to the rumor that we had surrender requests stacked clear to the ceiling. I responded, "Not much, but don't forget our building has very low ceilings." Fortunately, he didn't quote me. As a result of the run, the rank and file in the Policy Holder Service area were stretched to the limit. In addition to the surrenders, there were thousands and thousands of phone calls from worried annuitants, most of an advanced age, and genuinely frightened about the security of their retirement. At the height of the crisis in March 1990, 25,000 phone calls came in per week company-wide. For many senior citizens, their only source of income, other than Social Security, was their annuity with Executive Life. It was always Fred's position that none of us, including himself, was too important to talk to a concerned customer. Fred and the rest of senior management took a substantial number of phone calls from worried policyholders, some of them downright tearful.

As the rash of annuity surrenders peaked in April, there were discussions by the company's senior management that we might consider a special bonus, sort of a combat pay, for those who had gone the extra mile during this difficult period. Instead, Fred declared Friday, July 27, 1990, Employee Appreciation Day. Each employee got an Employee Appreciation Day T-shirt. A special luncheon with exceptionally good cuisine was thrown in our company cafeteria. Fred and Alan Snyder, Executive Life's new president, gave heart-warming speeches about employee performance during these difficult times. They expressed sincere gratitude and optimism about our future. In the afternoon, everyone was surprised when the newly appointed president, Alan Snyder, appeared pushing a balloon-laden ice cream cart, dressed up like a Good Humor man and passing out Dove Bars. Fred was breaking Alan in right on his "ballons instead of bucks" philosophy.

In the past, employees had pretty much gone along with Fred's approach to employee morale problems. By 1990, however, people were a bit jaded. Their stock options were worthless, they had recently lost their 125 Plan, and there were persistent rumors (not to mention documentation in the press) that the holding company was going to go bankrupt and they would soon be taken over by the California Insurance Department.

Fred's solution to employee productivity would hardly make the textbooks of modern management, especially those we now read focusing on the Japanese approach to employee relations. The fact is, however, that these tactics worked reasonably well, especially when it was a smaller company. If one wants to judge Executive Life solely by results, there can be no doubt that it was among America's most cost-efficient life insurance companies. Year in year out, Executive Life ranked number 1 in the annual *Forbes* survey in the area of employee productivity. I should point out that the measures for the survey, like so many of those business journal assessments, were not exactly accurate. The argument can be made that it was not the employees that were efficient, it was the product they sold. Executive Life was ranked first by *Forbes* among insurance companies based upon the number of employees per $1 million of revenue. The fact is that revenue per employee was high, not because of the efficiency of our employees, but because of the size policy they sold. What *Forbes* didn't realize was that year in year out, Executive Life sold the highest average premium in the life insurance industry. Its average insured person was fifty-four years old and bought about $300,000–$400,000 worth of life insurance. This compares with an industry average of less than $50,000. The average premium was $6,000, as compared to an industry average of less than $1,000. Although their policies were cost-effective, this measure was skewed in their favor.

From an employee perspective, there were some good things about working for Fred Carr and Executive Life. First of all, it was for all purposes a lifetime employment situation if you wanted it (assuming the company's longevity exceeded that of the employees). He rarely fired anyone unless they did something downright dishonest or immoral. At the senior level, employees who were incompetent usually were turned out in as benevolent a way as possible. In the mid-1980s, a couple of officers generally regarded as incompetent by the sales force and most people in the home office, could have easily been discharged. Instead, they were set up in business by Fred, who gave them an opportunity to have an Executive Life franchise in the Southern California area. Armed with the hottest franchise in the industry and a shoe box full of agent leads that Fred allowed them to take with them, it was fairly easy for these individuals to build an MGA-type distribution system for the company overnight. In both cases, the people in question were highly compensated for a number of years before the bad publicity and strong competition caused the Executive Life franchise to fade into the mainstream of life insurance offerings. Once there was no magic to the franchise, these people were forced to compete like everyone else and wound up performing about as well as they did in the home office environment. Yet, for a while, they enjoyed artificially high compensation for the abilities they brought to the assignment. Of course, instead of being grateful for their brief good fortune, they became bitter about the turn of events. My predecessor, Joe Suske, who was not incompetent but just burned out by the situation, was given the Hawaii region. This plum included an income well into six figures, even though it had been developed from the mainland with no on-site management! He flew off into the blue horizon for what turned out to be one of the better deals anyone ever got out of Fred Carr. Of course, when the company went in the tank, so did Joe's sales organization, leaving him in the same boat as the rest of us.

Remarkably, some of the most senior positions in the corporation were awarded by Fred to clerical-level people who simply happened to be within arm's reach when he needed somebody to do a job for him. There were several examples of people who were simply not qualified by education or background for the six-digit-income jobs in administration that Fred eventually doled out of them.

Like his confidant Mike Milken, Fred liked to take ordinary, run-of-the-mill people and vault them into positions of exceptional responsibility. In doing so, he was assured, above all, of absolute loyalty. Other than Jim Cox, who is an enigma we will discuss later, the best example of this practice was Cheryl Wada. Until 1986, Cheryl was Fred's chief operating officer and the only executive vice president the company ever had. She started out with Fred in the early 1970s as his personal secretary. As the company grew, Fred heaped more and more responsibility on Cheryl, which was a way of maintaining control himself without it actually being apparent to some. His seemingly unlimited confidence in Cheryl Wada was a mystery to everyone. We were certain there was no romantic connection, as one might suspect in such a situation; rather, she was completely loyal to Fred, which obviously meant more than anything.

A kind and gentle person, Cheryl had little background for any of the operations, data processing, underwriting new business, marketing, and other responsibilities she oversaw. She literally ran the company for Fred—except she knew practically nothing about the life insurance business. We were all confident that Cheryl never aspired to nor asked for any of the responsibilities she wound up with. She would sit through our senior management meetings (in place of Fred, who rarely attended) motionless and silent. Her only movement was to gather information on a yellow legal pad, taking copious notes from our comments and suggestions. In time I realized that the notes were her efforts to try to piece together what it was we were talking about. Action was rarely taken on any of the matters we brought to her attention—or, if it was, it came from Fred's direction, not our guidance. For the most part Cheryl seemed genuinely bewildered by her role in the company and Fred's apparent confidence in her. I used to watch her in meetings when she would resort to her secretarial instincts and take notes; I assume she went back to her office and tried to make some sense out of them. If there hadn't been so much at stake, it would have been funny.

As the company grew explosively, Cheryl and several other members of the management team became hopelessly eclipsed by the ever-increasing demands of their jobs. When the field force grew in size and sophistication, they put more and more pressure on Fred to do something about the quality of his management team and the caliber of employee the company hired. The situation was exacerbated by the fact that Fred is a very non-confrontational person. He had a lot of difficulty hauling employees on the carpet or reprimanding them in any way. His solution was to psyche himself for a difficult meeting ahead of time; then he would gear up mentally with a series of statements that worked him from a casual conversation into a frenzy. It was quite something to watch, and someone always got to watch, because he would never do it without a third party present to witness and tell others what he was capable of. After a while, I would know when he was going to go into one of his ass-chewing routines. He would start out by commenting on some minor issue and begin to blow it out of proportion, swearing profusely, and eventually screaming and jumping up and down as if it were the most critical issue in the history of the company. It was very reminiscent of the old John Belushi shtick where he would begin in a low-key criticism of an individual, then pause and say, "But oh no, not you. You couldn't do it this way ..." at which point Belushi would begin ranting and raving like a lunatic. I think Fred borrowed this routine solely for the purpose of those occasions where he had to force himself to be tough with someone. It was totally out of character and really didn't wear very well with him. At first, those he used it on were shocked; eventually, they just took it with a grain of salt as one more example of Fred's eccentric behavior. Although he chose me for the role of witness on several occasions, I was fortunately never the subject of one of his onslaughts.

In time, it became more and more apparent that Cheryl Wada was hopelessly over her head with almost every aspect of her job. However, with a substantial salary and significant stock options, which at that time had great value, it was difficult for her to think of going elsewhere unless she wanted to take a significant pay cut. Finally, one day, Fred called her into his office with me present. He started explaining to Cheryl how the agents in the field were fed up with the poor service and administrative performance of herself and her staff. He began calmly but quickly started to build momentum. It was apparent that he was going into one of his Belushi shticks. When it finally reached the crescendo, with Fred pacing around the office flinging his arms about, Cheryl was close to tears. I'm fairly certain Fred had never done this type of thing to her before. Until then, he had never used the routine on his favorites, rather he liked having one of us present as a witness, just to see what might happen if we displeased him.

A few days after that, Cheryl announced she was resigning from Executive Life. Of course, Fred acted remorseful and said he didn't know what he was going to do without her. In fact, he never did replace her and I am certain she did leave by her own choice. At the time, only our chief legal counsel, our chief actuary, and myself reported to Fred. After Cheryl left, the rest of the senior vice presidents, the chief financial officer, the chief operating officer, the chief of Data Processing, and the vice president of Personnel all reported directly to Fred. In other words, they reported to no one. Fred had no interest in any of these disciplines and allowed each of the department heads to go their own way. We tried to have regular management meetings, but there really wasn't much point to it since Fred rarely attended. Without him there to make decisions on the information we presented, the meetings were more of an update to ourselves than an exercise of the management process. Even though

Cheryl had been just a buffer, at least we could count on her to read her notes on major issues to Fred and get back to us with his response.

One of the disadvantages of running a Fortune 500 sole proprietorship is the lack of checks and balances. Fred believed very strongly in checks and balances, but had to develop his own way of handling them in our unique environment. Executive Life had no budgeting. None. It had no serious internal controls. Instead of detailed budgeting, expense management, and management reports, Fred liked to encourage his executives to be watchdogs over one another. He didn't exactly pit them against one another, but he certainly made sure that each of them had an interest in the activities, expense management, and overall productivity of at least one other division of the company, headed by someone they perceived to be a competitor for higher stations in the organization. Actually, it was a pretty good system, except that we tended to focus only on those areas of the company we had some feel for. Consequently, if I were keeping my eye on Operations, for example, I was interested in reporting to Fred on those elements of that division that affected my area directly. This would include new business and underwriting, commission accounting, and so on. Things like investigating the validity of claims were not really an important area to me and, therefore, I didn't act as an effective watchdog. Obviously, in a large corporation, there is no substitute for internal controls. We simply didn't have enough of them, and in the long run, as is true of many of the areas in which we saved money in the short run, it wound up costing us a great deal. When people at all levels discover a company is vulnerable to financial abuses, they test it. When the word gets out in the industry that a company is easy to take advantage of, it is taken advantage of. In the case of Executive Life, it was easy, it was known, and plenty of advantage was taken by field and home office personnel alike.

The greatest inefficiency in the company, however, was not internal. First Executive Corporation had an addictive reliance on outside consultants. Much of what Fred gained by skimping on quality people internally was offset by the incredible fees paid to outsiders who ostensibly worked on our behalf in various capacities. To be sure, many of these individuals were essential to the success of the company, notably Al Jacob of Actuarial Analysts in New Jersey. He was the architect of the product portfolio which was central to the whole success story. But even he made Fred pay and pay and pay again for his contribution to the success.

In the Accounting Department, Fred repeatedly resisted the outside auditor's requests that they staff up adequately to meet the company's needs for annual and quarterly reporting. Usually the first quarter of the year when they were working on the annual financials, the company would spend hundreds of thousands of extra dollars on last-minute personnel to help pull the numbers together. They even paid double and triple for the printing of their many financial and annual statements because they worked the printers around the clock. It was as if they were doing a securities offering. The outside accountants at the time, Deloitte Touche, had great revenues in their Consulting Department from the Executive Life account in a number of areas. Most noteworthy was the fact that because Fred refused to have an adequate staff in the Accounting Department, they had to have consultants from Deloitte Touche come in and, in effect, do much of the work that should normally be done by the client's accounting staff. When Bill Sanders, the partner in charge of the First Executive audit for Deloitte Touche, joined the company as CFO, he told me he felt that First Executive Corporation spent about $2 million a year more than it needed to on the annual audit. He said that each year he would encourage Fred to add additional staff so that he wouldn't have to use his people at four and five times what the cost would have been to the company if they used their own employees. Finally, he joined the company and brought most of his auditing staff with him on the premise that he could save the company about a million dollars a year, even though he would be adding a million dollars or so to the payroll.

It was the same thing in the Data Processing Department.

Because the company either couldn't or wouldn't hire enough adequate programming help, they were constantly having to hire programmers from the outside. On one particular new product we developed in a subsidiary I managed, First Delaware Life, we spent $500,000 on outside systems modifications and programming work. Our product actuary later explained to me that if we sold this product successfully for the next ten years, we would never recover that investment. This was not the result of poor systems choices; rather, it was the tendency the company had to be so product-driven that when a new product was conceived, little consideration was given to the administrative and data-processing systems necessary to support it.

For product development and much of the administration associated with the policies themselves, they used Actuarial Analysts of New Jersey—an independent actuarial firm owned by the ubiquitous Al Jacob. For services rendered, Actuarial Analysts' average bill each month ran about $200,000. They could have probably done a lot of the less creative element of this work within the company, but perhaps it seemed that by farming out this less important but very profitable work to Actuarial Analysts, they were able to repay Al for his monumental contribution to the company. Some of Al's biggest bucks came in the early days, when he negotiated a number of reinsurance treaties that reportedly made millions for him. Many of these agreements later had to be undone because they failed to pass the smell tests of the California and New York Insurance departments. Al was probably better at product development than he was at negotiating reinsurance treaties—except of course for the fees he negotiated for himself.

Fred's favorite response to an employee's request for advancement or more compensation was "It will never be enough." He really believed that once you start giving in to people, it never stops. Once again, this isn't an approach to management one would find in a textbook, though it's hard to argue with in the real world. My own case was a good example. I had an ongoing annual sparring contest with Fred about my compensation. Having negotiated away some raises and bonuses in favor of stock options, I was in a losing spiral from the time I joined the company in 1986 when the stock was at its all-time high. As the stock price drifted down, I would double up like a Black Jack player thinking my luck had to change. It was sort of like dollar-cost averaging. When it didn't work out, I was understandably unhappy.

As always, Fred was gracious and sympathetic, but like a good Black Jack dealer, he reminded me we can only play the hand we are dealt, and a deal is a deal; had it gone the other way, I wouldn't have given back options in favor of other compensation. Of course he was right, but every year I would go to the mat with him on the inadequacy of my compensation, and every year he would invite me to plead my case to my heart's content. One year I thought I would try to bluff the dealer. I sent him a note saying, "Fred, it's that time of year again. Time for our annual confrontation over my compensation. This year, rather than argue, I am enclosing the first résumé I have ever prepared. Review it and decide what you should pay me. Make me the right offer and I'll tear it up. Otherwise, you may assume the obvious." Fred charged into a meeting we were both attending the next day and shook my hand. He said, "Gary, you get better every year. I can hardly wait until next year to see how you top the résumé tactic!" I got a good raise that year, but I am 100 percent sure my threat made no difference. Fred was simply not intimidatable.

In fact, his "It will never be enough" theory is probably right. Most of us think we're worth more than we are paid. Whether we are correct or not is not the point. When you work for someone else, it is not their goal to pay you what you're worth. If you paid everyone enough to make them happy, you could never succeed in a business. Therefore, one must conclude that if you're running your business properly, most of your people feel underpaid, but not enough for the good ones to leave. The way Fred saw it, the right compensation for an employee is one dollar more than what it took to keep them. Harsh, but especially true today.

8

The Rules of the Game

"First Executive was in the right place at the right time, and management had the foresight to capitalize on opportunities."
—Frederick S. Townsend, Jr., Partner, Townsend & Schupp Co., *Broker World*, November 1988

Despite Fred's idiosyncrasies in the way he ran his company, managers really should take an interest in his practices. Some of his tenets were unorthodox and totally without basis in social or management principles. Others, were as basic as the Ten Commandments. Given what he accomplished in a single decade, it would be a mistake for people not to consider that some of his views, though unconventional, may have a place in the management philosophy of other companies.

Fred Carr's Ten Rules for Running a Fortune 500 Sole Proprietorship

1. No one gets fired. One of the great things about working at Executive Life was you had to either do something dishonest, immoral, or downright stupid before you were fired. This was not a conscious principle as it is in Japanese companies. Part of it simply arose out of Fred's non-confrontational nature. More of it was probably due to the fact that Fred was almost paranoid about getting sued. He fired his exclusive national distributor of annuity products, Vince McGuiness, in about 1980, which was disastrous. He didn't go through the standard procedures most of us in corporate life know. There are a number of legal quagmires you can fall into if you're not careful about severance, especially in California. People must be treated consistently and fairly, not just in our eyes, but in the eyes of the law. Fred, having a sole proprietorship mentality, simply wrote the individual a letter and told him he was through representing us as a distributor of annuity products. Vince was his biggest producer, and apparently Fred was not too kind in the letter. Furthermore, when Fred hired him he forgot to tell him he didn't have an exclusive deal and his franchise was not forever. Executive Life got sued big time and lost. The final settlement was reportedly for $5.5 million plus legal fees. Fred made as many mistakes as the next guy, but he never made them twice. Vince McGuiness was the last person Fred Carr ever fired.

An important adjunct to this rule is that almost no one got hired either. When it came to staffing, Fred loved to remind us that "You can't solve any problems by throwing people at them." Fred hated adding people; he challenged, resisted, and procrastinated on every request for staff. He believed that most people were just not productive, and was always trying to explore ways to increase productivity—except, of course, for the conventional approaches of better wages and benefits. He believed that once staff was added, management could not deal with the pain of reducing it if need be later on. So, his solution was to make it as painful for us to get additions to staff as it was for us to reduce staff. Most of his executives would rather go through a root canal than go in to ask Fred for more staff. It just wasn't worth the grief he gave us. As a result, we had one of the lowest expense ratios in the life insurance industry, second only to the notoriously niggardly Northwestern Mutual.

2. Use the Chinese restaurant approach to customer service.
In Fred Carr's organization, one person was as good as the next
and, although everyone had a job, there was no job in the company that was less important than another. No one was permitted to wear their stripes. Furthermore, if an agent needed
something done, anyone could feel free to try to get it done for
him, regardless of whose responsibility it may be. The lines
between jobs were very blurred. Employees could assume
almost any responsibility that presented itself if they wanted to.

Fred was famous for carrying people's luggage at the conventions, serving them coffee, chasing down waiters to serve
his guests, or doing whatever it took to make his guests happy
when he was throwing a party. He was the same way around
his office, fetching beverages, cookies, popcorn, and carrot
sticks, all of which were part of almost every meeting. He never
had a guest he did not walk to the elevator when they left. Fred
expected the same attitude from all of his employees when
dealing with agents. I called this *Fred Carr's Chinese restaurant
approach to customer service.*

When the Chinese first arrived in America, they started out,
as do most immigrants, trying to fit into our culture. I assume
some Chinese people worked in lowly positions in the traditional restaurants of the day, learning the way the business
operates, including the hierarchy (maître d', headwaiter, waiter,
busboy, etc.). Then, when the Chinese opened their own restaurants, they tried to apply what they learned to accommodate
the ways of the typical American. My guess is that the
American approach didn't work for Chinese restaurants, and so
gave birth to the most efficient method of operating a restaurant, which to this day, for some odd reason, is the purview of
the Chinese.

It probably went like this. The typical patron would ask for
service during his meal: "Oh Chong, may I have more soy
sauce?" The person to whom he addressed his question would
then reply: "Excuse sir, my name Fong. Chong maître d'. Your
waiter name Dong, but if you want soy sauce, must ask busboy.
His name, Wong!" I postulate that the typical brusque

American, to whom the employees all looked alike and were named alike, eventually wore down the inscrutable proprietors. Finally every employee answered to any name ending in "ong" and delivered the requested service. Today, one of the great things about eating in a Chinese restaurant is that you can ask any employee for almost anything. If you want a beer, you just flag down whoever is passing and they bring it to you. The lines of responsibility are blurred; as a result, the service is efficient and responsive, and the tables turn over quickly. That may be one reason it seems Chinese restaurants seldom go out of business. In the case of Executive Life, this approach was not used so much to provide efficient service as to maximize the productivity Fred could wring out of his employees; the result was greater expense control, rather than better service.

Nobody at First Executive Corporation was allowed to assume any type of superior demeanor in the corporation due to their rank. There were never clearly defined lines between officers, and no one person was treated much differently than anyone else. The idea of referring to someone as "Mr.," "Mrs.," or "Ms." was unheard of. I never heard any employee refer to Fred as "Mr. Carr." In recent years, the first-name approach has been awkwardly adapted by a number of companies because the fad management books have said it's the thing to do. At Executive Life, it just never occurred to anyone to call another by anything other than their first name. That's the difference between a corporate climate that fosters openness and top-down management that mandates it. Like the people who run Chinese restaurants, Fred took a different tack in building his business than the establishment recommended.

3. **Manage conflict like a matador.** Before the events of 1990, I was going to write a book on Fred Carr entitled *Matadorial Management*. The term best describes his uncanny ability to sidestep almost any potential conflict or problem until it dissipates from the pure exhaustion of never being attended to. Fred believed that most tough issues are best left undealt with until they either work themselves out through attrition and changing circumstances or become full-blown crises. His view seemed to

be that the time, energy, and other resources needed to handle the problems on everyone's daily list, the way most companies do, through meetings, committees, budgets, and the like, exceeded the value of the end result.

Meetings and committees tied up groups of people, for all of whom the payroll meter was running, while they sat around, usually making decisions that involved spending more money. For this reason, Fred discouraged any committees within the company and forbade any meetings before 4:00 p.m. (he used to say that that way he knew they would end by 5:00 p.m., when people wanted to go home). Instead, people in the company who had problems were encouraged to bring them directly to Fred. If the solution to the problem involved spending money, he usually said, "No," or, "I'll get back to you," meaning, "I'll put it off until it becomes a crisis." His style was to let issues smolder until they either went away or became a roaring blaze. Thus, he never dealt with smoke, only fire. This was a major weakness in the view of some of us, especially Jerry Schwartz, who felt Fred's "no response, no information style" was a main cause of the company's undoing.

If it was a non-monetary problem, he would usually tell the individual to check with another party he felt could offer some perspective (by telephone, not by meeting), or he would just say, "Do what you think best."

The amazing thing was that most of the problems he brushed aside did eventually work themselves out. Fred felt that at the point when most problems are identified, you seldom have enough information to make a good decision. By the time you have enough information, the solution is obvious, so there is no need to meet on it. This approach often worked with things like setting interest rates on our policies or doing a securities offering, for which he would always wait until the very last minute to make a decision. It also worked on issues like the defaults we were experiencing in 1989, which he avoided sitting down and discussing until the rights offering was closed and he had the $285 million it raised in his pocket. In areas like data processing, where we needed top-down strategic decisions on some fundamental issues, it was interesting to watch. A number of software vendors had insisted they could solve the company's problems if Fred would engage them to build a customized system for the company. Fred told them that when they could show him another life insurance company whose problem they had solved at the quoted price and in a way that had improved the company's profitability, he would sign a contract. None of them ever came back, and executive life never upgraded its D.P. system. Fred often stated that, at least in the insurance industry, "twenty-five years of ever-increasing computerization has failed to eliminate the first job." Where, he wanted to know, was the cost benefit of automation? As a result, he dodged every possible big decision in this area.

Once in a while, like the brilliant matador he was, Fred would surprise a problem by burying a sword between the shoulder blades. That was his response to a crisis. A good example of this was when he was negotiating with Jerry Schwartz and his partners for the purchase of their agent owned reinsurance company (AORC). The group, at one time, was thinking in terms of $50-60 million or so as the purchase price, based upon their analysis of what companies were selling for at the time and the high quality of their book of business. The understanding was that Executive Life would make an offer to purchase their AORC at the end of its tenth year of operation Jerry and his partners started working on the capitalization plan eighteen months ahead of time, but their activities were basically unilateral. Predictably, Fred waited until the very last minute to sit down with them in late 1989. Waiting paid off for Fred. Things were tense by then, and the overall appeal of insurance companies to potential buyers was fading fast. After some negotiating, Fred offered a price that, depending upon how their business persisted, would be between $40 and $50 million. No concessions. Take it or leave it. They took it.

4. Give balloons instead of bucks. We have already discussed this management tactic in some detail. Nobody was better at making you feel good about your relationship with your company than Fred. We would regularly receive kind notes from him, comical little cards offering an apology for a tiff you may have had with him, or phone calls on special occasions such as your company anniversary.

On this count, I must say it is unfair just to say he was gracious only as a substitute for spending money. Fred is a naturally gracious and considerate guy. I remember limping around the office one day because I had thrown my back out playing tennis. Fred noticed and inquired. Then he called me later that day and urged me to go to a doctor. I informed him I had an appointment with a chiropractor the following day. Then he called me at home that night to tell me he was worried because he didn't have confidence in chiropractors; he wanted me to visit his physician, who had taken care of his bad back in the past. This was typical of the kind of interest Fred took in many of his close associates. That was the paradox of his personality: he never opened up to us the way a true friend might, yet he showed the concern of a true friend if we had a problem. Not at all in keeping with the image of him portrayed in *Barron's* and *Forbes*.

5. Manage on a need-to-know basis. Tell people only what they need to know to do their job. To tell them more is superfluous and can lead to a lot of communication problems within the company. The thing Fred most hated about being a publicly traded corporation was the fact that he had to discuss his business activities publicly. For Fred Carr to stand before a bunch of analysts or reporters and discuss his business life was as uncomfortable as most people would find answering questions about their sex lives in the same forum.

Fred was a master at pigeon-holing relationships. Each individual operated independently of the rest of the management of the company to whatever extent possible. Fred seldom attended management meetings and rarely chaired the few of which he was a part. He discouraged interaction between his senior officers, preferring instead to have them deal with him privately about their activities and problems. We seldom used a collective approach to solving problems or devising strategies. It was always every man for himself, subject to Fred's approval. It is important to note, however, that his approval was easy to get if you came prepared. Fred did not second-guess his executives or look over our shoulders. When we visited with Fred about our plans and projects, he seldom changed a thing. We ran our units of the company as if they were free-standing subsidiaries. This approach can be beneficial, but for it to work, there must be some networking. The left hand must know what the right is doing. This is where our management team fell apart. We seldom interacted in meaningful ways about our activities and priorities. The area that suffered most because of this was the Information Systems Department, which never knew what our priorities were, only what the latest crisis was. Raul Cruz, who ran the department, continually pleaded with Fred to give him his marching orders so he could let us have what we needed; but even when he did, the priorities would shift momentarily.

Still, managing on a need-to-know basis had one advantage that was very important to Fred: he was the only one who knew all the components of the formula for running the company. This way he maintained total control without ever having to assert himself.

6. If it's important, never put it in writing. In the five-year period I worked for him, I received three memos from Fred. One of them was to remind me that anything I put in writing was a matter of public record and could never be taken back. Therefore, all managers should communicate with him verbally before putting down their thoughts on paper. Fred was almost fanatical about this. I had learned in my business career to communicate by memo; it was a way to put my thoughts down on paper and allow feedback from my superiors as to whether or not I was going in the right direction. Memos were also an excellent way of preparing for an important meeting—they give everyone an overview of the issues to digest before the meeting. Fred preferred a spontaneous meeting or, better yet, a simple phone call to discuss any pressing issue.

Part of this had to do with Fred's phobia about being sued. He believed that in every business relationship, if there was a way people could take advantage of something you told them or misinterpret something you said or wrote, you should assume they would. He believed fervently that any written memo or letter to an employee, field person, or policyholder was wide open, and could be interpreted as they saw fit should the relationship at some point turn adversarial. I guess part of this came from the termination letter he sent Vince McGuiness, which reportedly wound up costing the company close to $6 million. I suppose that would make a lot of us paranoid.

Appreciation was the one important thing that Fred Carr always put in writing. Thank you, congratulations, and "just thinking of you" cards and notes were regularly received by many home-office people and salespeople. In this notable exception to his "never put it in writing" rule, Fred was almost prolific. A lot of us have a drawer full of kind remembrances from Fred that we greatly value.

I must say that I've been surprised at the number of high-level executives I have known who keep careful documentation of everything their CEO or president sends them. I also know several executives who even keep a record of telephone discussions with their CEO, in which they carefully document every subject covered in each discussion and file it for future reference. Fred is probably right. When you're the boss, it's best to assume you're always on camera, and that everything you say or put in writing will eventually be used against you in the worst possible light. That's the litigious society in which we are living today.

7. **The telephone is the most important tool in your business life.** This rule is no secret, but Fred used the telephone with far more skill than anyone I've ever known. He even used it to the almost complete exclusion of travel. Fred managed to travel only rarely—for example, when he was doing a road show to promote a capital-raising effort. Other than such major items, since he never took vacations, he was in every day. I guess Fred was in his office 50 percent more than the typical CEO, and usually on the telephone. Some of his ability in this area must have come from his mutual fund days when, although he was running the hottest fund on Wall Street, he seldom left Los Angeles.

He was a master of time management. Little time was wasted in meetings or unnecessary activities. When you did meet with Fred, it was concise and to the point. Meetings seldom lasted more than twenty minutes. I used to go to Fred's office with a hit list of eight or ten items that, in my previous company, would have inspired a month of meetings and deliberation. Fred would go down the list with me with a consistency that never varied. "Yes" meant "Run with it and do what you want so long as you keep me informed." "No" meant "No." He never reversed a no, so there was nothing to do but move on to the next subject. Because he was so consistent in his logic, I usually knew which would get a yes and which a no before the meeting. The third answer was, "I'll get back to you," which meant, "Let me handle it in my own way." Most of these last issues were ones Fred did not want to deal with—nor did he want anyone else dealing with them.

While meeting with you, no matter who you were, Fred always took all phone calls. This got to be irritating in that one could barely get through a conversation without three or four interruptions. On the other hand, given the level of telephone activity he had to deal with, it probably made good sense. At any rate, one thing he was known for was always being accessible and always returning calls on those rare occasions where he was unable to take them.

Fred's greatest skill with the telephone was to call people almost daily just to check in and see how things were going. It's very difficult to stay in daily touch with all the key people in one's organization. Yet Fred used to call me daily if he hadn't heard from me first. He'd find some reason to call, usually something remarkably unimportant to which he seemed to attach significance—a minor complaint from an agent or a policyholder, a casual remark by an employee that was disturbing to him. Almost anything that one would normally expect to slip through the cracks always came to Fred's attention. Very little escaped his notice. Yet he seldom acted on anything he heard about.

Although always happy to meet with me, when I called for an appointment he would say, "Of course, unless we can handle it over the phone." Even though we met almost daily my first few years with the company, frequently we would avoid a second or third meeting that day by using the phone. He also would call us at odd hours during the day and weekend. It wasn't uncommon for all of us in senior management, and for that matter many of our field force, to get calls from Fred early on a Saturday morning or late on a Sunday night. He never seemed to rest and was always an arm's length from his own telephone when we called him. Rarely did I get two rings off before he would answer his private line at home.

Another surprising thing was that telephone conversations never had to be terminated unless you wanted them to be. He was willing to listen to whatever you had to discuss until you had completed your thoughts. Frequently, there would be the noise of papers rustling in the background, which meant he was probably reading or doing some work while talking to you, but still you got as much time as you wanted when you called him. Fred is a person who automatically has at least two things going on in his head at once. During meetings there was always a legal pad in front of him, on which he would periodically scrawl a key word or phrase to remind him of something. People thought he was taking notes on the meeting, but this was rarely the case. Usually the notes were on an entirely different subject he was thinking about while sitting through the meeting. Many of us try to do two things at once, but Fred really could. He never missed a beat or lost his place in a meeting just because of the second meeting going on in his mind. I think one of the reasons he loved the telephone is that it wasn't so obvious what he was doing while he was talking with you.

8. Turn the other cheek at all costs. Nobody, but nobody, is more reluctant to criticize his fellow human being than Fred Carr. You simply cannot coax a negative remark out of him about even the most distasteful of persons. His tolerance of his enemies is almost Lincolnesque. Take Joseph Belth, the editor of *Insurance Forum*, which regularly attacked Executive Life. Belth was certainly someone Fred had good reason to dislike, and for whom he must have felt contempt. Yet, when we discussed

Belth's latest attack on the company, Fred would shrug his shoulders and say, "Well, he's found a way to make a living and I guess everybody needs to do that. Unfortunately, we make good fodder for him and help build up his reprint sales. He's discovered a business that's working for him, and I suspect it will continue to do so for a long time."

Fred was oblivious to bad behavior. People could behave boorishly, rudely, even vulgarly toward him and he would shrug it off. At sales conventions, agents might buttonhole him after having too much to drink and behave in ill-mannered or insulting ways, still without much response. They could show a lack of respect for his station and position, without ever eliciting a response. He would just remark mildly, "People are people, what can I say?" He simply was unoffendable. I sometimes think that he viewed people with a benevolent condescension that caused him to hold them not responsible for their poor behavior. He seemed to feel as if most people didn't know any better. Therefore, why get angry at them?

I remember sitting in his office one day when a particularly damaging article had just come out in the *San Francisco Chronicle*. The reporter had interviewed Fred under the guise of an objective, balanced article he was researching on junk bonds. In reality, all he really wanted from Fred was to work a quote or two into a piece he had already completed. Fred went to great lengths to be helpful when the reporter called for a telephone interview. He even violated his own rule of using the telephone for interviews and invited him to fly down and meet at the airport for a few hours, so he could present him with the most current facts on the company. Fred showed up at the Admiral's Club at LAX with a shopping bag full of documentation on the company and the junk bond market. He also gave the reporter a glimpse of his eccentricity as he produced the customary bag of celery and carrots he always keeps to munch on during meetings. From the account of Jerry Schwartz, who was in attendance, it was an upbeat and enlightening experience for the young reporter, who acted as if he was interested in learning the facts instead of perpetuating the misconceptions about First

Executive. Then, of course, when the article came out, it was just another standard job of First Executive bashing. It turned out the reporter had been working with Joseph Belth on the piece for some time.

Fred smiled when we discussed it and said, "Well, I suppose I could call John up and ask him how he could do such a thing; how he could take advantage of my confidence and pose as somebody who was fairly neutral, when in fact he had no intention to do anything other than a hatchet job on me. I could scream and holler and cuss him out. But what would that accomplish? It probably wouldn't accomplish anything except let him know that he had gotten to me. I don't think I want to dignify his attack on us by letting him know it's disturbing to me. Because, in fact, it isn't. He's got to do his job and I've got to do mine." I really believe that Fred meant that. I don't think he took anything personally, no matter how frequently people seemed to attack him on that basis. He understood that being a public figure made you an "item" rather than a person.

Agents regularly became furious with Fred over his refusal to respond to the attacks on his character and on the company. In time, they began to wonder if the reason for his reluctance to retaliate had something to do with possible validity to the charges being made. I don't believe that. Fred simply was above the business of mud slinging and innuendo and the type of thing that was being practiced against him. In the broadest sense, his attitude was virtuous, but in the practical world of the agent trying to save a sale, it was all wrong. He believed that in the long run, history would prove that him and his strategy with First Executive to be right. He was counting on posterity being his judge, rather than a bunch of uninformed, biased reporters and detractors. He's still counting on it.

9. Use the ethereal carrot as a motivational tool. I swear Fred Carr doesn't own a checkbook. He doesn't need one. When it's time for Fred to shell out money, whether it's a bonus to an employee, cash for an AORC, or an overdue dividend to stockholders, he always manages to get them to take some of his "Chinese paper" instead. Chinese paper is a term originally used to describe the debt of the highly leveraged conglomerates of the 1960s, vis-à-vis LTV Corporation. At Executive Life, the term was revived by general agent Mike Gilman—who had been with Fred the longest of any of us—to describe Fred's penchant for putting together convoluted deals to restructure and push back any obligation for which he had to write a check. The deal was always too good to refuse, or so it appeared. He used stock options to lure key executives to the company rather than pay market wages. When the options appeal faded, he instituted a unit share program that gave us the actual stock. Several of us were given awards with a market value of six digits the first year we had the plan. The zinger was that there was zero vesting for five years.

When the company's first agent owned reinsurance program started, they planned on a five-year production commitment, after which the agents would sell or capitalize the company and go their own separate ways. At the end of the fifth year, Fred put together various incentive and loyalty plans to get agents to re-up for another five years in exchange for stock, warrants, or other non-cash goodies. Everyone re-upped. The package he put together for the sale of Executive Life of New York was so circular that in the final analysis, even if the deal had gone through, it was a non-sale sale. And of course, his most notable and bold Chinese paper was the 1989 rights offering, which we will discuss elsewhere.

After three or four personal experiences with Fred, where he got me so excited about my future rewards that I would probably have worked for him for next to nothing, I became a bit wily. Not because the deals he offered weren't fair. They were. They just didn't work out. None of them. Toward the end, when our AORC deals fell apart, a lot of the field people felt they had been snookered. I don't believe that was anyone's intent, especially Fred's, and had things worked out, I'm sure nobody would be complaining. Fred's approach has always been to offer bigger rewards on the back end with as few as possible up front. That way, you only reward those who have earned it—providing everything else works out. He even did this with our

Irreplaceable Life^SM policies; they were back-end-loaded contracts that worked best only if the client kept them for twenty years or more. Everyone who quit before then paid a heavy surrender charge.

10. Always be accessible, but never influenceable. If you had a scheme, a pitch, a million-dollar idea for the life insurance industry, or almost any idea you thought was worth listening to, the one CEO who would always give you an audience was Fred Carr. Clearly, he was the most accessible CEO in the industry, but influencing his judgment by anything other than cold, hard evidence is a virtual impossibility.

Many days Fred's office looked like that of the Godfather on his daughter's wedding day. There would be two or three major sales personalities, investment bankers, or product gurus in the reception area waiting for their audience to share their multi-million-dollar idea with Fred. Anyone in the industry who thought they had a way of doing business profitably could get an appointment to talk to him about developing a product or sharing a market with them. He would listen to a hundred ideas and reject ninety-nine. But occasionally that one in a hundred would ring right with him. In fact, most of Executive Life's big sales ideas came from the field. A whole series of markets were virtually invented by the field force. They would sell Fred on the concept, then he would give it to Al Jacob to turn into a product. One of the reasons this would happen was because of the encouragement of feedback and creativity from the field by Fred.

For many agents, it was the first time in their career that they could sit down and share their marketing ideas or product ideas with a company CEO, knowing they would get a receptive ear. If the agent could make the sale—and again, that was the hard part—he could actually have some type of a founder's fee on the premiums developed from his idea. This happened more than once and made a lot of money for some agents. Most amazingly, if Fred liked an idea, he'd go to press with it immediately. The agents would literally start selling the product before the company had administrative support or the ability to issue a policy. Fred used to say that if we waited around until all the administrative and operations people were ready to give us the green light, the window of opportunity for most markets would have long passed. Therefore, when an agent invented a new product that Fred liked, he ran with it and sold it, administration be damned. The price of this philosophy was, of course, poor service. When the agents complained about service, Fred would always remind them that if they wanted him to adapt the product development practices of their former companies, he would be happy to do so, but this would mean that as far as agents were concerned, the patent office was closed!

On the other hand, if you had a position you wanted to sell Fred on that was more hype than substance, look out. When it comes to a business decision, he is the most dispassionate person I have ever known. Basically, no matter who you were, how capable you were of persuading others, how eloquent your argument, Fred could cut to the center and make a judgment call in record time. I've never known anyone so consistent in his resistance to influence by emotions, salesmanship, or other passionate pleas. Yet those who wanted to sell Fred on an idea seemed never to get the hang of it. They'd keep coming back to the well, hoping they could persuade him to go in their direction rather than the one he had chosen. I'll never understand why he kept seeing people over the same issues, knowing there wasn't a chance in hell he'd ever change his mind. Yet this was Fred. If you wanted to come back to re-argue your case, you could do so. You could do it again and again and again. But never would you make one inch of progress in dissuading Fred from his position unless that's where he wanted to go. And if he had wanted to go there, he would have done so the first time.

In the five years I worked for him, Fred Carr never once deviated from any of these ten principles.

I Get By with a Little Help from My Friends

William L. Morris, founder of the world-famous William L. Morris talent agency in Los Angeles, used to say, "The most important quality in a business relationship is loyalty, but you have to be willing to pay for it!" When I first heard that quote, I thought it was a witty cynicism. After getting to know Fred, I realized that William L. Morris was probably right on the money in many situations. Fred did not expect loyalty from most of his people. It never seemed to surprise him when someone turned on him or the company in a given situation. Although no one was intimate with Fred, those few people who were very close associates were expected to be loyal. And Fred understood what Mr. Morris was saying. He paid for it, and paid well.

Perhaps the hardest thing about running a publicly traded Fortune 500 sole proprietorship is the issue of accountability. Fred hated being held accountable or having to explain his position or actions. This was evident at annual shareholder meetings and press conferences, which he only participated in reluctantly, because he had to. One place Fred managed to keep his accountability at least minimal was his board of directors on the holding company level, First Executive Corporation (this being the *real* board, not the nominal boards of the subsidiaries on which I served).

The reality of the corporate world is that board involvement in company management is usually a myth. Most boards I have observed go through great pomp and ceremony but have little understanding and even less real say in the day-to-day operations of the company. Much has been written in recent years about the lack of hands-on involvement of most corporate boards; these accusations have led to a number of suits by angry shareholders, who feel board members accept fat fees for prestigious positions to which they seldom bring anything in the way of management performance. On this issue, one could say Fred didn't waste time putting up a front. He put together a three- or four-person board consisting of the few people he regarded as competent and whose contribution he felt would be worth what he paid them. In addition to his friend Al Handschumacher, he had his close business associate George Rosenthal. George and Fred were involved in several real estate deals together. George is the owner of Raleigh Enterprises, a real estate firm with considerable office building and hotel holdings in the Los Angeles area. Most of Fred and George's dealings were kept private, but George's company and its affiliates did manage the Executive Life complex in which they also resided, for which, along with their other dealings with First Executive, they collected fees in excess of $1 million in a typical year.

To balance the board out there was Ben Nelson, a former Insurance Commissioner from Nebraska whose law firm Fred kept on a surprisingly large retainer for various helping hands it gave the company with lobbying efforts at the Insurance departments around the country. Ben and his law firm, Kennedy, Holland, DeLacy & Svoboda, collected over $900,000 in fees in 1989, and more than a million dollars in fees in 1990. Exactly what they did that warranted a million-dollar year in fees was never very clear to many of us.

Periodically, Fred would respond to the criticism that the board was tilted in his favor by appointing a prominent outsider. In 1987, Al Handschumacher convinced Fred to appoint an old friend, Norman Barker, retired chairman of First Interstate Bank in California and a very prominent figure in Los Angeles. They got more than they bargained for with Norm, who took the job seriously and hung in there until the end, challenging some of Fred's tactics along the way.

In 1986, Fred appointed Warren Bennis, the former Harvard and MIT professor who is currently at the University of Southern California, where he has distinguished himself, among other things, as a best-selling author and nationally known speaker on the subject of leadership. After three years on the Fred Carr Express, Warren decided he had had about all of Fred's brand of leadership he could stand, and resigned. Keeping people of Warren's stature and integrity on a board as unusual as First Executive's was a constant struggle.

When ICH, the Louisville Insurance holding company, acquired a 20 percent interest in First Executive Corporation, Fred grudgingly permitted them to have representation on the board. ICH Chairman Bob Shaw chose his own low-profile board member, ICH's senior vice president of corporate relations, who basically was there to keep Shaw informed of what Fred was up to in the chess game the two of them had played for four years.

Officers were never invited to attend board meetings; nor did we ever make periodic presentations to the board about our various divisions, as most of us had grown accustomed to doing in our previous experience. In fact, during my five years with the company, I was never even introduced to a board member. Instead, I figured out who I needed to know, and made a point of building a relationship with them. Ben Nelson was one of the key players. Now governor of Nebraska, Ben was very highly regarded by Fred and was seriously considered as a candidate for the presidency (of Executive Life, not the USA), but Ben had other candidacies in mind. He knew his way around the regulatory community, which was a big help to Fred, who had notoriously strained relationships with the NAIC. Unfortunately, the evening I flew to Nebraska to have dinner with Ben, in hopes of gaining his confidence and learning more about the goings on at the company, he told me he had decided to run for governor and that if nominated, he would win. This meant he would have to resign from our board. The other board member it was important to know was Handschumacher. Even though he, like the rest of the board, played little role in the operational decisions, Fred had a permanent loyalty to Al for having brought him to the company, and kept him generally better informed than the rest. Eventually Al and I became pretty close.

When Caroline Hunt's Rosewood Financial acquired a 10 percent stake in First Executive Corporation, the principals of the firm became outraged at the structure of our board. As the situation deteriorated in 1988 and 1989, Rosewood repeatedly tried everything it could to gain influence with the board in its well-publicized quest to oust Fred Carr. It had no notable success until it challenged Nelson and Rosenthal, based on a conflict of interest due to the seven-digit fees they were collecting from the company for services rendered. Both men resigned from the board about the same time, supposedly for other reasons. In the case of Ben Nelson, running for governor was a good one. His opponent, incumbent Kay Orr, chose to make First Executive junk bonds and Mike Milken the central issue of her campaign. Ms. Orr blasted Nelson for his role as chairman of two First Executive subsidiaries, First Stratford and Regency Equities, in which Mike Milken had a major stake. Meanwhile, Ben distanced himself from First Executive by focusing on local issues, questioning why the people in Nebraska should care about what goes on between the high rollers of Beverly Hills, California. Ben won the election by the narrowest of margins.

In addition to key board relationships, some of the outside consultant relationships had overtones that were disconcerting to me and others. I'm surprised that with all the scrutiny and innuendos First Executive Corporation has been subjected to, no one has challenged some of these relationships. Although I have no reason to believe Fred did anything dishonest, the inconsistency in the way he spent the company's money in these as opposed to other areas is a mystery.

Al Jacob was always the best-known outsider when it came to asking the question, "Who has Fred made rich?" Actually, Al made Al rich. He just took charge, billing the company $200,000 per month and more in fees, and making huge sums on his reinsurance contracts and product development ideas. The fees and expenses Al charged the company for his services were probably the highest any company ever paid for similar actuarial work. Al's personal expenses for MGM Air, hotel suites, and a VIP reputation with the wine stewards of Los Angeles' finest restaurants were a constant reminder of his powerful influence in the company. Al knew that Fred was very non-confrontational and would rather pay a bill than argue it with a key person in the organization (he'd always argue with outsiders, or more likely not pay at all if he felt overcharged).

Bud Warner was Fred's personal accountant and long-time business associate. His accounting firm, Warner & Corbette, did the leasing and limited partnerships which Fred put together on

the new home office buildings on Olympic Boulevard for partic-
ipation by company officers. For his role, Warner's firm collected retainers of $50,000 per month in a typical year. As was
the case with George Rosenthal, Fred had a number of private
dealings with Bud, who profited substantially from services
rendered to First Executive Corporation for which he seemingly
never had to compete.

The most mysterious of Fred's inner circle was unquestion-
ably Jim Cox. An old friend of Fred's from his stockbroker days
in Los Angeles, Jim worked at the company as a one-man
investment department until he left to form his own company,
Sallis Securities, whose only significant client was First
Executive Corporation. When Jim left, he simply moved up to
the tenth floor of the building at Wilshire and Santa Monica and
suddenly started collecting fees that were five times greater
than his salary had been. Jim was a chain-smoking bundle of
nerves, and I never met anyone as seemingly uncomfortable
about his role. A nice fellow, he was not especially impressive to
other investment people who met him. This was surprising
when one considers that the company paid his tiny three-man
firm $75,000 per month for his advice. This was only the tip of
the iceberg. Sallis Securities received huge fees on many company transactions and securities offerings that ran into the millions. Jim's specialty was the private placements that Drexel
brought to the company. These were loans to smaller firms
which did not warrant a public offering. Jim put together the
deals, usually involving transactions of $5 million to $25 million, on which his fees were netted from the loan proceeds. Why
he needed a retainer on top of his considerable fees was questioned by some of us privately.

It's hard to say how much Jim was paid in fees, but every
time I poked my nose into the subject, I was surprised by what I
learned. In 1989, when Executive Life did its $750 million collat-
eralized bond obligation (CBO), Sallis made a deal to manage
and market the package. Basically, the transaction involved the
packaging of various holdings of the company, which ranged
from junk to investment grade, into six companies that in turn

would be offered for sale to outside investors. When the company got a barrage of bad press because the structure camouflaged the junk and won an investment grade rating for the CBOs, it reached an agreement with the California Insurance Department to unravel the deal and reverse the transaction. Cox, who by mid-1990 was the most stressed-out-looking man I have ever seen in my life, wanted out. Not just out of the CBO deal, but out of his relationship with Fred Carr. I was jolted, along with other Executive Life board members, when we were asked to approved the payment to Sallis Securities of $2.7 million for undoing the CBO deal and related fees that were promised. When we questioned the amount, we were assured that Alan and Fred had negotiated long and hard with Cox, and this was the best settlement they could attain. One thing I was sure about was that Alan Snyder was a tough negotiator, and notoriously tight with a buck. He was very emphatic that he went to the mat with Cox on this issue and settled below the contractual rights Jim was entitled to. So we okayed the payment. After that, Jim Cox promptly retired. Few of us in the company have seen him since.

While Fred was skillfully waving the ethereal carrot at most of us, he was making a chosen few of his associates rich. There's a lot of speculation about the nature of these relationships. I choose to believe that Fred felt the company was better served by having these individuals involved in the various projects I have described. One outside consultant and friend who was privy to much of the financial data was having lunch with me in mid-1990. After discussing some statistics on the kind of money the otherwise tight-fisted Carr paid his outside consultants, especially Jim Cox, my friend said: "You know, it boils down to this. Fred Carr is either stupid or he's crooked." I responded: "Whether or not Fred is crooked is something I honestly do not know. Whether or not he is stupid is something I know for certain." Still, I don't think this fellow would have made the statement if he knew Fred as the rest of us did.

9

The Sayings and Antics of Chairman Fred

---

*"Watching Fred Carr maneuver is like watching Picasso paint.
You have to take off your hat and acknowledge that you are in the
presence of a master."*
— Allan Sloan, syndicated financial columnist,
New York Newsday, July 30, 1989

Most people would agree that, in general, there has been a lack of leadership in the life insurance industry at the top level for quite a while. There were plenty of greats in the sales arena; Marshall Wolper, Norm Levine, Barry Kaye, John Todd, John Savage, and a host of others come to mind. But in the executive suites, the dearth of talent has persisted. In the 1980s, if you held a gun to the head of many of us in the industry, we couldn't tell you the name of a single CEO at a Top 25 company other than the one we represented. The sole exception was Fred Carr.

Just about everyone knew who Fred Carr was. There were a number of reasons for his notoriety, but I believe the most important one had to do with his unique style of leadership.

Fred was the leader of the interest-sensitive revolution. Even though many of its leading participants held him in the greatest contempt, he was at the forefront of the movement, and Executive Life was ahead in most of the key areas. Fred is nothing like the stereotype leader we have all read about. He is understated, almost bashful, and clearly not charismatic, nor is he an impressive speaker. He is the opposite of the staid, eloquent, and distinguished types who lead many of the large companies. The ones no one seems to remember. Fred's bald head, round, jowly face, and gentle voice are more reminiscent of one's favorite uncle than the high-flying financial whiz from Wilshire Boulevard he is portrayed as in the press.

Former First Executive Corporation Board Member Warren Bennis has devoted much of his life to the study of leadership, and has written several best-selling books on the subject. In *Leaders*, he redefines leadership for the 1990s: "The new leader is one who commits people to action, who converts followers into leaders, and who may convert leaders to agents of change. We refer to this as `transformative leadership.'"[1] Although no longer a Fred Carr supporter, Warren would have to admit that Fred Carr is a perfect example of his definition of the "new leader." Fred's style was to commit others to action, anointing followers to become leaders and act as agents of change, in an environment where change was something everyone knew had to happen but *no one wanted to be responsible for making happen*. No one, that is, except Fred Carr, who assumed the role of harbinger of change with characteristic aplomb.

Fred Carr, like many bigger-than-life figures, is a complex collection of contradictions. He can be prophetic one moment and profane the next. Just when you think you have him figured out, he surprises you. Usually soft-spoken and avuncular, he could burst into hysterical anger over seemingly minor issues. As we have seen, I'm not sure this was a personality quirk so much as a contrived way of reminding everyone who

1. Warren Bennis and Burt Nanus, *Leaders* (New York: Harper & Row, 1985).

was boss. His expectations of hard work from those who reported to him were unrealistic; yet when people delivered, they were seldom praised or rewarded. Other times he would lavish unexpected gifts on undeserving recipients with little or no explanation. Although he was noted for the low wages he paid employees, he would pay a consultant almost anything they asked.

Fred's personal life is full of contradictions, too. He lived in a small upper duplex which he rented in a mediocre West Los Angeles neighborhood. He drove a seven-year-old company car while the rest of us traded ours every three years or so. But his *was* a Porsche. Whatever his personal wealth, which has been estimated to be all over the map, he was earning $2 million per year in salary and bonus at the time. For a man who worked so hard to accumulate it, wealth seemed to serve no useful purpose in his lifestyle or habits. There were some indulgences to accommodate his passion for fitness. He had his personal tailor drop by frequently to refit his suits to adjust for minor fluctuations in weight. He also had a fitness consultant visit him each morning for an individualized workout (Fred shares him with a number of celebrities, including Ronald Reagan). No matter how prestigious his visitors—and he had a lot of them—Fred always lunched in the company cafeteria, the Garden Cafe. He took great pride in the health-oriented food they served, which he assumed would thrill his out-of-town visitors. He never took anyone out of the building to lunch, no matter who they were. At dinner, however, he loved to go to the Bistro Gardens, an all-time favorite of the Beverly Hills celebrity crowd, where they had a special table reserved for him. Of course, as a vegetarian and non-drinker, he didn't go to enjoy their sumptuous offerings, so I assume he went there solely for the pleasure of his guests.

The Best of Times

Agents were always angry at Fred over the terrible service they and their clients received from the generally low-quality staff and limited resources he tolerated in the company. Just when he felt the agents were about to revolt, Fred would give me a call and tell me to pick out twenty or so couples for a little party he had in mind. He would usually be very cryptic, only hinting at what he had in mind. I would dutifully pick out a group and ask if they were available on a given weekend for a "little gathering" Fred was putting together. Knowing him as they did, few declined even if they didn't know what we would be doing. On a couple of occasions, everyone was told to meet at the Santa Monica Airport on a Friday morning for what turned out to be a "summer weekend in Aspen." We were met by a fleet of five or six private jets (six to eight passengers per plane) and off we went to Colorado. Of course we stayed at the exquisite Jerome Hotel.

If it was Laguna Beach for sailing and shopping, it was the Ritz Carlton. If it was Santa Barbara for scenery and artistry, we stayed at the Four Seasons Biltmore. When it was Boston for a fall weekend of watching the leaves turn, it was the Four Seasons on the Common. Always spontaneous, just to "hug the agents" and apologize for the way they got beat up by the service issues and bad press. The agenda was jammed with the best the area had to offer—hot-air ballooning, skiing, helicopter rides, chartered sailing yachts. All you had to do was let Fred know your preference, be it a massage or facial in the health club or a private limousine tour of a local attraction. We did it the way the rich folks did, with no detail unattended to.

Then there were the special Fred Carr touches. Each night his guests returned to their rooms to find an expensive gift, beautifully wrapped, with a note from Fred thanking them for sharing this wonderful time with him. Next to the gift they might find some milk and chocolate chip cookies. Smaller gifts would follow weeks after the trip, just to say "thanks for being with us." The value lingered and, to a degree, offset much of the grief agents experienced with the bad press and poor service. It was awful tough for an agent to call me the following Monday and chew me out about a service problem he was having. Of course, to our type of agent, business is business and fun is fun.

Usually, after a few weeks, the glow had worn off and they had no compunction about blasting us for our bad press and service problems.

Sometimes Fred arranged some very special surprises. In February 1988, we took about twenty couples for a weekend to Park City, Utah, where we skied Deer Valley and Sundance during the day and went to a film festival at night in the Sundance Complex, which is owned by the actor Robert Redford. During our private cocktail party, the ladies and most of the men were momentarily paralyzed when Redford joined our party for chitchat and a personalized photo session with the ladies present. Knowing how Mr. Redford shuns the spotlight, I can't imagine what Fred had to do to get him to schmooze with a bunch of insurance salespeople.

On occasion, Fred's penchant for the unexpected seemed downright weird. In June and October 1986, we did two trips to the Jerome Hotel in Aspen, one each for our two biggest producer groups, Windsor Insurance Associates and Exceptional Producers Group. The afternoon of our arrival, we had a high tea, a favorite event of Fred's. The Jerome Hotel is turn of the century, restored to the kind of resplendent elegance that can command $300 per night. They served fantastic cookies, scones, cakes, and cappuccino, along with a bunch of exotic teas and champagne, all against the backdrop of beautiful chamber music provided by a local orchestra. It was a moment of tastefulness and class that gave everyone a sense of euphoria. Fred asked me to get up and welcome everybody, then introduce him for a few remarks. I waxed on about the beauty and serenity of the place and introduced our host to a round of enthusiastic applause. Fred then proceeded to show what an eccentric kook he can sometimes be.

Rather than the usual gracious remarks to which we had become accustomed in previous gatherings, Fred told the group that he had been pondering the many uses of a word that, in his view, was the most versatile in the English language. "A word," he went on, "that is near and dear to us all. A word, the very mention of which conjures up images of passion, love, and lust, as well as anger, scorn, and insult. By now," he continued, "you've probably guessed that I'm talking about the word `fuck.'" Fred then went on to demonstrate how in the English language you could use the F-word as a noun, a verb, a pronoun, an adjective, or as an adverb, and so on. The talk continued for about ten minutes, frequently punctuated by hysterical outbursts of laughter from Fred, at his ribald joke, which in turn were accommodated by polite laughter by some of his bewildered audience. Here he was, chairman of one of the industry's largest companies, talking in this elegant setting to some of the industry's top producers and their wives about derivations on the F-word. David Downey, Don Mehlig, Greg Pellet, and a number of other known industry speakers were getting a dose of the audacity of Chairman Fred. This was one time these guys didn't lift any of Fred's material for their next speech!

That evening, after we returned from dinner, Fred threw a pajama party—another favorite theme of his. Everyone *had* to show up in p.j.'s or a bath robe to be admitted. It was a typical Fred Carr party. Tons of goodies. An ice cream fountain, entertainment, and a lot of coziness. Fred mentioned to me that we had a few late arrivals and perhaps I would like to greet them and introduce him to say a few words. I did so, and when Fred got up, he explained that some of the group had not arrived in time for his opening remarks. For those who were present, he hoped they wouldn't mind hearing them again. Off he went on his derivations on the F-word shtick. By this time, most were over the shock and, since they'd had a few drinks and it was quite late, it went over a little better, but not much.

We all thought, given the feedback we gave him, that we had heard the last of the F-word speech. We were wrong. A couple of months later, we took Jerry Schwartz's Windsor Insurance group on the same trip to Aspen. Exactly the same, including Fred's welcome. This time it really bombed. Jerry had a number of pretty conservative people in his organization, including a group of Bible Belters who referred to themselves as such with pride. Although he was the closest to Fred of any of us and a constant Fred Carr analyzer, Jerry was stymied by Fred's bizarre attempt at humor. As a person who shared Jerry's and my principle that, other than on moral or ethical issues, you should never take a stand or make a statement that could cost you business, we were both surprised that Fred would risk offending someone unnecessarily. We understood that we all regularly offended someone by our beliefs about the way we ran our business, but we never wanted to be more offensive than we had to be. Fred had always been the best example we knew of this, with his refusal to criticize even the worst of his many detractors and his well-known aversion to confrontation. The only explanation I have been able to come up with for this stark deviation from Fred's usual courtly, understated manner is that he felt it would add to the growing interest among his public in his eccentric personality.

Fred got one of his best promotional ideas back in February 1983. He invited all of the company's leading managing general agents from the brokerage division to Los Angeles for what he called the Beverly Hills Shopping Spree. It was a four-day party during which the group was wined and dined in splendiferous fashion. It took place at the Beverly Wilshire Hotel and was inspired by the Drexel Burnham bond conference (more commonly known as "the Predator's Ball"), which Mike Milken started hosting for his customers about the same time down the street at the Beverly Hilton. The activities were back-to-back in typical Fred Carr fashion, offering more than anyone could have time to do. The ladies always got a day-long make-over at a popular Beverly Hills salon, followed by their own private photo session with a portrait photographer. Everyone had a limousine and driver at their disposal all day to transport them from activities that ranged from horseback riding along the beaches of Malibu to private cooking lessons from the greatest chefs in Los Angeles or private matinees of the hottest show in town. Or, if they preferred, there was shopping along Rodeo Drive, for which Fred would always give them a few hundred dollars "walking-around money." The evening involved taking over a Los Angeles landmark such as the Magic Castle or the MGM Studio Commissary for a party, followed by a midnight pajama party back at the Beverly Wilshire Hotel. Once, the group even attended the Hollywood premiere of a George Lucas film in a caravan of limousines. The place was loaded with major stars just as one would hope, most of whom were very cordial to us. The 1983 Beverly Hills Shopping Spree was such a hit that Fred decided to make it an annual event.

At the 1984 Spree, as it became known, Fred held a special meeting to which he arrived with two armed security guards and a briefcase containing $1 million, which he spread out dramatically on a table. He then told the group of about thirty MGAs present that the money would be divided up among them in five years, based upon their relative percentage of new production during that period. Meaning if a person produced 15 percent of the group's total production over the five years, he or she would receive $150,000. The idea created great enthusiasm and later became the talk of the industry, creating even greater demand for an Executive Life franchise. Several MGAs over the next few years became obsessed with their relative percentages of the million-dollar prize. The two leading MGAs at the time were Marty Greenberg of Los Angeles and Max Gomberg of Pittsburgh, both of whom were determined to find a way to get the entire million dollars. Marty and Max were good friends and probably the two highest-profile MGAs in the life brokerage business. The proclamation by each that they would win the lion's share of the $1 million added a lot of excitement to the contest. As it turned out, Marty got the biggest piece of the pie, about $250,000. Max, on the other hand, did find a way to get $1 million from Executive Life, but not by winning the contest. Instead, he intercepted a check for the purchase of a $1 million annuity policy payable to Executive Life and somehow diverted it into his personal checking account. For this and similar infractions perpetrated on other companies, Max Gomberg was convicted of theft and is currently serving two to ten years in a Pennsylvania prison. The throngs of big producers who were Fred Carr devotees ran the gamut, from the likes of Max Gomberg to the pristine Don Mehlig, 1991 president of the American Society of CLU (Chartered Life

Underwriters). All had big stakes in the House of Carr.

During that same Beverly Hills Shopping Spree, it rained unusually hard for Los Angeles, even for February, which can be a wet month. On Valentine's Day, they had a Dine Around party in which all of the couples were allowed to select from a list of six of L.A.'s finest restaurants. Fred then made an appearance at each of the restaurants, dressed in a trench coat, with an arm full of long-stemmed American Beauty roses, which he graciously passed out to all the ladies present. By the third restaurant, he looked like hell. He was completely drenched by the pouring rain and very rumpled, having gotten in and out of his car several times to make his rounds. Since Fred looks like a sixty-year-old Homer Simpson (the cartoon character), complete with five-o'clock shadow, he was a sight soaking wet. Undaunted, he persisted to the last restaurant. When he approached the first table, one of the MGA's wives refused the rose, thinking Fred was trying to sell it to her, and saying sadly to the rest of the party: "It's terrible how they treat the homeless here in Los Angeles. But still they shouldn't allow them to wander into restaurants and do this type of thing. Least of all a place like Chasen's where the company is spending a fortune to entertain us!" Fred never said a word, he just walked away. The table burst into laughter and the mistake was explained to a very embarrassed guest.

In 1989, after five years and the awarding of the $1 million, the company discontinued the Beverly Hills Shopping Sprees, as well as the "Hug an Agent" trips. In light of the company's emerging troubles, the expense of these extravaganzas was excessive even by Executive Life standards. Especially when one considers that these functions weren't even the main event.

The "Hug an Agent" trips and Beverly Hills Shopping Sprees were nothing compared to Executive Life's annual sales conventions. These were the talk of the travel business and the envy of every competitor. The Fred Carr spectaculars in Rome, Paris, London, Hong Kong, and Venice were the social event of the life insurance world. Even the company's most vocal detractors could hardly wait to hear the stories from their peers who had "done Paris or Rome with Executive Life."

Fred understood what he was up against when he went after the industry's leading agents. At their previous companies, they had been top gun. They were used to the preferential treatment at sales conventions that was reserved for the company's leading agent. So, what do you do when the entire convention body is composed of people who led or virtually led their previous company? What Fred *didn't* do was almost as important as what he did do. He knew that in their previous environments, most of these agents spent long evenings seated at the head table of an awards banquet, where blustering home office officials passed out plaques and trophies; meanwhile, everyone else had to listen to boring acceptance speeches while watching their Baked Alaska melt. At Executive Life conventions, each agent got a beautiful gift every night upon returning to their room. Instead of another useless plaque, they might find a piece of Ralph Lauren luggage or Baccarat crystal. Not just one night, but every night. Not just the leading agent, but every agent. No plaques, no speeches, no meetings. Executive Life conventions were fun!

They did actually schedule one business meeting at the conventions, which was mostly a question-and-answer session with Fred Carr, more at the behest of the agents than because of any feeling Fred had that they should meet. The agents loved this time with him during which he passed on pearls of wisdom and industry insights. He would hold their interest with his every utterance, all without ever answering a single question directly. No one ever left with any specific answers, no matter how insistent they were about getting them. Yet they always left feeling Fred was in control of the future, theirs and his.

Mostly, these trips were designed to create unique memories for a constituency of affluent sales heavyweights who had been everywhere and done everything. One thing that made this seemingly difficult task easier was Fred's passion for showmanship and gamesmanship. For the London trip, there would be auctions set up in the tradition of Sotheby's or Christie's, where play money was issued to agents, based upon their production,

which could then be used to bid on valuable items such as auto-
mobiles and works of art. In fact, he once even held a drawing
for a Rolls-Royce.

Then there were the games, Fred's specialty. He loved scavenger hunts and mystery games, which he would create for the
entire convention body. Unlikely as it might seem for so upscale
a crowd, they got into these activities in a big way. Before the
San Francisco trip, for example, everyone received a copy of
Dashiell Hammett's *The Maltese Falcon* at home and was asked
to read it. On the opening night of the convention, a magician
showed the group a stunning crystal creation of a falcon, com-
missioned by Executive Life from Gumps, the prestigious San
Francisco gift emporium. He then made it vanish before their
very eyes. The rest of the week, each couple followed clues as to
the falcon's whereabouts. The clues were delivered to their
rooms nightly. Along with the clues would be expensive gifts,
including trench coats, gold inlaid magnifying glasses, and
Houndstooth detective hats. For the couple who solved the
mystery, the prize was, of course, the Gumps falcon.

There was always a film crew present on each trip to com-
pose a video of all these activities, which they turned into a
hilarious and entertaining collage of the trip that was then
given to every participant as a keepsake. Each video always
closed with a self-demeaning comedy routine featuring Fred as
a dishwasher, a Chinese tailor, or a panhandler. The agents
never could get over Fred's earthiness, when compared to the
conduct of the CEOs of the other companies they dealt with.

The conventions were never held at the hotel sites picked by
most companies. Instead, Fred would choose a four-star,
smaller hotel like a Ritz or Four Seasons. In spite of the group's
size, they were able to do this because Fred insisted on intimacy
at our meetings. Instead of one huge group of 500 or 1,000, like
the other leading companies, Fred had four separate groups of
150 to 250 people. This way he felt he could "get close to the
agents." Usually, they went to two cities in the same area for
three days each, which enabled them to stagger the groups and
get through all of them in about two weeks. They might have

three days in Rome and three days in Venice, or three days in Barcelona and three in Madrid. For Fred and me, the trips were grueling, in that he would usually be stationed in one city and I in the other. Every night we would have some spectacular function whereby we would take over a museum or castle for a spectacular evening of dining and entertainment. At our respective locations, Fred and I would have to host the identical evening for four separate groups.

I remember one year when we took over a theater in San Francisco and hired Tony Bennett to do a private concert for us. Because our groups were small (150 or so), Fred hired a "rent-a-crowd" of about 400 people to stand outside the theater and wildly cheer each couple as their limousine pulled up. Then, as the couple got out, the rent-a-crowd would seek autographs and snap pictures with flash cameras. Afterwards they joined us in the theater for the show because Fred felt it would work better if Mr. Bennett was playing to a full house. By the fourth evening, I was so tired of hearing Tony Bennett sing "I Left My Heart in San Francisco," I had to slip out to the lobby. I can't imagine how, at this point in his life, Tony must feel when asked to sing that song. I guess the ability to be consistently enthusiastic about a difficult task that one has mastered to the point of monotony is the mark of a true professional. I used to wonder the same thing about the Houston heart surgeon Michael DeBakey, who did ten by-pass procedures a day. He had to be on automatic pilot most of the time, yet he never made a mistake. I suppose one could beg the question one step further and ask how an investment officer handling billions of dollars of other people's money, single-handedly as Fred did, can stay as focused as he would if it were his own life's savings. Probably tough to do.

Another Executive Life trademark was the surprise side trip that no other company in the industry would even dream of trying. In London, the group had a mystery trip for which everyone had to report to the hotel lobby at 6:00 a.m. on a Sunday morning. They were all bused to Heathrow Airport, where two Concorde jets were waiting. On the first Concorde, the qualifiers were whisked off to Copenhagen for lunch and an afternoon of tours. When the group arrived in Copenhagen, the airport was jammed with well-wishers and press because it was the first time ever that a Concorde had landed in their country. As many people had been encouraged to bring their children on that particular trip, there were a lot of kids that needed baby-sitting that day. No problem. That's what the second Concorde was for. The children and their chaperones were taken to Paris for lunch and their own activities, returning that night at the same time as their parents to share adventures.

At the April 1990 trip in Spain, when the group left Barcelona for Madrid by chartered jet, there was an unannounced departure from the itinerary. Instead of Madrid, we landed in Marakesh, Morocco. We went to the unbelievable five-star La Mamounia Hotel for a gourmet feast and entertainment. Then we were given a whirlwind tour of the city, and entertained by every kind of merchant from snake charmers to Persian rug salesmen. In the evening, the group was taken to the country-side for a Moorish feast. We were entertained by horseback Bedouin warriors, who put on the exact feast and show they had done for the now famous Malcolm Forbes seventieth-birth-day party just a few months earlier. I don't believe in omens the way much of this region of the world does, but given how things went for Malcolm and for Executive Life almost immedi-ately after these extraordinary indulgences in entertainment, I suggest others enjoy them vicariously through our accounts rather than firsthand.

On one occasion, the most memorable surprise was some-thing even Chairman Carr couldn't take the credit for, although it had its genesis in the deeds of another chairman named Mao. In 1989, Executive Life held its convention in Hong Kong and Beijing, in four groups beginning in late May. The world watched as the momentum of the student protest in Tiananmen Square grew. We had previously arranged to hold the farewell banquet in the Great Hall of the People, located in the center of the square. Starting with the first group, the protests were reaching their peak. As we drove through the streets, the agents exchanged victory signs with the thousands of students. By the time the third group arrived, martial law had been declared and we were sequestered in our hotel. That didn't keep us from going into the streets and taking pictures of the action. Dan Rather and his CBS crew were stuck at the same hotel with us. We all stood around as Dan had his cable cut by the authorities in the hotel courtyard. He bid a tearful goodbye to his Chinese counterparts and pushed past us to go home to the United States. We, on the other hand, were detained for another day before getting clearance to go on to Hong Kong.

Stories about Executive Life agents and their Tiananmen Square ordeal were printed in the local newspapers. Of course, Fred issued special "I was there" T-shirts, with the names of all in attendance printed on them. Executive Life trips were always the experience of a lifetime; sometimes they were also a once-in-a-lifetime experience.

But for many long-time participants the most memorable trip Fred put together took place right here in the United States. Fred launched our 1987 sales campaign with a special sense of mystery. He hinted there would be a once-in-a-lifetime trip for those agents who did over $300,000 in first-year commissions. For most life insurance companies, this would be too short a list to do anything with other than hang their portraits in the boardroom. For Executive Life, Fred and I felt we could attract up to 150 qualifiers for such a contest if the prize was exciting enough. Fred had the answer: "Around the World in Eight Days." Executive Life would charter two Concordes and take the groups to the finest hotels in the world, on a whirlwind tour they could tell their grandchildren about. They would start in Los Angeles, visiting Honolulu, Tokyo, New Delhi, Cairo, London, and New York. With typical impetuousness, we announced the trip out of pure excitement for the idea. Eventually the supply of available Concordes fell through, and the sheer exhaustion of such a trip on commercial airlines made it unrealistic. Fred opted to take everyone who did at least $100,000 in commissions to our regular convention in China in May, then promised a special additional trip that fall for those doing over $300,000 in commissions. We had no idea what we were going to do, but again, Fred had the answer: "Executive Life Trumps New York." Well, that went over like a lead balloon, especially since many of the top producers were New Yorkers transplanted to Los Angeles. As usual, they were underestimating Fred.

The New York trip may have been Fred's finest triumph in a history of great trips. It most certainly was his swan song, since it took place in October 1989, on the eve of closing the controversial $300 million rights offering, and three months before we went into free fall. We took over the best rooms in the newly renovated Trump Plaza. Of course, Ivana Trump was on hand to greet us when we arrived. The trip was a dazzling array of unforgettable events. Some highlights: Day One—breakfast at Bloomingdale's (two hours before opening time), gourmet food, and then an envelope for each couple containing $2,000 in cash for a personal shopping spree, plus specially marked items throughout the store, normally worth hundreds or even thousands of dollars, that were marked for purchase by our people for a few dollars; an evening with the legendary Bobby Short Quartet—not in their perennial habitat in the Carlyle Hotel, but with us exclusively in the Plaza ballroom; an evening at the opera, *Phantom of the Opera*, that is. Not just going to the musical, but taking over Sardi's afterward for our own private cast party. The cast stayed with us until 2:00 a.m., taking turns at the piano, singing favorites from the many Broadway shows in which they had appeared. Cast members told me that such private parties for outsiders just weren't done—especially at Sardi's. Cast parties were for casts. Apparently no one told that to Fred Carr! A few months later, we repeated the same cast party in Los Angeles, with the *Phantom* cast there for another of Fred's agent gatherings. I had the pleasure of introducing the original Phantom, Michael Crawford, who spent about fifteen minutes with us, bolting down some pasta, for which I had to take him aside and peel off $3,000 in hard cash. This was the type of experience I was once enamored with, but by that time I accepted it as just part of life with Executive Life.

Fred knew that the typical top agent did enough business with various companies to qualify for three or four trips per year. Because the agent didn't have time to take that many vacations, he'd have to pick one or two. Since our trips were in a class by themselves, Fred always knew the spouses of the agents would press them to qualify for the Executive Life trip first. It was a strategy that worked like a charm.

I suppose those who invested in First Executive Corporation or bought a policy from them might be a bit miffed when they read about these extravagances. But such outings were not abuses in self-indulgence, like those practiced by many of the savings and loan industry, whereby corporate funds were diverted and squandered on yachts and artwork for the pleasure of the management. These incentives were what attracted the best agents and the best quality of business in the industry to Executive Life. Furthermore, they were a calculated investment by Fred, which he felt made his dramatic savings on company overhead tolerable to the agents.

To go on such a trip, an agent had to do at least $100,000 in first-year commissions over a one-year period. This was about twice the qualification requirement for the conventions of most of Executive Life's competitors. There was a good reason, though. First of all, Executive Life spent an average of $10,000–$12,000 per couple on the trips, which was easily two or three times that of other competitors. Secondly, most of the agents were involved in agent owned reinsurance companies whereby the company was giving them back half of the profits on their business. Executive Life had to pay for the trip out of its half; the company never allocated trip expenses to its AORCs. In hindsight, I think this may have been an expensive mistake. Yet, when one looks at the overall result the company got from the money spent, it's hard to argue with. A trip may have cost $10 or $12 million more than it would have at a competing company; but Executive Life's total operating expenses were only about $80 million or so, which was probably half that of the nearest company in its size range. The agents hated the service problems, but still kept giving us their business. And although the trips weren't the only reason, they were definitely a factor. This trade-off of a good party in exchange for lousy service was the best example of Fred's trademark "balloons instead of bucks." Not a textbook approach; but for the boy raised in a family grocery store in Watts, the technique served him well.

Words of Wisdom

Each year at the sales convention, the highlight would be Fred's business session, which was mostly a question-and-answer session with the agents. Usually he would deliver a brief message first, in which he coined a phrase or made an observation that would become a theme for him that was replayed from then on. Some of Fred's favorites became popular views for all of us. Here are just a few examples of these insights:

"These Are the Good Old Days." In 1986, at the San Francisco convention, and throughout the balance of the 1980s, Fred never stopped reminding agents that the tax-advantaged products they sold would not last forever. He claimed not to know what they would be selling in a few years, but promised that whatever it was, it would not be nearly as good as what they had. It certainly motivated agents to be reminded that there was a time limit on the availability of their products, just like a sale at a department store. They needed to move all the merchandise they could while they could. "Trust me on this," he'd say. "Someday agents will look back at 1986 and say, `Wow! Those were the good old days.'" He was right, especially for those agents who sold for Executive Life!

"The Penalty of Leadership." When things heated up over the junk bond issues, while at the same time Executive Life had the best product in the industry, Fred opened one of the conventions by reading from the seventy-year-old copy of an advertisement he uncovered entitled "The Penalty of

Leadership"—used by the Cadillac Motor Car Company in 1914. It talked about the price one pays for excellence in the form of criticism, jealousy, envy, and slander that eventually gives way to imitation and praise. It became a standard source of comfort to new agents who, upon joining the company, were hammered by the negative sales tactics of the competition. All of them got a firsthand taste of the Penalty of Leadership.

"Ten Great in '98." In 1988, Fred promised his followers at the sales convention in Italy that there would be ten great life insurance companies in America in 1998, and Executive Life would be one of them. Shortly after that I noticed that the license plate on Fred's car read IRPTO98, which I took to mean Irreplaceable until 1998. That would complete Fred's twenty-fifth year with the company, and if Executive Life was one of the ten great companies, I suspect Fred would feel his work was done and he could retire at age sixty-eight. He would then become the elder statesman of the industry he had changed, and enjoy the long-overdue recognition he so justly deserved. It was a noble vision. Somehow the prophecy "Nine Great in `98" doesn't have the same ring to it.

"Junk Bonds Have Become un-American." Fred introduced this theme at the convention in Spain when things had fallen apart in 1990. He felt the relentless criticism by the press had become a self-fulfilling prophecy for the junk bond market. Reality aside, Ivan Boesky, Mike Milken, Drexel Burnham, and junk bonds were all evil and contrary to the American way of life. Perception had become reality. A lot of us listening to that talk thought back to 1986. Fred was right; they *were* the good old days.

Fred used to say, "Executive Life is not just a company, we are a culture." Some went further and called it a cult—a word which, were it not for its negative connotations, would be appropriate. The Executive Life marketing force had a unique and intense admiration for Fred Carr and the principles he

preached: competitive, innovative products, long-term partnerships with agents, maximum value for the consumer, being the
industry's low-cost provider, and a sense of dynasty about
Executive Life's role in the industry's future. They bought into a
set of core concepts which were valid and exciting, and which
would lead the industry into a new era. Fred was considered
a visionary whose every word gave some glimpse into that
new era.

Fred's power as a leader lay in two areas: his ability to look
over the horizon and see the big picture, and his discipline in
giving only glimpses of what he saw to his followers, leaving
their imaginations to run wild with speculation about his true
agenda. These powers made Fred the embodiment of the new
leader described by Warren Bennis. Yet, unlike most pundits, he
was unimposing, accessible, and easy to talk to. A real mensch.
He was, as he liked to put it, "Just a salesman who knew how to
read a balance sheet." And when agents were entertained by
Fred, it was always an event they could count on remembering
the rest of their lives. Dazzled by the entertainment, stuffed
with the finest food and drink, indulged with beautiful gifts to
remember the occasion by, on the way home they would recall
the wisdom and insights shared by Chairman Fred, usually dis-
tillable into a single exciting thought like "Ten Great in `98." It
was a wonderful feeling.

III
THE MOMENTUM SHIFTS

10

The Irrepressible
Professor Belth

"I'd rather have Fred Carr running my company than the people who run General Motors."
— Peter Lynch, Magellan Fund, *Barron's,*
February 2, 1987

In 1977, the Million Dollar Round Table, the 15,000-member organization of the life insurance industry's top producers, formed an elite inner circle called the Top of the Table, which eventually had its own separate annual sales conference. To qualify, for example, in 1991 for the Top of the Table, an agent had to earn $252,000 in first-year commissions, exclusive of renewal and other compensation, which for such a producer would typically equal their first-year commissions. In other words, those at the bottom of the Top of the Table earn a half million dollars a year! Just as eagles never flock, producers of this magnitude do not usually affiliate themselves with a single carrier, even though one company often does get a majority of their business. At almost any given time in the 1980's, Executive Life could boast a lead company position with as many members of the Top of the Table as any other company in the industry. This was a stunning achievement for a twenty-year-old West Coast firm in a fraternity of elite producers whose other companies were all hundred-year-old bastions of the East.

The typical Executive Life agent was among the leaders in his or her field nationwide, and usually a standout in the community. Most Executive Life agents were in their late forties and fifties, with a lot of experience in the business. Because of their upscale, high net worth market, Executive Life agents were by definition successful, in that purchasers and their advisers in this market are likely to select agents whose credentials warrant their doing business with them.

Once an agent crossed over to Executive Life turf and began giving them significant business, a number of things changed in his life. First, he almost always fell in love with the products. They were fun to sell—flexible, profitable, and innovative. Most importantly, competitive. All of a sudden the agent could go after a big sale, where there is always competition, and know that he'd have the best performing illustrations. Not sometimes, or often, but always. Not the second best, but the very best. Executive Life didn't beat the household names by a little bit, either. Its products generated internal rates of return that were 15 to 25 percent more than the next competing illustration. Executive Life agents always won; or so it seemed. As if great products weren't enough, the Executive Life agent could also look forward to great compensation in two ways: not only were the first-year commissions and renewal commissions among the best in the business, but he or she also got to share in the company's profits on the business through ownership of an agent owned reinsurance company.

Still another change the Executive Life producer experienced was that the usually prominent and foreboding line between field and home office became blurred. Access to Fred and the rest of us in senior management was as easy as walking into a convenience store. At Executive Life the agent was the customer long before the notion became popular. None of us at the senior level was allowed to wield influence because of our position.

No one was ever treated better than anyone else—except for the agents. It was a truly egalitarian environment. The agents recognized this, and were very responsive to the fact that they were held in genuine high regard by their company.

Most good things in life involve trade-offs, and Executive Life was no exception. What the agent gave up in exchange for more competitive products and commissions, a piece of the profits, and an elevated status with the company was considerable. Ultimately, the cost to most was beyond the benefit. First and foremost, when an agent joined Executive Life, he (or she) broke ranks with the establishment. He was making a statement, just as Executive Life was, that the industry was out of touch and inefficient. He was rejecting the industry—something that wasn't often done by agents in the upscale and advanced markets at the time. The other agents with whom he competed had to explain why their products were not as good as Executive Life, and explain they did. The issue became one of integrity and the business practices of our company versus theirs. They didn't have to look hard to find ways to attack Executive Life: Fred Carr's integrity, an upstart company, poor service, and so on. But ultimately it was the junk bond issue that became the club with which the competition relentlessly beat Executive Life agents over the head. Junk bonds, junk Carr, junk policies equaled junk agents. Agents choosing to represent Executive Life were never again treated quite the same by their industry peers.

I believe the source of the disapproval that eventually turned to contempt and hostility could have been greatly diminished with some public relations and involvement in industry activities by Fred Carr and Executive Life. A commitment to Executive Life by an agent often turned out to be rather more of a commitment than he or she bargained for. The press and competitors cast a pall over the company that unavoidably sloped over to the agents and eventually wilted their image within their communities. The attacks on the company intensified over the years, with notable success, primarily since Fred's style was to ignore all negative press. The agents also sought to have at least private comfort, if no P.R. support, on these issues. The Marketing Department provided this well in agent seminars and company-prepared handouts.

We developed a good deal of point-of-sale material showing comparisons between Executive Life and the rest of the industry on key financial statistics. The contrast between the actual facts and what the press said was presented to the agents in stark fashion. There was no room for any gray areas: someone was full of bullshit. The agents concluded it was the press. Not just some of the agents, but almost all of them. Although plenty of significant producers eventually got worn down and left the company just for relief from the debate, I recall none going because they decided Executive Life was the House of Cards the press portrayed. These people were true believers. Once they bought into the Executive Life concept, they burned their bridges with much of the establishment.

The attacks became a rallying point for some—kindred spirits in a movement to bring the industry out of the dark ages. They knew they were right and that their detractors were short-sighted, uniformed, and above all envious of their success. These detractors couldn't compete fairly with their numbers, so they resorted to trying to undermine Executive Life's numbers. As far as the Executive Life agent was concerned, their critics were the ones with the integrity problem. It was a classic case of carrying a sound argument to the extreme and having both parties hurt themselves and their cause in the process. There were no winners in the Executive Life controversy. Except, perhaps, the man who probably did more to fan the flames of the debate than any other.

A Friendly Conscience

Executive Life had a good many detractors and enemies in prominent places in the industry. Guardian Life agent Alan Press, a past president of the National Association of Life Underwriters (NALU), and New York Life agent Stanley Liss, a past president of the Million Dollar Round Table (MDRT), were just two of the agent leaders who were vocal in their disapproval of Fred Carr and his company. Leading companies, such as Northwestern Mutual, the Guardian, and New York Life had competitive Information departments which systematically gathered and disseminated press and other materials to their agents that were unfavorable about Executive Life. This was the type of response Executive Life inspired by its products and practices. Those of us there at the time didn't like it, but I can't say it wasn't expected. What was *not* expected was the campaign mounted against the company by Joseph Belth, which started in 1986. If Fred Carr is the protagonist of this story, then his antagonist was most certainly Indiana University Professor Joseph M. Belth.

Joseph Belth is owner and publisher of *Insurance Forum*, a monthly newsletter published and distributed for the benefit of agents and other insurance industry personnel. His campaigns against Executive Life made the efforts of its other adversaries look sophomoric. And with good reason, because Executive Life was probably the best circulation booster Dr. Belth hit on in the history of his publication, which coincidentally started in 1974, the same year Fred Carr took over at the helm of First Executive Corporation.

Joseph Belth graduated from the University of Pennsylvania in 1958 under a fellowship from the S. S. Huebner Foundation (Huebner is the father of insurance academia). After a brief stint at the American College and the American Society of Chartered Life Underwriters at Bryn Mawr, Pennsylvania, he joined the faculty of Indiana University. By his own account of his early days, as told in the January 1984 issue of *Insurance Forum*, Belth's was an early voice against controversial and questionable industry practices. After having his opinions suppressed by the industry press on some thirty-odd occasions by such publications as *The Actuary*, *The CLU Journal*, and *The National Underwriter*, he came up with the idea of the *Insurance Forum*. Getting no industry support, he funded the project with his own money. Early issues of the *Insurance Forum*, as the name suggests, encouraged the submission of others' ideas and criticisms, but the *Insurance Forum* soon became, as Belth puts it, "a primary vehicle for my views, even though ... that was not what I intended at the outset."[1] Although there have been a few exceptions over the years, *Insurance Forum* has remained primarily a platform for Dr. Belth's criticisms of the industry, its practices, and certain of its companies. The early objectives, as described in the January 1984 issue, were the open discussion of industry problems, the encouragement of insurance reforms, and to make the *Insurance Forum* self-supporting financially. In this same issue, Belth goes on to complain that the biggest obstacle to financial sufficiency "is that most of the people in the insurance industry don't care about the problems of the business."[2]

No one, in my opinion, can justify a negative attitude about the overall career and mission of Joseph Belth in his role as insurance industry observer. Put quite simply, he is a man whose whole life has been dedicated to the maintenance and promotion of integrity in an industry he loves and believes in. During the early years, Dr. Belth served as the conscience of the industry and certainly rankled much of its leadership. Balanced and undiscriminating in its views, the *Insurance Forum* occasionally targeted both the mighty Prudential and the sanctimonious Northwestern Mutual, as well as most other household names.

In these earlier, less than prosperous days, the *Forum* crusaded for a number of laudable causes and acted as watchdog of the industry, no matter who the offenders were. Titles of early articles in 1974 and 1975 tell us that Dr. Belth was out to right all wrongs and wasn't about to compromise in his views: "How to Pay Premiums for a 'Piece of the Rock' and Have No Insurance Protection," "What Equitable of New York Does to Beneficiaries," "The Northwestern Mutual Wildcatters," "The Flight of Old John Hancock Policyholders," "New York Life's Tontine-like Arrangement for Agents," and "How MONY

1. *Insurance Forum* (January 1984).
2. *Ibid.*

Handles Orphan Policyholders" were but a few of the monthly exposés on the practices of the Eastern establishment. In those days, Belth was truly an unbiased investigative reporter. He showed no favoritism and took no prisoners. If there was an impropriety at a company that came to his attention, he reported on it. No doubt he was a breath of fresh air to the few consumers who read his offerings, on an industry that had always cloaked its less than ideal practices with confusing jargon and small print.

But the role of critic to an industry by way of trade newsletter, the purchase of which is of little interest to those outside of that industry, is a noble yet flawed concept. Dr. Belth could have left the industry and attacked it from the outside, as a number of others had done, to their own enrichment. Instead, he remained an inside critic who stopped short of muckraking, choosing instead to push for reforms from within that he clearly believed in. As a result, *Insurance Forum* limped along as a respected, but thinly read, voice of fair play.

Boosting Circulation

Then, in the April 1982 issue of the *Insurance Forum*, the lead article, "The A. L. Williams Replacement Empire," changed all that—including, in my opinion, the apparent priorities of Dr. Belth. The article was the first in a decade-long series exposing the practices and sales tactics of the A. L. Williams replacement machine, which had become the bane of the old-line giant companies specializing in the lower- and middle-income markets. Williams's organization specialized in replacing the permanent insurance policies sold by the old-line Eastern giants with term insurance. But Williams's operation was not just another buy-term-and-invest-the-difference scheme. He built up a gigantic sales force based on a pyramidlike hierarchy that had about a dozen layers. This made for a very costly distribution system and therefore an extremely uncompetitive term policy that his agents, who were mostly part-timers, peddled to the middle-

and lower-income markets. Demands for reprints of the first article from agents to be used to sell against A. L. Williams exceeded 60,000. At only 20¢ apiece, that was hardly a windfall for the fledgling newsletter; but Dr. Belth had discovered a new business that might at least pay his overhead. One in which he could still attack the bad guy, but also finally earn a buck for himself.

No one could seriously begrudge this. After all, for years Belth had nurtured the *Forum* along, giving balanced criticism as it was deserved. Furthermore, A. L. Williams was an organization on which most of the industry felt someone needed to blow the whistle. Best of all, attacks on the A. L. Williams organization offended no one other than those targeted. So, over the next few years, the *Forum* format changed, with more and more space devoted to A. L. Williams. There were ten feature articles on A. L. Williams in 1986 alone, and at the same time, a noticeable tempering of views about the Eastern giants, whose agents reportedly were buying up reprints faster than Belth could fill the orders.

The *Insurance Forum* had discovered a market at last, and with it, Joseph Belth became an industry celebrity and sought-after speaker. A. L. Williams was the nemesis of those companies whose policyholders were blue *and* gray collar, middle America; agents for those companies urgently needed to have something with which to counter Williams. Dr. Belth, in effect, provided them with the third-party influence they wanted to fight A. L. Williams at the point of sale.

In 1986, Dr. Belth discovered that the nemesis of those companies specializing in the upper-income markets was Executive Life. Its explosive growth, which led to a number of careless practices for which the regulators clubbed the company's wrist, gave him excellent new subject matter. Between A. L. Williams and Executive Life, Dr. Belth was in the third-party influence business, selling reprints by the thousands. A study of the objects of his criticisms over the period 1986–91 shows an alarming decline in any meaningful criticism of any company other than A. L. Williams and Executive Life. They were virtually his only targets, while massive financial problems at companies like the Equitable and the Travelers began to smolder unmentioned in the *Insurance Forum*.

The largest writer of ordinary life volume in America was not the Pru or the Met or the Equitable in 1986; it was A. L. Williams. Williams was buzzing through the big companies' books of old profitable policies like pine bark beetles through a pine forest. It was literally an epidemic. Many of these old policies had traditionally given poor value to the consumer. It was this weakness on which A. L. Williams preyed. He gave them a less attractive value than was currently available, but argued it was still better value than that the insurance industry had given the policyholder in years gone by. It was this arbitrage—the spread between the old, profitable, but uncompetitive policy and the newer, perceived better deal—on which Williams built his empire. He didn't need to go all the way to the forefront of the product revolution; he only needed to go far enough to make the old debit policies sold by the door-to-door salesman of the old-line companies look bad.

On the other end of the scale was Executive Life which, in effect, was doing the same thing to the upscale companies that had catered to the high net worth individuals. Names like New England Life, Massachusetts Mutual, and Connecticut Mutual were viewed as the blue-chip companies, catering to individuals and businesses with a high net worth. Executive Life agents went to that client base and replaced their business, just as A. L. Williams did at the lower end. The big difference here, however, was that to get this business, Executive Life had to provide the absolute optimum value. The profit margins came from the spreads in its bond portfolio; everything else was razor thin or less. This is where the Executive Life advantage was, which unfortunately led to its being perceived in a similar light to that of Williams and his crowd when they replaced the lower-end policies. The Executive Life agent's belief was that there was a big difference. He was offering true, long-term value in a product which, year in year out, performed better for the policyholder than anything in this market. (This was true for

Executive Life policyholders every year throughout the 1980s.) Williams was trading third-rate policies for second-rate policies at best.

To those who used Dr. Belth's material to sell against them, however, the issue was not just saving an existing policyholder, it was beating out Executive Life on a new sale. Executive Life did a lot of replacement, but its bread and butter was the new policy—sold in the emerging market of those who viewed the new-wave policies as an investment and cash accumulation vehicle. When a businessman was installing a deferred compensation plan for his executives that was to be funded by life insurance, he would usually get several quotes. More often than not, Executive Life would be among the companies bidding for the business, and more often than not, it would have the best performing product. The competing agent would usually try to turn the sale into a due diligence issue, in which he would use Belth's materials to impugn the financial integrity of Executive Life. It was a powerful counterattack to their competitive proposals, and much of the time it worked.

In all of this, Joe Belth saw an opportunity to become propaganda minister to the Eastern mutuals. Every one of them was being relentlessly antagonized by these two "Johnny-come-lately" companies, which had exploded onto the scene, writing more new business and generating more profit than almost anyone else in the industry. Most importantly, these two companies engaged in practices that the rest of the industry questioned. Their views, when the same as those of Dr. Belth, were obviously given credibility when aired in his newsletter. Make no mistake; the views were always those of Dr. Belth. This was a man who had paid a big price to remain the independent conscience of the industry. There was no doubt, however, that Dr. Belth had finally found his place under the sun.

The *Insurance Forum* clearly served a valuable purpose in calling to everyone's attention the weakness of these nouveau life insurance companies that were putting the industry in a state of disarray. The problem was that there were inherent deficiencies and incompetencies in the life insurance industry to begin with.

It was these inefficiencies and poor values to the consumer that made Executive Life and A. L. Williams possible. They, in fact, played on the weakness of the industry, which had not done a good job of delivering value to the consumer, just as the industry eventually played on their weaknesses when they failed to do the same. Live by the sword, die by the sword.

Dr. Belth first jumped hard on Executive Life in 1987, when the New York Insurance Department disallowed a number of reserve credits taken in 1985 by way of a series of reinsurance treaties put into place by Al Jacob. A reserve credit is basically a transaction that frees up (credits) monies that are required to be put aside (reserved) by the regulators to meet future policy-holder obligations. One way it may be accomplished is by surplus relief—the method whereby the assets of another company are borrowed to put up the reserve, thus freeing up the money within the company. The transaction in question involved $119 million of reserve credits Executive Life of New York (ELNY) took for insurance ceded to three Bermuda companies, which were backed by letters of credit from Alexander & Alexander, the huge casualty company, and twelve banks—mostly of national prominence. This incident, along with examinations by the New York Department of much shakier transactions entered into in 1984 and 1985, led to an agreement whereby ELNY admitted to violation of eight sections of the New York code and agreed to pay a $250,000 fine, equaling the largest ever imposed by the New York Department.

The incident was embarrassing to Executive Life, showing that it clearly had not behaved in a responsible way in its financial reporting practices during the period of most rapid growth. Due to the disallowance of the treaties, it was necessary for ELNY's parent, Executive Life of California, to make an immediate downstream capital infusion of $151 million. This, of course, put some strain on the statutory surplus of Executive Life of California, which eventually had to turn to its parent, First Executive Corporation, to raise capital. It did so in the form of a loan from a consortium of Japanese banks, which we will hear about later. From this incident Belth was off to the races, featuring Executive Life in almost every issue for the next couple of years. His reprint sales were reportedly reaching record levels. Meanwhile, any meaningful criticism of the Eastern establishment was all but quelled, while the sale of reprints to their agents who used his materials as point-of-sale propaganda soared.

After several monthly rehashings of the New York reinsurance fine, Dr. Belth found a new theme. In his October 1988 issue entitled "Executive Life and the California Insurance Department," he postulated that on December 31, 1987, Executive Life of California was, for one brief instant, insolvent on a statutory basis. His claim had to do with the mechanics of gaining approval from the California Insurance Department for the $151 million capital infusion into our New York company after its surplus relief notes were disapproved. Belth maintained that there was a moment during the transaction at which they were technically insolvent. The issue here was a complicated one, having to do with the timing of approved transactions on which both the California Department and Executive Life of California were in total accord. In my own unsophisticated view, I would say that it was analogous to mailing your house payment the day before you deposited your paycheck into your checking account to cover it. However, the facts did not even support that the transaction was as improper as that.

Belth turned the issue into a headline on Executive Life's solvency, which generated reprint sales for him and a lot of unnecessary surrender charges paid by policyholders whose agents apparently used Belth's materials to convince people to drop their Executive Life policies. The articles were reportedly used by agents to frighten a number of policyholders into paying heavy surrender charges to move their insurance, based upon implications about the safety of their funds. The reality was that this issue was an accounting one and had little to do with policyholder safety, because the funds in question were securely in place long before the *Insurance Forum* got hold of the issue.

Out of frustration over the problems these articles created, one Executive Life agent, Larry Osiwala, wrote California

Insurance Commissioner Roxane Gillespie on October 12, 1988, to ask her point blank about Belth's aspersions regarding our solvency in 1987: "I would like a short (one word, yes or no) answer to this claim." Ms. Gillespie in her own hand wrote "No" across Mr. Osiwala's letter, which she then initialed and returned officially stamped as having been received by the Department of Insurance. Another agent, John Donohue, Jr., wrote a similar letter to the Chief Financial Analyst of the California Insurance Department. In his response, the analyst flatly refuted Belth's claim when, on October 20, 1988, he wrote: "This Department does not concur with Dr. Belth that further adjustments [to capital and surplus] were necessary to that surplus." Both letters were sent to Belth by me and several others. His only response was to question their authenticity and completeness in a letter he sent back to the agents. This was especially upsetting to many of the people at Executive Life. Belth's crusade on the issue continued, with no acknowledgment in his newsletter that the California Commissioner and her Chief Financial Analyst had just refuted his charges in writing.

The agents were getting murdered by reports on the rumored insolvency, yet because of Fred's lack of response to the critics, those of us in the company were able to do little other than circulate the two letters from the California Insurance Department, which countered this accusation. Then the idea struck me that Belth would be very vulnerable to some good-natured satire. I viewed him as somewhat humorless and by this time possibly a bit egotistical over his newfound status. I suspected he might rethink his tactics if he thought people were not taking him seriously. My disappointment with Dr. Belth was that, in my opinion, he had crossed the line from an industry watchdog with balanced views to a promoter of partial truths, which led to competitive practices that were not in the industry's best interest. I might add that when he was attacking A. L. Williams, I thought it was fine, so I'm the first to admit my opinions are tempered with some bias. At any rate, I got an idea for a spoof on the *Insurance Forum*, which I called *Insurance Bore'em*. I wrote two issues, which I think may have had more underground circulation than even the actual *Forum*. The satire revolved around the seeming obsession the *Insurance Forum* had with Executive Life, while other controversial issues in the industry went unreported. Although I was proud of the idea, I had to remain anonymous because of my corporate role and the fact that Fred had specifically prohibited any written response to criticism. Obviously it would have not looked good for First Executive Corporation if it were known that I was the author of a silly spoof like the *Bore'em*.

Dr. Belth was predictably upset at the smashing, although brief, success of the *Bore'em*, which was even commented on in a *New York Times* article. He went so far as to offer a $100 reward in his newsletter for the identity of the "anonymous culprit" who authored *Insurance Bore'em*. It was a great relief for our sales force to have the humorous diversion the *Bore'em* provided from his attacks. To my pleasant surprise, although almost every agent knew it was I who penned the *Bore'em*, no one turned me in. My hope is that although Dr. Belth may not send me the $100 reward, he at least will accept a good-natured dose of his own medicine. Especially since he ultimately had the last laugh. A laugh that will no doubt be a rewarding boost to his career for years to come.

Dr. Belth eventually began reaching a little far for issues when in the January 1989 *Forum* he did a piece called "Executive Life and the Redwoods." In it he contended that Executive Life was somehow responsible for Pacific Lumber Corporation accelerating the harvesting of its giant redwood forests because it needed the money to pay the interest on bonds it had sold to Executive Life to finance its leveraged buyout. Following Dr. Belth's logic, I guess if you over-mortage your house and can't feed your family as a result, it would then be the fault of your mortgage company. The article was his lead story, at a time when at least two Top 15 companies were struggling to remain solvent on a statutory basis and a host of other industry issues were the topics of the industry press. I harbor no malice toward him for making a decent living; it's just unfortunate that the materials he produced on Executive Life were used to convince policyholders they should surrender their contracts, resulting in a double hit of a surrender charge on the old policy and a commission load on the new policy.

In my view, between the reserving requirements, the industry's strong sense of responsibility to protect all policyholders, state guarantee funds, and other regulatory safeguards, no Executive Life policyholder was, or is, likely to lose significant policy values. By far, the most significant losses experienced by Executive Life policyholders were those incurred by surrender charges and commissions paid when competitors, with the aid of material such as the *Insurance Forum*, convinced them they should move it or lose it. In my view, this represented the real injustice to the consumer and is the basis for my concern about the way in which Dr. Belth's work was used. As the perception of Executive Life continued to deteriorate and the prophecies of the critics began to materialize, Dr. Belth became the recognized authority on the subject of statutory accounting issues and other complex aspects of insurance regulation. Rarely did a reporter do a well-researched piece on the industry without quoting Dr. Belth. More often than not, the quote included a jab at Executive Life. It was clear that he wanted his opinions about the company on record, so that when it finally went down, he would enjoy elevated status for his foresight. Of course, that is exactly what has happened. Today, Dr. Belth is widely praised for his tenacious pursuit of the issues that plagued Executive Life and eventually led to its undoing. Not to take anything away from the glow of Dr. Belth's success due to his predictions about the demise of Executive Life, but one must wonder if the company might have survived, had not the press provided so much fuel for those trying to convince people to surrender their policies.

For his entire career, Joseph Belth has been a consistent ally of the insurance industry community, while reminding them of their obligation to regulate themselves with intelligence or find themselves regulated by those who may not have their best interests at heart. Furthermore, many of his criticisms of Executive Life were well founded, and no one can deny that his reports were factual in base. I do not question the contribution Joseph Belth has made to the life insurance industry, nor do I doubt that he believes he is acting in the industry's best interest—even when he limits his criticism to those areas most remunerative to himself. But I do believe he has lost sight of the mission he stated in an early issue of the *Insurance Forum*, which was to provide "a vehicle through which insurance problems could be discussed openly [and] to accomplish insurance reform." Of course today, he has little choice but to finally comment on the disasters at companies like Mutual Benefit and Mutual of New York, which have been covered elsewhere for some time. Joseph Belth started with a valid concept and he has already contributed a great deal. Now, like much of the rest of the industry, he needs to get back to the basics.

11

The Real Problems

"What I did violated not just the law, but all of my own principles and values. I deeply regret it and will for the rest of my life,
and I am very deeply sorry."
—Mike Milken to Judge Kimba M. Wood before
sentencing, November 21, 1990

The Junk Bond Issue

Few professionals could have gotten so swept up in a *cause
célébre* like the junk bond issue as did most of the agents representing Executive Life. Those who have successfully sold life
insurance for a living know that we must spend much of our
time doing those things that the failures don't like to do—
prospecting and getting appointments with people who really
don't want to see us, to talk to them about a product they really
don't like to buy. To succeed, we need a purpose big enough to
overshadow the negative aspects of the job. We need a cause to
champion. In many ways, the industry's reaction to Executive
Life and its agents was a replay of most of our early careers as
agents. At a cocktail party, when a life insurance agent mentioned to someone that "I sell life insurance for a living," he

would experience the inevitable step back and the defensive remark, ``That's got to be a tough way to make a living," or, ``I've got all the life insurance I need." As an agent, I remember responding, as most did, by digging in my heels and proving to the world that I had made the right choice by coming into the business. I would succeed in spite of their cynical attitudes. Joining Executive Life was very similar to that. The situation caused agents to relive these same types of conversations and rekindled many of the same feelings, only this time it was with their professional peers. At industry functions, when an agent said, ``I write for Executive Life," he could count on a slight step backward from the person he was talking to, and at best, a cynical remark like ``Interesting company." Sometimes the response would be downright offensive.

Nobody ever led a group of people in this type of environment better than Fred Carr. Fred knew his audience. They were at least a decade past the traditional ``positive-mental-attitude" Dale Carnegie or Zig Ziegler hype. These were sophisticated, thoughtful business executives, highly successful in their own right. They were master salespeople, although few could rival Fred's understated sales genius. They wanted substance behind the hype. Fred gave it to them. He became their tutor on the inner workings of a life insurance company, something that had never been shared with them by the management of previous carriers they had worked with. He became their futurist on the industry, regularly predicting changes that he saw on the horizon, doing so with alarming accuracy, and always in his typically Delphic style. To some he was a mentor, to others a celebrity, whose name they could drop with friends and associates. When with a peer group, agents loved to say things like ``Well, I was talking with Fred Carr the other day and Fred thinks...." It was like one of those old E. F. Hutton commercials. Even many of his detractors believed he had a crystal ball. To all of us, he was cryptic and enigmatic. He always left us with the impression that he was about to move the earth with his next blockbuster idea or concept. We knew we were part of something big. Fred was making insurance history and we had a front-row seat. It was a potent lure, even for the strongly independent agents he attracted.

As the attacks on junk bonds intensified, Fred developed the series of themes that helped strengthen the agents' convictions about their association with the company. Sophisticated audience or not, Fred knew that in orchestrating a movement, the essence of the cause must be boiled down to a few simple statements like ``The Penalty of Leadership'' or ``Ten Great in '98.'' He knew how to blend just the right amount of hype into an otherwise believable call to arms.

The message he wanted to deliver was that we were ``reinventing the life insurance industry,'' and that, like most purveyors of change, we would be criticized, attacked, and belittled by those upon whom the change was being perpetrated. But ultimately we would prevail. Posterity would be his judge. As it turned out, this big picture approach was a major problem for many agents, who eventually realized that Fred's time frame was much different from theirs. They were working on next month's production, and were shattered when some adverse press caused the biggest case they had bagged that year to go sour. Fred, on the other hand, focused only on the big picture. He was working on the epitaph they would inscribe on his tombstone. He had no reaction to the daily events that would soon be forgotten when contrasted against the long shadow of the man who changed the direction of an industry. Although Fred never seemed so to the casual observer, he was very egocentric. The more the debate raged on about whether or not Executive Life was a house of cards with no real value, the more clearly the battle lines were drawn. Eventually the competitors' files on Executive Life bulged. Every time their agents made a sales call, the competition would bury the prospect with anti-Executive Life propaganda.

Most agents have to make three sales: first they have to sell themselves; then they have to sell the prospect on a need; then they have to sell the product. The Executive Life agent had to make the additional sale about Executive Life not being what it was portrayed to be by the press and by the competition. But it didn't end there. If he was successful and won the client over, then he had to go back periodically when disconcerting news about Executive Life appeared in the press. Eventually, agents had to use the ultimate sales tool: they had to put their reputations on the line for Executive Life every time they sold an Executive Life policy. They were strong and, because of their stature in their community, highly regarded by their clients. They had a lot of control with their clients, because of the long-standing, trusting relationship typically built up over the years. Still, sooner or later they had to grab the client by the lapels and say, ``Look, all this stuff you're reading in the press about Executive Life is bullshit. Trust me, I know what I'm talking about!"

By the time the company took its first catastrophic write-down of $550 million on January 19, 1990, most of the agents had already had that lapel-grabbing conversation with their key clients at least once. They had no choice but to stand their ground, even though most were sick about the turn of events. They had good reason to feel as they did about defending the company. A. M. Best, the industry's leading rating agency had given Executive Life its top rating, A+, for a dozen straight years. When Standard & Poor's went into the rating business, Executive Life was one of the first companies to earn its AAA for claims-paying ability. Out of some 1,400 companies in the industry, only 32 had attained both of these coveted credentials. The investment portfolio of the company had not only passed the scrutiny of the experts, it had been given their highest grades. What's more, most agents had gone a step further and spent a lot of time listening to Fred Carr's explanation of what a junk bond really was, and why it was such an ideal investment for the properly balanced portfolio of a life insurance company.

Fatal Attraction

On Thanksgiving morning, 1990, like many business executives, I passed on watching the holiday parades on television and pored over the *Los Angeles Times* and *New York Times*, reading about the sentencing of Michael Milken, which had occurred the day before. Judge Kimba M. Wood, who gave Milken ten years in jail for securities fraud, had postponed the sentence for a few days; I can't help but wonder if she did it so a lot of business people would spend this reflective holiday thinking long and hard about the gift of a free enterprise system, and what happens when they abuse it.

We won't spend much time analyzing the Milken–Drexel–junk bond saga, since it has been the central topic of the business press for several years, as well as the subject of several best-selling books. What we will do is look at these issues as they affected First Executive Corporation, and its agents and policyholders, roughly a quarter million of America's more sophisticated consumers who bought their products, and another quarter million participants in pension plans who wound up depending on their ability to perform when their plan managers bought Executive Life Guaranteed Investment Contracts (GICs).

From a marketing perspective, the thing that made it all work for First Executive Corporation was the most competitive life and annuity products of any company in America. Nobody could touch them. Nobody. What made it all possible was Fred's investment strategy. And what made Fred's investment strategy work was junk bonds.

That fact that junk bonds were the single most important contributor to First Executive Corporation's success formula is no secret. Yet, in spite of all of the publicity they have received in recent years, most people, including many insurance people, have little understanding of what a junk bond really is. For years Fred Carr resisted calling them ``junk bonds,'' preferring to refer to them by their original name, ``high-yield securities.'' This indeed is what they were known as, before being popularized by Michael Milken and Drexel Burnham Lambert. Somewhere along the line, an analyst who has yet to step forward to take the credit coined the pejorative term ``junk bond.'' In many ways, that term became a self-fulfilling prophecy. The real problem is that, like most bigoted terms, it is a generalization about a perceived flaw in one area that is applied erroneously to all within its class.

First, let's clarify what it is that constitutes an investment grade bond. These are bonds issued, typically by Fortune 500 corporations, which are rated BBB- or higher by Standard & Poor's, or Baa$_3$ or higher by Moody's. In a given year during the 1980s, there were between 750 and 800 companies in all of the United States whose debt qualified as investment grade. The debt of every other corporation in America qualified as junk! These bonds have ratings that range from BB or lower from Standard & Poor's and Ba$_1$ or lower from Moody's. The general distinction, however, remains that between investment grade and junk. If the world worked in the black and white way that the press often paints for it, this would be a simple delineation, by which we could distinguish very safe from very risky bonds. The truth is that many bonds that are investment grade when purchased later become junk. Jim Anderson of Towers Perrin, the nation's largest actuarial firm, made this prediction at the annual meeting of the American Society of Actuaries in 1990: ``The financial crisis of the next decade will be centered around the deterioration of credit risks and the probability of a replay of the `80's with dramatic increases in interest rates and inflation." On the other hand, one is hardpressed to believe that the debt of all but a relative handful of American corporations should be saddled with the moniker of junk.

To lend perspective on how inappropriate the term is, one only has to look to the banking industry, which uses the term "prime rate" to refer to the most favorable interest rate it makes available only to "prime customers." Ironically, both terms, "junk" and "prime," often refer to the same corporation. Many corporations that qualify for a prime interest rate at their home town bank would be assigned junk ratings by Moody's and Standard & Poor's if they floated a bond issue. Before Mike Milken, raising capital through bond offerings was chiefly the purview of America's leading corporations. The rest had to go to their local banks rather than Wall Street. The junk bond market Milken created took away many of the prime customers of the banking industry, considerably weakening their portfolios. And arousing their rancor toward him and his better customers.

Except for a handful, most states have only a half dozen or so corporations whose debt qualifies as investment grade. So, to a bank in Princeton, New Jersey, the home of Prince Corporation (Prince tennis rackets, etc.), or to a bank in Southern California, the home of Mattel Toys, these companies are probably prime-rate qualifiers. Yet, when these and hundreds of other similar companies raised capital through bonds sold to Executive Life, their credit was rated as "junk." The local car dealership, the tool and dye shop, and of course, you and I, are all the junk in the portfolios of the local bank. The cream of one financial institution's portfolio is the trash of another—that is, if you want to paint everything with the same broad brush. Clearly, the issue is more complicated than the line between investment grade and junk. Let's take a quick look at the facts.

It all began back in the early 1970s when Michael Milken, then a very young investment banker with Drexel Firestone, identified an opportunity in bonds trading at a deep discount due to the fact that they were non-investment grade (Ba_1 or lower by Moody's, or B+ or lower by Standard & Poor's). Such bonds were thinly traded, and of little interest to Wall Street until Milken convinced Drexel Firestone to begin publishing listings and commentary on them. Milken promoted these credits because he recognized that the spread between the prices and effective yields they offered far exceeded the risk. He cultivated a clientele among pension fund managers and institutional investors such as life insurance companies.

Interestingly, when Milken started to make his mark, these bonds really were not originally junk. At the time, they were more "fallen angels" in that they were once companies successful enough to sell an investment grade bond issue, but who had fallen on hard times and whose bonds had been downgraded and were trading at big discounts. Milken focused on the credits of bankrupt or near-bankrupt companies like Penn Central Railroad, eventually controlled by Carl Lindner, and Reliance Insurance, eventually controlled by Saul Steinberg, as well as a number of real estate investment trusts (REITs). It was not just that he recognized a type of credit whose yield was greater than the risk warranted; he jumped in at a time when the market was overreacting to prevailing conditions. Often these types of bonds were available at 20¢ and 30¢ on the dollar. The yield at these prices could not be offset with any default rate as long as they lasted three or four years on average. (It is indeed ironic that in 1990 the same kind of overreaction occurred after Drexel's collapse and comparable values were again available.) What Milken did next was to begin expanding the market by offering new issues of non-investment grade securities. Rather than looking for companies whose bonds had sunk to the non-investment grade, he found the companies whose credit started out that way. Many of them, however, were companies which used the money for the right purposes—to grow their businesses. It was a sound and worthwhile strategy.

The trouble started when Milken began to carry a good thing to the extreme, which usually makes it a bad thing. First, he began to do deals that were not sound because the long-term ability of the issuer to service their debt was questionable. Then, of course, the leveraged buy-out (LBO) wave hit, opening up huge opportunities to finance management-sponsored purchases of companies, using the company cash flow to service the debt and in theory ultimately retire it. Many LBOs were done with strong companies in stable industries and worked out just fine. Others were doomed from the start because the only way the debt could be serviced was if everything went well for a long time. Through these expansion strategies, the annual public offerings of junk bonds grew tenfold between 1979 and 1986, to $40.8 billion. These later types of junk were what brought the whole market for non-investment grade securities crashing down. This was the bad junk, or what should all along have been identified as the real junk—LBOs that were underfunded and companies lacking cash flow to service the debt.

Just as Wall Street had spat upon Fred Carr a few years earlier for tainting the analysts' image by becoming a market maker in his "emerging growth stocks," so Milken was scorned for "peddling this crap," as one prominent analyst of the 1970s put it. In general, it is neither crap nor junk, although the junk market contains some of both. Mostly it is the debt of a medium- to large-size corporation that, for various reasons, does not qualify as being among the very safest among its peers and on which the issuers must pay a premium interest rate to offset the perceived risk. The junk bond market contains the credits of more household names than does the investment grade market. Companies like Revlon, Holiday Inns, Chrysler Corporation, and Safeway supermarkets are typical junk bond issuers. To lump these and dozens of similar corporations under the banner of "junk," by definition disqualifies the appropriateness of this term.

The issue, then, is the deterioration of credit risk, which we talked about in Chapter 4. It all comes down to due diligence on the part of the company buying the bond. Just as a bank makes a determination on a mortgage loan to an individual based upon his or her earnings and past performance, so the purchase of a corporate bond should be based upon similar criteria. However, earnings and cash flow of corporations can experience far greater swings than those of us who work in them typically experience. Furthermore, companies that are heavily leveraged have far less adaptability to the increasingly changing environment in which we all operate. Whether you enter a recession where cash flow is diminished, or a boom where additional capital investments are important, the burden of heavy debt is a competitive disadvantage. Just as it goes with the individual, debt is an encumbrance both in tough times, where you want to weather the storm, and in good times, when you want to plow capital into your enterprise.

Nobody understood this better than Fred Carr, who had an aversion to debt financing for his own corporation. One of the paradoxes in Fred's strategy was that although he abhorred the dangers of debt on his own balance sheet, he built his whole company by investing in companies that were often heavily indebted—to him! He was on the other side of the problem, but the result was the same. Their not being able to pay their obligations was passed through to Fred, until—irony of ironies—the burden became so great he was unable to pay his.

Mike Milken published a number of statements and made many speeches on the virtues of junk bonds, and few would argue his qualifications to address the subject. Furthermore, Mr. Milken now has plenty of spare time with which to polish his thoughts on the subject. I'm sure we can look forward to his story in a book and probably a movie.* Let's remember, however, that Milken *sold* junk bonds while Fred Carr *bought* junk bonds, plenty of them. By some accounts, First Executive Corporation did over $40 billion in trades with Drexel Burnham between 1982 and 1987. By 1987, First Executive Corporation had the largest junk bond portfolio in the world. The best qualified man in America to discuss junk bonds is the man who bought more than anybody else. In June 1990, Fred Carr was called before Congressman John Dingell's Subcommittee on Oversight and Investigations of the Committee on Energy and Commerce, at the U.S. House of Representatives. Fred's comments to the subcommittee, which are now part of the *Congressional Record*, focused on three of his most basic investment beliefs:

- A properly structured, high-yield bond portfolio is not "riskier" than one featuring real estate and mortgages.
- In a properly constituted portfolio, the higher risk of default for high-yield bonds is compensated for by the higher interest rates, producing the same net "safety."
- "Interest-rate risk" can threaten investor safety just as default risk can.

Fred's testimony in defense of his junk bond investment

---

* My choice for the role of Mike Milken in the inevitable movie would be the wrestling star Andre the Giant. Not only does he look like Mike, but his physical stature is the embodiment of Mike's role in the world of finance. Furthermore, the credibility with which Andre the Giant plies his craft apes that of the junk bond king.

strategy was flawless. He did such a good job defending his position and explaining what he thought were the issues that he wasn't invited back, which was his goal. Dingell wanted someone to make an example of, to validate the subcommittee's feeling that the insurance industry needed federal regulation. Before Fred's testimony, they had a good chance of it. After all, if the two Insurance departments that oversaw First Executive Corporation, New York and California, couldn't manage them, what must it be like for companies domiciled in the other less populated states, where the resources of the regulatory bodies were likely to be more limited? Fred's skillful and carefully prepared statement, along with his pursuant testimony, slowed the congressional momentum on this issue. If they wanted public support for federal regulation of the insurance industry, they wouldn't get it by showcasing Fred Carr as an example of a CEO who was asleep at the switch.

That was in June 1990. A year later, with the Executive Life companies insolvent and in the hands of the California and New York Insurance departments, it was quite another story. By that time it was painfully evident that Fred appeared not to have been practicing the due diligence he had been preaching with regard to his investment strategy. He clearly had not built the "properly structured, properly constituted" portfolio he described to the subcommittee. His portfolio was every bit as badly off as the market, and its profile showed no aversion to the defaults occurring in the market—if it was defaulting, one could almost rest assured that Executive Life owned some of it.

This was very disconcerting to the proponents of the "good junk, bad junk" theory, who had always believed Fred knew how to pick the winners. By that time, Congress had proposed the idea of a federal solvency regulator similar to that overseeing the banking industry. This would not replace the fifty state regulatory bodies, but would add another layer of bureaucracy at the federal level to look over matters of solvency. As it turned out, the Executive Life failure would be the focal point of the issue for the Congress and the state regulators. How well the California and New York Insurance departments handle these insolvencies will be the reference point in the debate on state versus federal regulation of the insurance industry. One good by-product of this contest would likely be that the industry and the NAIC will take every measure to see to it that policyholders are made whole, so they will not provide an example for Congress to point to, thus supporting their call for more federal regulation.

The *Los Angeles Times* columnist James Flanigan in his Thanksgiving Day, 1990, commentary asked: "What have we learned from Milken?" His answer could easily apply to Milken's main man, Fred Carr: "We have learned again that financial genius is before the fall. The Milken sentenced Wednesday is the same man who was hailed as the new J. P. Morgan, come to remake American business. Like scores of speculative geniuses before him, Milken turned out to be a fake prophet. Maybe the next time the public will be more skeptical and regulators will act more quickly to protect the financial system." Most would agree that those words could also apply to Fred Carr and Executive Life. Yet the issue is not junk bonds; rather, it is the responsible use of policyholder funds, which encompasses a lot more CEOs of insurance companies than just Fred Carr. Let's not call for the heads of those who gave us what we wanted. Flanigan goes on to quote Pogo's famous line, "We have met the enemy and he is us."

The sale of life insurance went from need to greed, and when it did so, some feel it lost its integrity. The companies, the agents, and yes, even the policyholders, all rationalized that they could optimize yield without increasing risk. It was just another example of trying to get something for nothing. Executive Life has probably gotten more than its share of the blame for a metamorphosis in which, although a leader, it was far from being the only player.

Executive Life projected performance based upon actual current yields, but underestimated the risks associated with those yields and fell short of its ability to meet projections. Other companies made projections they were not able to deliver on because of unsubstantiated optimism and also fell short. For both, the end result was disappointment. Over the long haul,

Executive Life policyholders will likely suffer the greatest trauma; but most buyers of insurance in the 1980s will be unhappy with the performance delivered compared to that which was illustrated by many companies.

Michael Milken is, of course, a convicted felon, who by his own admission "violated the law." There are no similarities in this regard between Milken and Carr, or the rest of the life insurance industry. Our violation was one of product integrity. We took a short-term period during which exceptional yields were available and applied them to a very long-term product. It was like shooting a birdie on the first three holes of a golf course and predicting a final score of 54! Whether we used high-yield risky investments to get there, or low-yield ultra safe investments, the result was the same. The industry's reach exceeded its grasp. As a result, there are a lot of disappointed policyholders.

It Takes Money to Make Money

The biggest problem that has faced American business in the past fifteen years is not foreign competition, nor various energy crises, nor the federal deficit. The real problem has been the lack of capital. Nowhere is the capital shortage more acute than in the life insurance industry. It takes money to grow any business, but the life insurance business is capital-intensive to the point of being self-destructive in the current environment, where it simply isn't doing well enough as an industry to attract much new capital. Back in the early 1980s when First Executive Corporation was soaring, most economists agree that the shortage of capital in American business played a key role in the twin spirals of inflation and interest rates. Obviously the junk bond market was a welcome contributor to help relieve this problem, but even the $40 or $50 billion it raised by mid-decade was a drop in the bucket compared to what was needed. More importantly, when the junk bond market really took off, the capital was mostly squandered on takeover and LBO efforts, which did nothing to help business grow.

Most businesses require initial capital to get started that is in excess of their revenues. Put simply, they start off in the hole and use the initial investment of the owners as start-up money until revenues create a positive cash flow. Usually this money is borrowed from banks (debt financing) or investors (equity financing) who buy stock in the company. Theoretically, when the business is up and running, the investors get appreciation on their stock plus dividends or the bankers get their money back plus interest, and everyone is happy.

Life insurance companies operate under an entirely different set of rules. The cost of putting a life insurance policy on the books usually far exceeds the first-year revenues, not just in the beginning stages of building the business, but on every sale you ever make. Thus, there is no positive cash flow in the early years with which to reward owners and investors, nor do you reach the point where cash flow on new sales becomes positive because the initial revenues exceed the initial outlay. Instead, there is, by design, a significant negative cash flow, which can take years before generating a profit to owners. The best way to understand it is to view a life insurance contract as a long-term installment purchase on which you make annual payments over many years—typically as few as six or seven large premiums, or much lower premiums that continue the entire balance of your lifetime, depending upon which type of policy you choose. This logic no longer applies just to accounting. Because of the new, unbundled insurance products sold today, it is also true from a consumer perspective. The company and the consumers are partners over the life of the policy, sharing in results that will vary from year to year. As the industry has learned, the results can vary a great deal from the projections used in the point of sale materials.

This is a change in recent years that has been difficult even for life insurance companies to understand. As we saw earlier, the consumer no longer "buys a life insurance policy." Rather, he or she is buying the life insurance policy over a protracted period of time. The performance of the company's investment portfolio, its expenses, its persistency and mortality experiences, are all a moving target that can be periodically adjusted—whether directly or indirectly. For the customer, the results of his or her purchase will vary from year to year based upon a series of factors built into the contract.

When the new policyholder makes his first installment on the purchase of his life insurance policy by paying the first year's premium, the cash flow is not adequate to cover the company's expenses. For example, in the case of a $200,000 life insurance policy purchased by a man at age forty, the cash flow might look like this:

Initial premium: $2,500

Agent commission:	2,000
MGA compensation:	500
Underwriting expenses:	400
Miscellaneous expenses:	100
Total expenses:*	$3,000

*For purposes of illustration, we are omitting taxes and similar considerations.

So, there's a shortfall of $500. To make the sale, we must then tap into our shareholder equity which, in a life insurance company, is called capital and surplus. Unlike a manufacturer, who can go to the well for an initial capital infusion to prime the pump to get his business going, a life insurance company must keep going back to the well every time it makes a new sale. The more successful the company, the more you bite into your capital and surplus base. This is true of industrial companies as they reach certain plateaus and must raise capital to build new plants and buy more equipment, but not with each and every product they sell. In fact, the opposite is true: as they reach certain levels of critical mass, their costs diminish on a per unit basis and their profits increase.

In an insurance company, eventually profits do begin to emerge on older policies because, although the premiums remain the same, the expenses are dramatically reduced in later years. For example, in the policy we are looking at here, the expenses in years 2 through 10 might be about $300 per year, including renewal commissions to agents and policy administration expenses. Of course, any death claims would go straight to the bottom line, but that's what the mortality charges are for. If claim experience is as expected, then there will be a profit left over from the mortality charges after all claims have been paid. Further, most of the remaining value that accrues is passed on to the policyholder—at least, that's the way it has been in recent years, thanks to the changes in products we have seen. Historically, insurance companies were aided by their accountants, who by using generally accepted accounting principles (GAAP) allowed the insurance company to amortize (spread out) certain expenses by deferring policy acquisition costs over the expected life of the policy. But these helpful practices are quickly drying up, and the once dramatic difference between GAAP accounting and STAT (statutory) accounting is narrowing dramatically. A company can still defer its acquisition costs, but it must also defer the profits it books on the piece of business in question, which greatly diminishes the benefit of cost deferral and affects the design and attractiveness of the typical life insurance policy offered today.

The new, higher-yielding policies sold in the 1980s created tremendous capital strain for many companies. As we have discussed, ironically, if the company paid its own agents to update their clientele, it got double-dipped. It lost the old piece of more profitable business that was generating surplus, then turned around and used up more surplus to rewrite that same piece of business on a much narrower profit margin. At least if it just lost the policy to a competitor, it only got hit once. In addition, when it lost a policy to a competitor rather than rewriting it, the lost policy freed up reserves that helped its statutory balance-sheet. Since regulators require very conservative reserving to meet future obligations, when the policy was surrendered, the reserve usually exceeded the surrender value. The difference went straight to the company's bottom line.

It isn't hard to figure out why the establishment in the life insurance industry hated this guy Carr and his peers. First they got beat at their own game by a new set of rules, then they got hamstrung when they tried to compete under those new rules. The nouveau companies had none of this baggage, they just went out and sold new products; which when you have no business on your books, looks pretty good even if the margins are thinner.

The critical factor for a financial institution that makes it possible to use borrowed funds to invest profitability is *leverage*. When First Executive Corporation borrowed $100 million from banks or in a Preferred stock or bond offering, it did so in anticipation of its ability to put that money to work. This means we had to sell products that used up the new surplus, and in exchange, offer spreads that significantly exceeded the cost of capital. For example, if First Executive had to pay 12 percent to borrow $100 million, that would mean it cost them $12 million per year for the use of the capital. If the annuities they were selling, due to excess reserving requirements, commissions, and expenses, generated a 10 percent surplus strain from extra reserve requirements and expense loads (mostly commissions), they then could sell $1 billion of annuities with the newly raised capital ($1 billion × 10% = $100 million of required surplus), which, in effect, is the cost of putting the business on the books. If the spread on this type of product was 250 basis points, they then grossed $25 million in year 1 and netted $3 million after paying the interest on the funds borrowed (12% × $100 million = $12 million) and putting up the extra reserve of $10 million for the surplus strain. In later years, with no commission loads and only modest maintenance expenses, the profits jumped to about $13 million after they paid the $12 million in interest to their creditors.

It's easy to see that if a company can make its investment spreads while still offering enough value to the customer to sell its products, it can be a very profitable business. Of course, this illustration assumes that the capital comes in just as you need it to write the business. In the real world, you may have the capital parked in low-yielding cash equivalents while you wait to get the business written. In such a case, there is no leveraging, and you may be paying 12 percent on the money and getting 6 percent on the short-term temporary investment. Or, as was the case with Executive Life in the mid-1980s, you may write the business first, then scramble around toward year end to find the capital necessary to satisfy the regulatory and reserving requirements, such as the last-minute surplus relief contracts they put on their books in 1984. Another problem can occur when the company writes a huge chunk of business all at once, such as in 1986 when Executive Life sold $1.85 billion of muni-GICs, which they won based on an assumed interest yield. They then had to find someplace to get high yields on this huge influx of cash. Many observers think it was at this moment that the company's need for junk to make good on its commitments to the muni-GIC holders caused it to buy anything put in front of it, most of which later defaulted. I do not recommend approaches this aggressive.

Surplus strain is obviously an important consideration in a company's growth plans. It also affects profitability, since the return on invested surplus decreases on a given product as reserving requirements increase. In other words, the more money you have to put aside in addition to the actual premium collected to get the policy sold, the lower your effective return is on that investment of surplus (assuming the premiums on one given policy are no more profitable than those of another). Obviously we have to go back to the well if we want to grow our business. Not just at expansionary plateaus like manufacturing firms, but with every sale. It's easy to see why rapidly growing life insurance companies become victims of their own success. This was never truer for any company than it was for the Executive Life Companies in the mid-1980s.

To all of this, one must add the fact that in the 1990s the life insurance business has not attracted outside capital even in the case of the healthiest companies. Uncertainty about further taxation on the inside build-up, as well as the loss of many tax benefits regarding deferred policy acquisition costs, are just part of the problem. The industry, in general, is in the doldrums, with sales flat and no new innovations occurring since the late 1980s. The portfolios of many major companies appear to be under water to the point that, on a statutory basis, some household names would be insolvent if they had to mark their bonds and mortgages to market. The life insurance industry had rocked along through the decades of the 1950s to the 1970s, enjoying steady growth with no particular boom or bust times. Now, after the go-go 1980s, it is in a real slump. Actually, the slump is more of a hangover from the 1980s, which were not so much productive as they were an enlightening time for the industry.

The underlying problem for Executive Life, perhaps as much as even junk bond defaults, was a constant shortage of capital. Because of the company's spectacular growth, and because of the shortfall on the liability side of the balance sheet created when some assets had to be marked down, there was a need for capital that even Fred Carr could not keep up with. It was an exaggerated example of the problem faced by the entire industry a year or so later. Even though other companies weren't growing as fast, they were plagued by many similar problems when their portfolios deteriorated in the wake of the savings and loan crises.

The world's largest life insurance company is Nippon Life of Japan, which reportedly has in excess of $100 billion in capital. The U.S. life insurance industry's Top 200 companies, which essentially constitute 95 percent of the entire industry, have about $100 billion in capital. As a financial services industry goes in the economic world in which we live, this makes the U.S. life insurance industry a minor player. The shortage of capital is the real problem. It was the real problem at Executive Life, and it is the real problem in the rest of the life insurance industry. This is the issue on which the industry and those who regulate it should be focusing for the balance of the century.

12

The Press Smells Blood

*"React swiftly, be decisive, take charge, don't be afraid to dele-
gate. Set a clear strategy and stick to it. Communicate. Communicate. Communicate. Executives take note. The President's
initial response to Iraq's invasion of Kuwait provides a textbook
demonstration of what to do when the going gets tough."*
— Ann Reily Dowd, "George Bush as Crisis Manager,"
Fortune, September 10, 1990

By the fall of 1989, members of the press were beginning to
assemble the bits and pieces of their various disjointed critical
analyses of First Executive Corporation into a mosaic of frightening disaster. They were now ready to forecast officially the
collapse of the House of Carr. Many insiders felt that the shorts*
who had made so many millions were orchestrating a campaign
in the press that would assure a crisis in confidence, leading to
the collapse of the company. Although I don't usually agree
with this common complaint for the decline of a company's
stock, one must at least pause and consider it. For all of 1990,
First Executive Corporation was the most shorted OTC stock!

*Shorts are securities specialists who speculate in stocks of companies they
believe will decline by selling stocks they don't yet own, then buying them to
fill the order at a later date and presumably lower prices.

200

Between the time of the annual shareholders meeting in July 1989 and the end of 1990, the stock fell from $16 per share to 16¢. That's a 99 percent drop in value, which has to be a record for a major corporation without first filing for bankruptcy. And judging by the size of the short positions held during that period, it's easy to see that huge fortunes were made. Eventually, however, it was the performance of the company rather than rumored problems that validated the market's opinion of First Executive Corporation.

One could further argue that the situation became a self-ful-filling prophecy. After all, the bad press can clearly be traced to declining sales and high levels of surrenders when there was lit-tle or no hard evidence that the company was anything less than healthy. Indeed, many of these foreboding articles appeared at the same time that Standard & Poor's, after exten-sive research, was issuing statements reaffirming its AAA claims-paying ability rating. Which did come first? Well, clearly the press was cynical about the whole junk bond market from the start. And as to Fred Carr, few major figures in the financial world have had a poorer image in the press over a longer period of time. Fred has been portrayed negatively for twenty of the twenty-five years he has been reported on. One could argue that the press may have contributed to the decline in pop-ularity of junk issues and therefore the market value. You couldn't pick up a financial journal after 1986 without reading negative articles about junk bonds. True, there was reason for concern; but as we have just seen, there was much more to the junk bond market than was reported in the press. Ten positive stories could have been reported for every failure in the junk bond market. Generally, in life, if only 10 percent of what you do goes bad, you're extraordinarily successful. In the bond mar-ket, however, a 10 percent default rate is disastrous, and that was the issue. Not the many successes of the junk bond market, but the unacceptably high percentage of irresponsibly con-structed deals that were pushed through along with the good ones, even though many were doomed from the start.

The truth is it wasn't the shorts and it wasn't the press that brought about the free fall. The ultimate cause of the market value decline of junk was the defaults. Bad press can put downward pressure on prices, and the shorts can certainly spread the bad news, but bad press doesn't cause defaults. Bad deals cause defaults. Poorly managed, overleveraged companies cause defaults, and this, all along, was the press's issue. They thought a lot of the companies issuing junk bonds would eventually lack the cash flow to meet their obligations. They and the shorts played their hunches. In the end it paid off. They believed it was only a matter of time before First Executive Corporation, with its overzealous appetite for junk, would stumble in the face of a recession or a liquidity crisis. All they had to do was keep fueling the prediction and wait to be proven correct.

It should be noted that the adverse publicity definitely exacerbated the situation and created a crisis in confidence without which the company might have survived; but in the end, the defaults vindicated the alarmists. For what it's worth, few corporate CEOs could withstand seventeen years of predicted fall the way Fred Carr did without sometime in their history fitting the predicted pattern. For most companies, when disaster occurs, it's a surprise, and as such, management has a year or two of reaction time to turn things around before the shareholders and critics bury them. In the case of First Executive Corporation, it was the long-awaited fall that many were cheering for. There was no reaction time, just enough time to cover up against the barrage of well-prepared critics who had only to push a button on their word processors to trigger their already written obituaries on Fred Carr and his company.

It was probably right next to the one they had on Armand Hammer, which had to have been written for as long and was activated about the same time. Press members who had been patiently waiting through seventeen years of Carr bashing now sensed that their time had come at last. It was all going to come unraveled at First Executive Corporation, and everyone was ready to say, "I told you so." Fred would be proven all they had said he was; and with a little help from Michael Milken, perhaps even more.

The first major sign that things were slipping out of Fred's control was in 1988, when he violated his own long-standing prohibition against debt and permitted Drexel Burnham to float a $275 million loan with a group of Japanese banks. Originally it was intended to be a bond deal, but when it was completed, it was the first outright loan Fred had taken since joining the company in 1974, and something he had always pledged he would not do. Prior to that had been the surplus note for $151 million in 1987, which he had to use as an infusion of capital into the New York company to fill the capital shortage left when the New York Insurance Department disallowed a series of surplus relief agreements. This, in hindsight, was another indication that Fred's hold on the tiger's tail was beginning to slip.

Then, in July 1989, came the complex rights offering that raised almost $300 million in capital through a typically convoluted Fred Carr transaction, which I suspect was not fully understood by many of the account executives in the securities industry who sold it. The offering was poorly received on Wall Street, and in the time between the offering in August and closing in October, the common stock lost 40 percent of its value. The deal was underwritten by Kidder Peabody and was eventually completed, raising $284 million of capital that was much more badly needed than anyone had imagined. A series of articles in the *Wall Street Journal* and *New York Times* described the transaction as more Fred Carr footwork and a ploy to raise badly needed capital to buttress up the company's sagging bond portfolio. Three months after the offering closed, First Executive Corporation announced its cataclysmic write-down, which eventually amounted to $776 million.

Also in early 1989, First Executive had announced its long-awaited deal to sell its New York company, which had been on the block, both officially and unofficially, for about two years. The deal involved long-time Fred Carr associate Martin J. Wygod, who had formed a partnership with recently ousted Equitable Life Chief Operating Officer Leo M. Walsh, Jr. (Mr.

Walsh more than anyone else has been held responsible in the press for the Equitable woes that occurred at about the same time). Again, the deal was very complex and, although valued at between $400 and $500 million, left First Executive Corporation with 20 percent control of the surviving company. Then, toward January 1, 1990, the deal fell apart. Many insiders never viewed it as a sale with much hope of materializing because the New York Insurance Department was unlikely to approve a fully leveraged transaction by two entrepreneurs to remove the New York unit from what, at the time, was a healthy and substantial holding corporation, at least as far as the regulators were concerned. One would have to assume that the New York Department would rather deal with a Fortune 500 holding company with $275 million in debt, warts and all, than it would a couple of guys like Marty and Leo, who would have had to borrow that much to control the New York company alone.

A painful side effect of the proposed New York transaction was that by placing a value on the company for tax purposes, whether they sold it or not, they now had given the IRS a basis on which to tax them on the gain between the book value at which they were carrying it and the market value established by the proposed sale. The result was a $135 million tax liability which came right off the bottom line, even though the sale collapsed.

The New York fiasco, the shoddiness of the deal and the tax loss it created, left a lot of supporters scratching their heads as to what Fred's agenda really was. The press moved in on the collapse of the New York sale as the beginning of the end for First Executive Corporation, which they maintained would now be desperate for capital.

While all of this was occurring, Fred got an ingenious idea for making a bunch of junk bonds disappear off the company's balance sheet. The concept was called a collateralized bond obligation (CBO) and it was closely modeled after the collateralized mortgage obligation (CMO), which was a popular vehicle on Wall Street at the time. Fred formed six companies and gave each of them packages of bonds, which they were hopefully going to sell in the marketplace at some future date. Jim Cox, Fred's long-time trusted associate, was CEO of all six companies. Each company packaged securities in classifications (tranches) falling into three categories. The type of securities were six-year bonds in tranche one, eight-year bonds in tranche two, and in the third tranche thirteen-year zero coupon bonds they had acquired at an 85 percent discount from their maturity values.

The idea was that although some of the packages contained junk, due to the diversification of the investments and the fact that some credits were of high grade, the overall package was investment grade, thus moving junk out of Executive Life's portfolio and freeing up the extra reserves (MSVR) required to be set aside to offset the higher risks associated with junk bonds. Because some junk bonds could now be classified as investment grade, Executive Life had a side benefit from the transaction, turning a liability (reserve) into an asset (freed-up cash). In the case of the CBO transaction, Fred eliminated about $725 million of junk and thus freed up about $120 million of reserves, which went right into the capital and surplus account.

When the press got wind of the transaction, it became big news and was portrayed as an evasive move by the company to reduce its mandatory reserve requirements, even though in December 1988 the NAIC rated the top two tranches as "yes" bonds (meaning investment grade). They reversed themselves on the issue in December 1989 on various grounds. The California Department of Insurance then ordered that Executive Life's reserve for 1989 should be adjusted to include the CBOs as "no" bonds (the NAIC definition of junk), which led to a $109 million differential in the company's extra reserves. It was a big problem from a public relations standpoint, in that it came at a time when the company's integrity was already being questioned. Obviously, although the California Insurance Department had been informed of the transaction, it was not explained to them in a way that would prepare them for the criticism it would receive in the press. These were the kinds of surprises that strained First Executive's relationship with the regulators.

Too Much Footwork

All of these transactions, viewed individually, may have been examples of Fred's creative financial genius. But when viewed collectively, they began to tell a somewhat different story—one that did not bode well for the future of the corporation. The press was starting to pull events together by December 1989: the $275 bank loan nearing default, the $400 million failed New York sale resulting in a $135 million tax liability, the $300 million rights offering bringing a pile of lawsuits, and the $756 million CBO transaction, which had to be reversed. Even the loyalists had to admit there was a lot of fancy financial footwork going on at First Executive Corporation in 1989. Joseph Belth was having a field day with these issues in his *Insurance Forum*, as were a host of columnists at *Barron's*, the *Wall Street Journal*, and *BusinessWeek*. The mosaic was beginning to take form and many were gravely concerned by what they saw.

While all of this was going on, there were two very interested spectators, who, although they were keenly interested in the turn of events, seemed surprisingly powerless to do anything about them. Bob Shaw, chairman of ICH Corporation, a large Kentucky-based insurance holding firm, had become intrigued by First Executive Corporation in the early 1980s. Shaw, who built his company through debt, greatly admired Carr, who had been able to raise capital to fund his growth through equity. Shaw's expertise was in acquisitions, which he consolidated into his base and paid for by the savings that occur when you shut a company down, let the employees go, and consolidate the administration of the in-force business, letting the cash flow from premiums create big profits. It is a simple process, but one that few can make work, due to the lack of strong administrative systems in the industry. Through the leadership of his arch-lieutenant Jack Gardner, Shaw had developed an acquisition machine that took inefficient dogs and turned them into cash cows. This milking approach to generating profits is not necessarily as glamorous as building a company from scratch by selling new products and marketing new concepts, but the end results for owners can be as good or better. In fact, many believe that the acquisition-oriented companies will be the big players until the year 2000.

What Shaw lacked and wanted from Fred was his skill in portfolio management. What Fred lacked and saw in ICH was administrative skills and a family of companies rich in cash and able to offer surplus relief. For these and other reasons, Fred agreed to sell Bob Shaw's ICH Corporation 20 percent of First Executive Corporation over a period of about two years. From a personality standpoint, the two were odd bedfellows, but no one could deny the business synergy. Fred sold Shaw his interest at an average price of about $15 per share. Shaw's rather transparent ambition was to gain control of First Executive Corporation, the ultimate acquisition. He could not contain his excitement over the prospect of someday owning Executive Life, and even used to allude to this in his speeches to the ICH sales force.

Fred played on the situation like a pro. He gave Shaw all the line he wanted; then, when he was ready, he set the hook. Of all of us who were smitten by the Fred Carr ethereal carrot, no one made a bigger reach for it than Bob Shaw. In fact, he bet his company on it, and lost. Although that was not part of Fred's plan, when our stock went into free fall, it burned through the bulk of ICH's capital base, leaving Shaw with huge losses, his company near bankruptcy and having to be restructured. For a while, ICH had essentially been gutted by its losses in First Executive Corporation, but today it is on the road to a modest recovery.

The other, much less silent partner was the Dallas oil heiress Caroline Hunt's Rosewood Financial, which owned 10 percent of First Executive Corporation. If ever there was an example of too much due diligence and not enough street smarts, it was Rosewood Financial's investment in First Executive Corporation. The firm boasted a staff of whiz kids who, after undergraduate work at Texas's better-known Christian institutions, went on to Wharton and Harvard for their MBAs. One of their key people, Jeb Terry, told me that after they decided to invest in a life insurance company, they eventually spent over $1 million on selecting and developing information on First Executive Corporation. They even commissioned Booz Allen to do a special survey of the sales force entitled "Agent Needs and Perceptions of Executive Life." Their enthusiasm for the company's future when they made their initial $100 million investment was almost uncontainable. Along with her oil holdings, Ms. Hunt had made a number of high-profile investments, including the Mansion at Turtle Creek, Texas's most exclusive hotel, and the Bel Air Hotel in Los Angeles, which she sold after a few years for the highest price per room ($1 million) ever paid for a hotel.

When Rosewood, at that time managing about $800 million of Ms. Hunt's assets, made its move into First Executive Corporation, it was the best endorsement of Fred's abilities as a CEO he had received to date. The stock moved up not just because of rumored takeovers, but because of the credibility that Hunt's name and big stake gave to the company. After all, until she met Fred Carr, Carolyn Hunt was rumored to be the wealthiest woman in America! On the other hand, one must remember that this was the sister of one of the infamous Hunt brothers, Nelson Bunker, who tried to corner the silver market earlier in the decade and wound up going from being one of the wealthiest men in America to bankruptcy. It is possible that, like her brother, Ms. Hunt had a bit of the family gambling blood for which their father, the legendary wildcatter H. L. Hunt, was so well-known.

Rosewood's experience should be a good lesson to outsiders who think they can research and analyze their way to expertise in the life insurance business. They failed, just as nearly every other non-insurance entity before them has, at trying to learn the business from the outside. Ours is an arcane business that can rarely be understood and effectively managed by outsiders. Indeed, for the moment, no one seems very interested in buying life insurance companies, except other life insurance companies. For those of us in the industry, if we have to be owned by someone, at least now it will likely be someone who knows the business.

As the situation at First Executive Corporation continued to deteriorate, the bloom on Rosewood's relationship with Fred Carr faded fast. It became clear after a while that Rosewood wanted Fred Carr out and new leadership in. The company even went so far as to announce in a *Wall Street Journal* story that it had engaged a retired Allstate Insurance president to head a new management team at First Executive Corporation.

Rosewood Financial and, to a lesser degree, ICH each tried their level best to gain control of First Executive Corporation in 1990, in hopes that by removing Fred and creating the perception of new management the company could be saved while there was still something left to save. I had no regular contact with ICH, but Rosewood representatives called me at home most Sunday evenings trying to engage my support and that of the field. I had to be very careful what I said. Although I wanted to hear their views, I always made it clear that I wanted Fred to stay, and that I supported him. I remember one night I got a call from one of their stronger guys whom I had gotten to know pretty well. It was 10:00 p.m. Los Angeles time, so 1:00 a.m. in New York, where he was trying to raise outside capital to support their takeover efforts. The guy was obviously stressed out and as I learned later was close to losing his job over the First Executive Corporation disaster. He spoke of Fred with malevolence, even though in the past he had frequently told me how much he admired him. He said things like "The dirty bastard. He had his foot on the throat of the industry and he let them get away! Now he's going down in flames and instead of stepping aside, he's going to take all of us with him." Interestingly, this individual, along with many of the Rosewood staff, was long gone when Fred Carr toasted in the new year in 1991 as First Executive Corporation's chairman. I don't mean to poke fun at him, because he happened to be a very bright, capable guy who, like many of us, bought a ticket on the Fred Carr Express. He just got tossed off the train a bit earlier than the rest of us. Before it was over, there was more than one occasion where otherwise strong people, myself included, cried in our beer over the battering we took.

When Ms. Hunt's $100 million investment in First Executive Corporation fell to about $14 million, the Rosewood people made several attempts to influence the market's perception of First Executive Corporation by cryptic press releases in which they would say they might increase their holding, decrease their holdings, propose an acquisition, or take over the company. Then, in late January 1990, in an act of desperation, they wrote Fred a letter in which they proposed an acquisition of the company for $6 per share subject to Fred's resignation. Rosewood tried to imply that it had financing lined up by engaging Chase Manhattan Bank and paying them a $250,000 fee to put the deal together. The bluff was immediately called by Fred and dismissed as a "non-offer offer," for which there was no financial backing.

It was surprising how naive the tactics of the Rosewood people were. They all looked like Dan Quayle, and when they tried to bluff or intimidate Fred, it was a laughable mismatch. On those occasions when they met with him, they were nervous and unsure of themselves, obviously intimidated by Fred's clever responses to their proposals and suggestions. It seems to me if Ms. Hunt wants to preserve what's left of her father's fortune, she should integrate her investment staff with some people who would qualify more readily for entry into her investment club than they would for her country club.

After several embarrassing failures at getting tough with Fred, the Rosewood people declared a truce and asked that, in exchange for their silence in the press and at the annual shareholders meeting, we meet with them and share information that would be helpful in their decision about the future of their investment. It was a weird truce in that, by now, they had to know Fred well enough to realize they wouldn't get any meaningful information out of him. Yet, by getting just some non-public information, they were now insiders and could no longer freely trade their securities. Anyway, we all met in downtown Los Angeles at the offices of First Boston. There were investment bankers, Rosewood's top officials, Fred, Alan Snyder, myself, and everyone's lawyers. We had a tedious day-long meeting, which was stiff, cordial, and a waste of everybody's time. After sending them a bunch of data on our investment portfolio, and another meeting, all communication ceased. A short while later, Rosewood Financial's unbelievably plush headquarters at the elite Crescent Court Complex in Dallas were dramatically downsized and much of the executive team terminated. Many said it was just another casualty of the collapse of First Executive Corporation.

Can't Buy Me Love

Through all these final cataclysmic events and during the years of endless criticism, inference, and innuendo directed at him, Fred remained steadfast in his commitment to silence as his tactical response. This was a continual source of conflict between Fred and the sales force, who desperately wanted him to fight fire with fire. To the end, he never really emerged from his silence, even though he eventually admitted it was a mistake. The best he would offer was to try to counter with occasional positive statements about the company or image-building programs.

Fred's one notable victory in fighting negatives by building on the positives was in 1987 when, in the wake of the Boesky scandal, he agreed to a three-year corporate sponsorship of the John Wooden Award. The Wooden Award—named for the legendary UCLA basketball coach whose teams won ten NCAA Championships—is the Heisman Trophy of basketball. By picking up the tab for various expenses associated with promotion of the award, given annually by the Los Angeles Athletic Club, Executive Life was permitted to do a number of promotions of their own involving Coach Wooden. My favorite was to bring him to sales and management meetings as the keynote speaker. His message is built around a concept he calls the "Pyramid of Life," which is the essence of his best-selling book a few years back entitled *They Call Me Coach*. The most complete gentleman I have ever known, John Wooden's very presence at one of our functions did a fantastic amount of morale boosting. The effect of the gracious eighty-year-old living legend praising Fred before his followers was as good as if Fred had appeared on the balcony of St. Peter's arm in arm with the Pope. Unfortunately, except at the nationally televised annual award presentation, where the Executive Life corporate banner appeared in the background, the aura of the Wooden association didn't extend much beyond the Los Angeles area. Despite the very positive results the company garnered from sponsorship of the Wooden Award, this was the only significant public relations effort Fred ever allowed the company to be involved with.

As Fred liked to put it, "Executive Life makes good fodder for the press." By late 1989 and early 1990, they were more than fodder, they were a major event about to happen. The beginning of the end was the collapse of the sale of Executive Life of New York (ELNY), which although not announced until the end of 1989 was known to have been in the tank several weeks earlier. The deal was questionable from the start in that it had to be financed with junk bonds at a time when the market was drying up. When the sale fell through, so did the attitudes of many investors such as Rosewood Financial. Just a few months earlier, analysts were setting the value of ELNY at $650–$900 million and there were repeated rumors that Fred might sell the whole company, but didn't like the talk he was hearing of $23 per share. The word was he wanted closer to $30. A year later, the stock was trading at $3; two years later it was at 30¢.

While Fred Carr was negotiating an awkward and generally unfeasible deal for ELNY with his friend Marty Wygod, officials at Rosewood Financial told me that he had turned down a good cash offer that would have sailed through the regulatory red tape. Rosewood was growing increasingly uneasy with Fred and began to refer to "the sleaze factor" as the company's main problem. When one looks closely at the various ill-fated deals that occurred in late 1989, questions do arise. Why did Fred's deals always have to be so convoluted and circular, so that when they were done they never seemed to come out as expected? Was it really just "Chinese paper" after all? Why, after all of the trouble they had had with regulators, did they continue to act as if officials wouldn't figure out that deals like the New York reinsurance transactions and the CBO transaction wouldn't pass the smell test? Whatever bureaucrats lack in brainpower, they make up for in perseverance. Eventually they will sift through every transaction and between them figure out exactly what the hell occurred. And even if the bureaucrats don't catch the scent of a questionable deal, they will always have the press to put them onto the right trail. In this case, the press in turn had a number of large shareholders, who felt unimpowered when dealing with Fred and his board, to steer them in the right direction if need be.

More to the heart of the issue is the question, why didn't Fred seem to understand that being technically correct in a transaction is not always enough? If you violate the spirit and intent of the code or doctrine under which you live and work, you are in violation, regardless of whether you are technically correct or not. We live in a subjective world. Perception is the reality. As an individual or sole proprietor, one can walk the fine line between what is technically correct but morally reprehensible, because it is your personal reputation and conscience you are dealing with. When you roll the dice in your own business, you are making a personal value judgment the consequences of which you alone must live with. In a publicly traded corporation, it is another matter. Even though others are not involved in complex financial transactions such as those discussed here, when the corporation's character becomes an issue, it reflects on the judgment of all associated with it—especially if they stay on past the airing of such concerns. This was the dilemma faced by many employees and agents at Executive Life. It's simple to moralize from the outside looking in, but ours was a complex relationship that could not be easily abandoned by those of us who had made the considerable emotional and intellectual commitment necessary to be part of it. Before we abandoned it, we needed to be hit over the head pretty hard. This, of course, is what eventually happened; but to this day, many of the integrity issues remain fuzzy, which is not a good place to be on such matters.

Whether it was the shorts, unhappy shareholders, angry competitors, or just the press acting on their own instincts, First Executive Corporation was beginning to crumble around the edges by the end of 1989. The voices of those of us defending the company were beginning to evidence the shrillness that accompanies self-doubt. Fred was becoming increasingly isolated and more pensive than ever.

Although I believe he had no specific knowledge of the upcoming $776 million write-down at the time, there is no doubt he sensed it, just as the press sensed the hemorrhaging it would bring when it, along with a series of other disasters, would finally send First Executive Corporation into free fall.

IV
FREE FALL!

13

An Unhappy New Year

"Fred, I've been listening to you for an hour and you sound to me like someone who's shorting the [FEC] stock."
—Peter Lynch, Magellan Fund, to Fred Carr at his road show presentation, January 1990 (Lynch liquidated Fidelity Fund's 11% ownership in First Executive Corporation the following day)

Traditionally, Executive Life's largest marketing group, Exceptional Producers Group, held their annual partners meeting on the Monday after Thanksgiving. The 1989 meeting was held at Century City in Los Angeles, just before their departure for the Hong Kong sales convention, because their original trip had been canceled in May due to the Tiananmen Square incident. Fred had agreed to address the group for a question-and-answer session, which was customary. In this case, however, the barrage of adverse press had made the situation a crossroads for many in their relationship with the company. The cracks in their wall of confidence in Fred were widening. It was a tense, angry session, at which Fred, for the first time since I had known him, lost his cool at the podium, becoming visibly shaken. It was not anger, although this too would occur at later sessions, but rather, as the agents took turns teeing off on him about his lack of response to the storm of criticism, he became defensive. His responses were weak and ill-prepared, and finally he called the session to an end, leaving the hotel rather than staying for the luncheon as planned. This scared the hell out of many of us who knew Fred to have more resistance to kitchen heat than just about anyone. Later that week in Hong Kong he held a second impromptu question-and-answer session, which was much more heavily attended than he had expected, given the last-minute notice. Again, Fred was almost weak-kneed in his responses. After a few minutes, he turned the session over to me, to discuss the company's new Agent Deferred Compensation Plan and other obtuse issues the agents had little interest in at present. Again, many of us sensed that things were getting worse rather than better, and that Fred, who so often at these meetings seemed to know what the future held for us, didn't have his familiar sagely grin. Instead, he looked sickened by what he saw.

Just when Fred's knowledge of the $776 million write-down occurred has been a matter of both speculation and litigation, as well as an SEC investigation. I was close personally to Merle Horst, the company's chief financial officer, who regularly dropped in on me to exchange thoughts about the crisis. On one such occasion, Merle told me about the planned road show whereby Fred was scheduled to go to Wall Street and meet with the company's institutional investors to allay their fears about the speculation in the press on our condition. He had scheduled the meetings for January 21, 22, and 23, 1990. Having just introduced Alan Snyder as his new president and chief operating officer of First Executive Corporation to us on January 8, Fred thought it would be a good time to introduce Alan to the investment community. Then, on January 11, Merle told me he had to sit down with Fred and break the news about the write-down. This corroborates Alan's story to me that the write-down occurred just three days after he took office. Of course, Fred had probably known there were defaults and problem credits, but the final word on what kind of hit a company takes in these

matters is usually hammered out between the internal accountants and outside auditors, and the outcome can vary significantly. At any rate, Alan Snyder couldn't have timed his arrival
more poorly. In fact, had he waited another week, I am certain
he would have chosen not to arrive at all.

Alan Snyder is a Wall Street guy all the way. He worked on
Wall Street, owned an apartment on Park, and spent his weekends at his Long Island residence. His great admiration for Fred
was obvious—he frequently referred to Fred as a genius and a
visionary. Fred looked at Alan as someone, although not well
known on the Street, who was respected by those who did
know him. The exact opposite was true of Fred by the time he
hired Alan. In that regard they did complement each other.

After he left college, Alan got involved in a business that
built pleasure craft—speed boats and the like. That company
went broke, and so did Alan. So he went into the securities
business, which required no capital investment, but a lot of
chutzpah. His boyish good looks and Harvard MBA (where he
was a Baker's Scholar) made Alan a natural for a business
requiring charm, an aggressive personality, and a good mind.
He started at Reynolds & Company, which was acquired by
Dean Witter, which in turn was acquired by Sears, Roebuck.
While at Dean Witter, he connected with Fred Carr in the later
1970s when First Executive Corporation was beginning to market its annuities through the securities industry. Alan had
gained his admiration for Fred from his earlier days on Wall
Street as a fund manager.

At the time they met, Alan was in charge of annuity and life
sales for Dean Witter, so it was through him that Fred gained
access to the Dean Witter sales force for Executive Life products.
It was a successful relationship, and hundreds of millions of
annuity premiums were put on the books. Alan was a very
good resource for Fred so far as getting a feel for what the
stockbrokers wanted was concerned. His product ideas and
keen mind for marketing helped Fred establish a footing with
other major wirehouses such as Pru-Bache and E. F. Hutton. But
the chemistry was bad between Alan and the Sears people. I'm

not sure if any of it had to do with the fact that he put so much of Fred Carr's controversial company's products on the books, but Alan really was entrepreneurial by nature and did not mesh well into the Sears corporate culture. So he left to form a consulting firm, the premiere client of which was First Executive Corporation. Probably out of gratitude more than need, Fred paid him a whopping $15,000 retainer a month, even though nobody in the company ever saw or spoke with Alan except Fred. Later, when he arrived on the scene, it was a surprise to everyone that Alan had been on retainer with the company for several years. Of course, upon further reflection, it was just another example of Fred's pigeon-holing of relationships. There was, however, one occasion in the fall of 1987 when Fred exposed Alan to other members of senior management.

Fred had decided that the company needed to think through some of our strategies. The term "strategic planning" was anathema to Fred, but he did manage to suggest we spend a few days sorting out the issues we faced at the time. The select group consisted of Ron Kehrli, president of our New York company, Alan Snyder, Fred, and myself. No one else in the company was aware of the meeting. Typical of Fred, he tried to extract as much extra mileage as possible out of us and then offset the inconvenience with a little Fred Carr pizzazz.

Fred hated to schedule meetings during work hours, so he put this one together over the Labor Day weekend. He scheduled the meeting at the recently opened Four Seasons Hotel in Beverly Hills (some may recall it has since been selected by Robin Leach of *Lifestyles* fame as the best hotel in the world). Alan came armed to the teeth like the good consultant he was. Thick ring binders jammed with key articles and essays from the *Harvard Business Review* and previous consulting assignments. Maytrixes and Gant charts; other charts showing networking opportunities within the life insurance and securities industries. And, of course, there was the format for a business plan to be developed by the management team. Alan demonstrated insights into the company and the life insurance business that were surprising to me. Of course, I did not know then that he had been in the wings working with Fred for a while. It was obvious that the feeling between him and Fred was special and, in fact, hindsight tells me there was a courtship going on for Alan to join the company. For a long time, many of us both from the field and the home office had been pressuring Fred to bring in a president of First Executive Corporation and a COO who could deal with the day-to-day operations of the company. Fred's indecisiveness about day-to-day management issues was becoming a bigger and bigger problem for all of us. We were more than ready for him to bring in some help—especially someone who could make the tough decisions.

The weekend at the Beverly Hills Four Seasons was an excellent example of the charming side of Fred's personality. The place was a showcase for the beautiful people. Celebrities were always wandering around the lobby and those who were not recognizable to us had the look and air of being important off-camera show-business types. We bumped into a number of big name stars, as well as rich and famous folks from the business and entertainment field. On Saturday evening, Fred took us along with our wives to Michael's, L. A.'s most exclusive restaurant at the time. While at dinner, we all commented on what a gem of a place the new Four Seasons Hotel was. Fred said that he had heard about an event coming up that evening. He told us it had something to do with the Four Season's 10,000th guest. It was a typical off-the-wall comment from Fred which no one could figure out, so we ignored him and went on with our dinner. Later, when our limo pulled up in front of the hotel, we were greeted by a brass band and a tuxedoed hotel manager welcoming us as their 10,000th guest. Our wives were presented with bouquets of roses and draped in beautiful capes. The band played marching music as we plowed our way through a gathering crowd into the lobby of the hotel; even the beautiful people wandering around rushed out to see which of their peers was being honored. Of course, the whole thing was staged by Fred. I'm sure the Four Seasons would never consider such a pedestrian display for their 10,000th or any of their other, much more notable, guests. It was a little embarrassing, but we had a good laugh, and Fred was very pleased with himself. He took great pleasure in doing special and memorable things for his associates. It was one of many examples of the type of event that became part of the Fred Carr lore. It wasn't just hype, either, it was the closest thing to an expression of love Fred could offer.

After our weekend of thought and planning, we agreed that it had been very beneficial and that we needed to do it quarterly. I knew we wouldn't because there weren't enough holiday weekends to accommodate that schedule. We never met again, although Alan called me a couple of times to try and follow up on what we had agreed we would do. Then the whole thing faded completely out of sight until Alan was introduced as our new president and COO at the Bistro Restaurant in Beverly Hills on January 8, 1990.

By that time, the company was clearly headed for serious trouble, although none of the management, including Fred and especially Alan, realized how bad things would become. The press was killing us, almost as if they were sure of our pending collapse. If ever a new president was dropped into boiling oil, it was Alan Snyder. Although he came ill-equipped, in most ways he performed admirably in the tumultuous months to come. Alan was one of those individuals who, despite great promise, had never realized his potential. His career at Dean Witter had been sidelined in a series of moves. He had been, if not in a staff position, then at least one ancillary to the line-marketing function. He ran the insurance product line, which in a securities firm is like the disability income division in a life insurance company or the truck sales division in a car dealership. The guy in charge of those areas is not really in the chain of command.

First Executive Corporation was Alan's Run for the Roses. It was his chance to fulfill his often-expressed dream to run a Fortune 500 corporation. The terms he accepted were modest, even if the company had been in better condition. A base salary of $300,000, a guaranteed bonus of $150,000, with options on 225,000 shares of FEXC stock at $8.875 per share. He had a two-year contract, which really wasn't worth much in the event of a bankruptcy or regulatory takeover. When, three days after he joined the company, the write-down of $550 million was announced, the stock fell from 8½˝229 to 3½˝. Alan told me that before joining the company he had reviewed the portfolio with Fred, credit by credit, and had been assured there were no surprises as far as anyone knew! He also said that Fred told him he had absolutely no idea the cataclysmic write-down was going to occur. Alan simply told Fred to reprice his stock options or he was heading back to New York. Some would argue, especially those who had options at $18 per share as I did, that this was not fair. I disagree. Given the situation Alan came into, he deserved to have his options priced at the bottom, because after all the turnaround was his job, and should it occur, he deserved to be rewarded. The board redid his option package in March so that he had options on 666,666 shares at $3 per share. Eight months later FEXC stock was trading at 30¢ a share. I'm sure Alan never would have come to Executive Life if he'd had any idea how bad things really were.

Yet here he was, realizing his dream to be at the helm of a Fortune 500 company, albeit a ship that was in very troubled waters, and with Fred Carr lashed to the wheel. Just what a burden his mentor would prove to be in the months to come was another thing Alan probably underestimated about his new job.

Fred, Tell Me It Ain't So!

The huge write-down, which proved to be the beginning of the end, was announced at the close of business on Friday, January 19, 1990. At the time, it was determined to be $550 million, but later accounting adjustments took it to $776 million. The following Monday, First Executive Corporation and all of those associated with it went into free fall. This state continued virtually throughout 1990, until things got to the point where no one cared any longer because the company's securities had become a penny stock by year end, and they had long been written off by the business world as dead and gone, though the obituary had not been printed yet.

The spate of adverse press was unlike anything even First Executive had experienced. The loss stirred a good deal of interest and awakened a number of other topical issues for legislators, regulators, security analysts, the SEC, and a host of other interested parties. The "failure" of First Executive Corporation became a focal point for the financial services industry crisis. A small sampling of the headlines in the major journals over just a two-week period between January 17 and January 29, 1990, sets the mood of the moment:

FEXC Stock Declines After News of Inquiry. State Legislative Committee Plans to Investigate the [Company's] Junk Bond Investment Strategies.
—*Wall Street Journal*

California Department of Insurance Commissioner Roxane Gillespie "Orders Executive Life to Recalculate MSVR and Clearly Disclose Its Junk Bond Investment Strategies." This was the result of the collateralized bond obligations that had to be undone.
—Gretchen Morgenson, "Dancing As Fast As He Can,"
Forbes

First Executive Sinks with Junk
—Floyd Norris, *New York Times*

FEXC Stock, Unit's Ability Receive Lower S & P Rating (Loss of AAA) U.S. Senator Howard Metzenbaum, Chairman of the Senate Labor Subcommittee, Announces That His Subcommittee Has Opened an Investigation into "Junk Pensions," Pension Benefits Provided Through the Purchase of Junk Bonds Provided by Executive Life
—*Los Angeles Times*

A. M. Best Lowers Ratings of ELIC and ELNY from A⁺(Superior) to A (Excellent)
—*National Underwriter*

SEC Launches Probe of FEXC. The SEC Launched an Informal Private Investigation of the Company
—Kathy M. Kristof, *Los Angeles Times*

FEXC Is Offered Merger Deal. [Offer] Specifies That Chairman

and Chief Executive Fred Carr Would Have to Resign
   —Scott Paltrow, *Los Angeles Times*

Executive Life of California Slated a State Probe. Under Prodding of Attorney General John Van de Kamp, a Major Legislative Committee Has Vowed to Investigate Executive Life, the State's Largest Insurer, for Their Heavy Investments in Junk Bonds
   —*National Underwriter*

Icarus Syndrome. Mounting Junk Woes Imperil First Executive Chief Fred Carr
   —Frederick Rose, *Wall Street Journal*

First Executive Expects Big Loss for 1989
   —*National Underwriter*

Of course, the bad press triggered an avalanche of surrenders among the book of annuity business. The stockbrokers who sold this block had a windfall. They moved the annuity business as fast as they could find it. A list of Executive Life annuity policyholders was worth its weight in gold to a stockbroker— several attempts were made to procure such lists, including employees being solicited. In one instance, an offer of $50,000 was made to one of our employees for the list of annuitants in the Los Angeles zip code. Other agents and brokers ran ads in local newspapers offering an Executive Life policyholder "rescue plan." Some held seminars for policyholders to help them out of their Executive Life "trap." By mid-February, the company was receiving 25,000 calls per week from nervous policyholders and concerned agents.

The write-down came as a shock to everyone. Reactions varied from the agents, who were shell-shocked, to angry accusations of fraud by stockholders, many of whom brought suits against the company for the $285 million rights offering that had closed the previous October and other financial transactions that occurred during 1989. All the suits also made big news in the press, which obligated the SEC to look into the matter. At issue was the question of whether or not the company had material knowledge of the default situation prior to the rights offering, which had been completed just three months earlier. If it did, or even if it suspected that it would happen, such knowledge should have been included in the prospectus filed with the SEC, so prospective investors would be aware of the situation. The SEC investigation, which eventually turned up no evidence to support these accusations, still made big news.

I have learned that with regard to damage caused by adverse press, there is very little difference between the terms "investigation," "subpoena," "indictment," and "conviction." In the eyes of the public, they are all more or less lumped together. The same goes for terms referring to the condition of a credit in one's portfolio. "Junk bond," "underwater," "mark to market," and "default" all mean about the same thing. Unbelievable as it might seem to anyone who understands the basics of finance, business journals frequently compared Executive Life's junk bond holdings, as a percentage of assets, to the defaulting or non-performing commercial mortgage portfolios of other companies as a percentage of their assets. One was a performing credit, backed by a reserve cushion, MSVR, in case it didn't perform; the other was in default, with no extra reserve to back it. One could easily say that responsible people don't buy junk bonds or get subpoenaed to appear before Congress in the first place, so what's the difference? It's only a matter of the degree of your guilt. That was pretty much the prevailing attitude toward First Executive Corporation. Where there's smoke, there's fire. Perhaps they were correct; but to me, it's scary when the system operates as it did on First Executive Corporation.

The $776 million loss was a very big number. Too big to be explained in any way that would preserve our argument that we were a well-balanced, well-capitalized, sound company. Still, the facts were not quite the same as the perception. They took a provision for loss reserve, they did not write a check to someone for $776 million. Most of the money never left the company! It did, however, leave the balance sheet, which was tantamount to saying we eventually expected it to leave. The provision consisted of three classes of security: those in default, which were marked down to zero; those credits which, in the company's view, were unlikely to be able to service their debt due to their current earnings or other difficulties within the company, which were marked to market; and finally those credits that were in the trading account, which, because they were expected to be sold within the next twelve months, the auditors felt should be marked to market. This third group was a new and very conservative interpretation that had never, to the company's knowledge, been applied to a life company's portfolio. Of the $776 million involved in the total write-down, only about $200 million had actually left the company by the end of the first half of 1990. Still, the total investment losses, which included common stocks and limited partnerships, were $951 million, which due to good gains from operating income put the company's net loss for the year at $776 million.

Executive Life learned very clearly at this point that in situations such as this, no one is interested in explanations. Once and for all, perception had become reality. It made no difference what was going on at the Equitable, Mutual Benefit, or the Travelers. Executive Life was finally taking its long-awaited fall, and the chorus was there cheering for it to stay down for the count.

Most observers felt that the January 22, 1990, announcement of the write-down was the shocking blow that led to the demise of the corporation. There is no doubt in the eyes of those who experienced it that it was a shock to everyone inside the company. Yet, from a marketing standpoint, the write-down was only the manifestation of our worst fears, which had been building for some time due to a series of articles in the press that were frighteningly detailed and confident in their predictions of disaster. This mood was best characterized in the article by Gretchen Morgenson that appeared in *Forbes* on January 22, 1990, the same day we announced the write-down. In it she listed the litany of problems besieging the "high flying Wall Street fund manager" who had "absorbed blow after blow in his new life as a life insurance C.E.O."—in which, she conceded, he had made a stunning comeback. But the tone of the piece was so negative, it ran chills down the spines of those of us who read it. It covered the slowing sales, the capital crunch within the company, the reinsurance problems with the New York

Insurance Department, the ill-fated rights offering, the collater-alized bond obligations (CBOs), the pending write-down, and every other sin committed by the company since its inception. Perhaps worst of all was the customary *Forbes* cartoon that appears in feature articles. This one depicted a statue of Fred on a pedestal with the arm and other parts falling off, while pigeons parked on his shoulder to watch. For many of us, this particular article was the one that sent a far-reaching hairline crack across the foundation of our confidence in the corpora-tion. We knew they couldn't print something this strong unless it was fairly accurate. The company's legal counsel wrote Ms. Morgenson and *Forbes* a letter correcting some significant inac-curacies in her article. But as things turned out, she had sized up the situation they faced fairly well.

One of the toughest situations was for the established Execu-tive Life agent who, at some earlier date, had typically beat out the Connecticut Mutual agent or the New York Life agent on one big sale after another. They now had to go to their country club, temple, church, or Rotary meeting and stand by while the competing agents played "I told you so" in front of the client, whom they were now going to rescue. Every surrenderable piece of business Executive Life had on the books was up for grabs. This was the moment much of the industry had been waiting for, and nobody, but nobody, had any kind words for those of us caught inside when the collapse occurred.

The devastation dragged on for months. When things finally subsided, the atmosphere of the company was like a battlefield the day after the conflict. The first quarter of 1990 was the toughest. They just had one unbelievable disaster after another: after the initial write-down of $550 million, the second, amount-ing to an additional $226 million; the loss of their A. M. Best A+ rating by both the California and New York companies; and the downgrade from Standard & Poor's from AAA to A. All of this triggered the biggest "run at the bank" ever faced by an insur-ance company. How Executive Life stayed afloat under such conditions is still a mystery to many.

By late January, the general belief was that Fred Carr was

only moments from resigning or being ousted. This feeling was amplified when the *Wall Street Journal* reported on a memo Jerry Schwartz, Fred's protégé and closest field associate, sent to his sales force calling for Fred's resignation. Jerry's position eventually proved to be correct, but at the time he was viewed with anger by most of the sales force for his rapid abandonment of Fred. After all, no one had made more money in their association with Executive Life than Jerry Schwartz. Most felt that if a call for Fred's resignation was in order, it should not have come from one who had profited from the association as much as Jerry had. Furthermore, at the time, there were enough people clamoring for Fred's head that he was well aware it was an option open to him. On the other hand, Jerry was, along with Fred and Al Jacob, a key architect of the whole Executive Life story, and his greatest wealth was yet to come from the sale of his AORC, the proceeds of which were now in doubt. Furthermore, unbeknownst to most of us, Jerry had already appeared privately to First Executive board members to urge Fred to resign, as well as to Fred personally—all to no avail. Fred understood only too well the business ethic that caused Jerry to ask that he step down. It was simple enough: the business comes first; when need be, even above the closest of relationships. Still, had the roles been reversed, I have no doubt Fred would have left it to Jerry's common sense to know that many wanted him to resign. And if he thought it would not occur to him, he would have told him to do so, only privately, as it should be with good friends—especially those who have helped make us rich.

A State of Liquidation

Money began moving out of the company like electricity almost the day after the write-down. By mid-1990, $2.2 billion, or about half of the single premium deferred annuity business, was gone. This business had been sold mostly by stockbrokers, and of course that made it easier to move. The feeding frenzy on the annuitants was another example of the abuses that sooner or later will bring more regulation to the sale of financial services products. Many of the agents and stockbrokers who moved $2.2 billion of business out of the company in 180 days did so by using the reports in the press as sales materials. The reports were not only very shrill in tone, but regularly confused the holding company issues with the life company issues. The write-downs that occurred in January and March were generally accepted accounting (GAAP) issues affecting shareholders' equity in the holding company. The life company, which is where the annuities reside, was protected by the special reserve, MSVR, which, although diminished, was still significant. For a number of reasons, there was a reasonable argument at the time for most annuitants not to pay the surrender charge and the commission to the broker to move to a new product that typically credited lower interest rates.

First of all, although the holding company was on the ropes, the life companies were still healthy. Secondly, if the life companies became impaired, as they eventually did, the California Insurance Department would step in and protect policyholders. It made pretty good sense for policyholders to stick around and see what would happen, even if another company were to assume the book of business. If that happened, they would probably wake up one day as Metropolitan Life policyholders or the like. If they didn't care for the credited interest rate or their treatment, then they could pay the exit penalties and move to another company. This way they were going to get one free change even if Executive Life failed. Of course, these arguments were made at a time when the hope was to avoid a run at the bank and the resulting pressures it creates. Given the way things turned out, the argument for "hanging in there" lost a lot of momentum toward the end of 1990.

I tried to stop the avalanche of surrenders by convincing Fred to establish a Consumer Advisory Unit, basically for the purpose of calming down policyholders and getting them to steer the course with us. We used business and finance students from UCLA and USC. I figured that Executive Life would be a strong topic for many a master's thesis in years to come, and that getting some of the kids a front-row seat to this experience would be attractive to them. I was right. We had more bright young students than we could offer jobs to. They worked the phones and talked to thousands of policyholders. It was a great education for them, and saved hundreds of millions in annuity business for the company. The amount of business that could be saved simply by holding the client's hand was surprising to me. Considering we were using untrained students to provide comfort levels, it is even more surprising.

When the students got in over their heads with the attorneys, accountants, and other advisers to the policyholders, they would refer the calls to management. In keeping with our no-excuses egalitarian culture, everyone in senior management—including Fred—routinely took phone calls from nervous policyholders. It had always been our custom to do so, even in better times when they were only occasional. But now the senior management in February and March 1990 were all taking at least a dozen calls per day apiece. We also handled the walk-in business, which was considerable. A good many of the annuities were sold in Southern California; with each wave of bad press, the lobby would fill with senior citizens. Seeing it from the inside scared the hell out of a lot of the employees and created a good deal of internal conflict for many of us doing the advising. Most of the callers and visitors were elderly, some in their eighties. Several were widows or widowers, relying primarily on their Executive Life annuity for income. But most of the walk-ins were couples, who sat nervously holding hands waiting for their audience with a company official. We quickly realized that it was unwise to have large groups of these individuals accumulating in the lobby. When they started talking together, they only became more upset. So a number of vacant offices around the building were turned into waiting rooms to separate the groups and at least give the impression that they were not part of a stampede trying to surrender their annuities.

Everyone who works in the financial services industry should go through what those of us at Executive Life did, just to get a sense of the importance of the work we do. In many cases, people had entrusted their life savings to the company; they had their Executive Life annuity and Social Security, and that was it. The responsibility of what to tell them that would be both truthful and reassuring was a difficult one. I quickly decided that regardless of the encouraging company data we had received, I needed to look them in the eye and talk about a worst-case scenario. I found it difficult to see the discussion from any perspective other than that of the insured. I saw my parents, aunts, and uncles all rolled up into one apple-faced doll staring at me with some instinctive trust and asking what she should do. I think I got a peek at myself someday, too. Well, no worthwhile professional could do anything other than talk to these people as he would his own family members, and that's exactly what I and most of the others did.

It was then that I began to accept the unavoidable reality: the company members had been seriously mistaken in their high-yield strategy. Not mistaken by reaching for yield that promised great value to the policyholder, but mistaken in that they took risks that, in hindsight, were not theirs to take. I have no sympathy for a person, no matter how elderly, who chooses to take risks with their savings out of greed for a higher than reasonable yield and then loses their money. But the problem was complicated by the fact that the Executive Life products were given the blessing of the two most credible rating agencies, A. M. Best and Standard & Poor's. Not just a blessing, but *the* blessing reserved for the elite. Not only that, but every major rating agency rated the company's securities as investment grade. Up until this point, when people put their savings with a savings and loan, a bank, or an insurance company, their perception was that it was above all safe. Very safe. Given the endorsements of the most prestigious rating agencies, those of us who sold clients on Executive Life felt reasonably assured we were doing the right thing for them. Then the events of 1990 changed all of that. It seems those who evaluate the insurance industry got caught asleep at the switch until 1991, by which time their downgrades seemed like reactions to yesterday's news clippings.

In the future, when insurance companies design products and rating agencies rate companies, perhaps they should also take into consideration qualifying the product and company by the type of customer they target. The fact is that when senior citizens buy annuities, they add a dynamic to the risk equation that isn't there for the rest of us. They have no recovery potential. This should somehow be factored into the rating agency's attitude about claims-paying ability. They should consider that this potential class of customer has ended their years of earning power and, should they lose the principal, has no ability to generate more income for future investments. These people typically are retired and through earning money. When it's gone, they can't just earn more to invest more wisely the next time around.

Perhaps even more important is the possibility that the senior citizen who has to reevaluate an investment ten years or so after making it may not have the judgment he or she once did. Many people choose this type of investment because they believe it will not have to be reevaluated or altered in later years, when they may not be as able to deal with such decisions. People in this position have no margin for risk. The no-risk perception is now the purview of government securities. The public sector—banks, savings and loans, and insurance companies—has lost much of its credibility with regard to the safety it was perceived to provide for the funds entrusted to it by its customers. This poses a great opportunity for the government: to issue new types of securities for this market, about which we in the financial services industry will no doubt complain.

Damage Control

In late January, just a few days after the write-down was announced, Fred and Alan went ahead and did their road show out East to try to calm the institutional investors. That, too, was a disaster, with particularly bitter attacks from the likes of John Lefrere of Delta Capital, who had invested heavily on behalf of clients, and Peter Lynch who, after attending, dumped his Fidelity investment's (Magellan Fund's) 11 percent stake in First Executive Corporation. No one in attendance could doubt that Fred Carr was through on Wall Street once and for all. He could never go back to raise one thin dime, no matter how hot his idea. This was terribly difficult for Fred, who had spent twenty years trying to reestablish himself on the Street since his gun-slinger days at the Enterprise Fund, when they had blamed him for that collapse, even though it occurred after he had left the firm.

When he returned from the road show, Fred was shell-shocked. The stock was at $3.00 and sinking, the board was par-alyzed with fear, the company was in meltdown, and the sales force could only be described as hysterical. The media, of course, were swarming all over the company. Executive Life was featured on two national television news shows and sev-eral local evening news spots in Los Angeles. The lobby of the building was full of anxious, elderly annuitants holding hands and pacing back and forth until we could get to them. Every-one's phone was ringing off the hook. There was no place to go for relief. It was a frightening, stressful, and terribly sad time for all of us. We just could not believe it was happening.

Fred was the original "positive-mental-attitude" CEO. He had always amazed me and inspired me with his cheerfulness and optimism. Whenever Fred was asked, "How are you?", his response was always the same, *"Today is the best day I've ever had!"* In fact, the company passed out T-shirts commemorating Fred's fifteenth year with the company embossed with this Carr-ism. After the disastrous road show, I never heard Fred utter those words again. Since his biggest loss had been his credibility, I suspect he didn't want it to suffer further by mis-representing his mood. The best day Fred Carr ever had defi-nitely was long passed.

On January 30, we had scheduled a nationwide satellite tele-conference to discuss problem issues with the field force. It also would be a chance for them to meet the new president, Alan Snyder. Fred really did not want to go through with the teleconference, which had been scheduled before the write-down, but it had become an industry event and was filled at all forty locations across the country.

The day before the teleconference, January 29, the *Wall Street Journal* ran a front-page article on Fred headed *"Icarus Syndrome. Mounting Junk Woes Imperil First Executive and Chief Fred Carr. Insurer, once Milken client, faces irate holders, probes by regulators, buy-out bids. Policyholders seek assurance."* The only flattering thing was their likeness of Fred, which was uncharacteristically attractive. The article provided the backdrop for a very tense setting at the teleconference, which made it extra difficult for Alan who, although he was brand new, was still game. I played the role of moderator, fielding questions from around the country for Fred, Alan, and Doug Marcian, our chief investment officer. The teleconference was modestly successful, but the real problem was that we were in a damage-control mode. It really became more of a forum for dramatizing the seriousness of the situation than for allaying fears and concerns.

The next challenge came when Norris Clark, Chief Financial Analyst of the California Insurance Department, wrote the company a letter in early February asking that they provide him with a comfort level about the situation. This time, Fred and Alan turned the request into a public relations opportunity. The Department specified thirty-two different scenarios under which they wanted to see how Executive Life would fare. Fred engaged Milliman & Robertson, the nation's second-largest actuarial firm, to conduct the study. They decided to add fifteen more scenarios to the format. The assumptions dealt with various assumed lapse rates and declines in the high-yield market. Under the harshest scenario, they assumed a 50, 40, 30, and 20 percent lapse rate on our policies in 1990, 1991, and 1992, respectively; in addition, a permanent decline in the high-yield bond market of 20 percent. Even under these conditions, the company developed a book value of over $1 billion by 1994. The Milliman & Robertson report provided credible reassurance that the company would come through its difficulties, especially for those of us who were not financial people.

After showing the results to an NAIC task force appointed to oversee Executive Life's situation, the California Insurance Department still wanted to see more, so Fred put Milliman & Robertson to work on Phase II of the study. This time they added twenty-two extra scenarios and a series of seven interest-rate scenarios, including ones whereby interest rates increased by 100 basis points of each of five years and then decreased by 100 basis points for five years, and about everything in between. These stress tests proved that the company Fred Carr had built was like the beach ball in a swimming pool: you can push it down as much as you like, but it just keeps popping up. The closest they could come to a scenario that would put the company under was to try to statistically solve for a point at which defaults, lapses, and interest rates would take its net worth down to zero. The answer was for 64 percent of the annuities to lapse, 40 percent of the life business to lapse, a 20 percent permanent decline in the market value of high-yield bonds, a 50 basis point decline in interest for each of ten years, and an annual default rate in the bond portfolio of 4.53 percent, which was about twice their experience over the previous five years. Even some of Fred's harshest critics were amazed by the resilience of Executive Life's balance sheet, which has to have been the best example of asset/liability matching the industry has seen. Of course in the end, even the skill with which Fred constructed his balance sheet could not offset the poor quality of materials he chose to build it with. It was the quality of the assets—which apparently even Milliman & Robertson overestimated—that caused the results of the study to be so encouraging.

One humorous moment occurred when, after presenting the results to the NAIC committee, one particularly cynical regulator complained that perhaps Milliman & Robertson had not been harsh enough in the some fifty-five scenarios they had incorporated into their stress test of First Executive Corporation. Fred looked at the guy incredulously and with typical dry wit responded: "I'd like to put together a scenario that gives you the answer you're looking for, but unfortunately, I'm operating under the constraint that each customer can only surrender his policy once."

Fred Carr had boasted in his 1985 annual report that he had

built a balance sheet that was "bulletproof." When put to the test of fire in the spring of 1990, he was almost proven correct. No other life insurance company, or for that matter, no other U.S. financial institution of the time, could have withstood the barrage of disintermediation (movement of funds) and portfolio collapse that First Executive Corporation did during 1990. Even after the write-down, he could point to $859 million of capital, surplus, and mandatory reserves in the California company alone, which ranked sixteenth in the industry, just behind Lincoln National. Their net investment yield, also post-write-down, was still the highest among the Top 15 companies at 11.22 percent. Executive Life had almost 13 percent of its assets in cash or cash equivalents, making it the most liquid Top 25 carrier. The 1989 cash flow corporatewide had been $4.7 billion. The average maturity of the bonds in the portfolio was between six and seven years, meaning that as the company burned through the huge cash reserves, between ongoing cash flow and bonds reaching maturity, it was hard to imagine a scenario whereby it could not meet its obligations.

Unless, of course, one wanted to ignore history and assume a catastrophic collapse in the price of junk bonds and default rates that was literally off everyone's chart. I guess the analysts at Milliman & Robertson should have considered in their research that history repeating itself is an incomplete basis for projecting into the future. After all, there has to be a first time for everything.

Fool Me Once, Shame on You...

The symmetry with which Fred Carr had constructed his balance sheet caused even his critics to take their hats off to him. The unsurrenderable assets, like GICs and structured settlements, exceeded the amount of junk in the portfolio. This meant that, in theory, he would not have to sell any junk prematurely to meet an obligation. More importantly, the expected duration of the asset was shorter than the expected duration of the liability, meaning the bonds would mature for their face value in plenty of time to meet the obligations they backed (unless, of course, they defaulted). Thus, in theory anyway, the underwater issue—that is, bonds trading below their face value—was mitigated because they would be able to hold them to maturity, rather than having to sell them in a discounted market to meet obligations. This was quite a different situation than that faced by many of Executive Life's competitors, who instead of investing in junk bonds, invested in junk commercial real estate, the mortgages on which tend to have a much longer maturity and thus match poorly against the duration of many of the liabilities they back. There is one crucial difference, however. When a commercial mortgage defaults, it does so with a whimper. When a junk bond defaults, such as TWA or Eastern airlines, it does so with a bang. Another factor no one counted on was that many bond issuers knew how to take advantage of a creditor that is on the ropes. Whether they themselves were in trouble or not, they knew that the timing was excellent for holding Executive Life's feet to the fire and negotiating a restructuring of their loan and bond covenants.

Truly one never to give up, armed with the facts and the newly completed Milliman & Robertson report, Fred decided to give Wall Street one last try. In an effort to dissuade the security analysts from the cataclysmic conclusion they were all driving toward, Fred offered to host a day-long meeting in Los Angeles on March 6 to update them on the situation. It was staged at the new Loews Santa Monica Hotel on the beach (who gave an embarrassing indication of our reputation when they insisted the company pay cash in advance before booking the meeting).

To Fred's pleasant surprise, about thirty-five of the various analysts and market makers who tracked First Executive Corporation stock showed up. It was a pretty prestigious group, including Fred Townsend of Townsend & Schupp and Herb Goodfriend of Prudential-Bache. Fred, Alan, myself, and others all went through elaborate presentations showing how well the company had withstood the $550 million write-down, and assuring them that we were on the road to recovery. They were skeptical, but could not help but be impressed by what they saw, and left at least not quite as certain as they had been at the Eastern road show that we were goners. Then, about two weeks later, the company was informed by its accountants that the final number for the write-down would be $776 million, instead of the $550 million originally announced. Fred Townsend called me and told me this was the final straw. Fred Carr's credibility was beyond gone. He told me he didn't know how Fred could have stood before them only a few days earlier saying that "The worst was over." I pointed out that it was unlikely Fred would have said what he did had he known about the further write-down. What purpose would it serve? Still, Townsend and the rest weren't buying. They had written Fred off for good. Nothing we tried seemed to be working. As Fred put it when I told him about Townsend's remarks, "Well, for the first time, we need a little luck." I couldn't help but wonder if the opposite weren't true. Perhaps Executive Life had had more than its share of luck for a long while, and the roll it was on was just coming to an abrupt end.

At the same time, the company launched a campaign to calm its sales force and try to get some more new business from them, which was declining dramatically. The results of the Milliman & Robertson study were presented all spring and summer in a series of road shows for field personnel, policyholders, and other interested parties. With the help of Steve Christopher, my vice president of sales, I did a series of forty seminars across the country trying to convince our constituency that all was okay with Executive Life. We spent most of February, March, and April doing these exhausting programs, and in fact we were very successful in convincing agents and clients to keep their policies on the books. Surrenders slowed dramatically for this and other reasons.

The hard part was that almost no one could be convinced to give us any new business. Executive Life's application count for new sales dropped from a high of 300 per day at its peak, to just 10 per day by the end of 1990. This was a problem not even the impressive Milliman & Robertson report could solve. With no new business, the company was in a state of liquidation, and eventually the surrenders would do it in. No matter how perfectly the assets and liabilities were matched, it was becoming apparent that without revenues from new sales, at some point the company was going to run out of cash and be forced to liquidate underwater assets to meet obligations. Once this started to happen, it was only a matter of time before the California Insurance Department would have to step in and put a freeze on everything. Thus, my appeal for new business was a Catch-22. Unless everyone bought in and new sales boosted cash flow past the flow of surrenders out the back door, the company was still in a state of liquidation. It was an appeal that the agents just couldn't buy at this point. No one believed we could ever again get sales to their previous level, let alone to a level that would offset the surrenders. Eventually I gave up on asking for new business and focused instead on getting the agents to conserve the business already on the books. At the time, I believed it was in their clients' best interest to do so, which seems to have turned out to be correct.

Much of our time visiting with the sales force, however, was spent mourning the demise of the hottest company in the most exciting times in the history of life insurance. Camelot was dead. The pain for many was almost unbearable.

14

Toy Weapons

"You know, once it finally happens, the worst ain't nearly so bad as you think it will be."
—B. Traven, *The Treasure of the Sierra Madre,* 1927

The situation at First Executive Corporation in 1990 couldn't have been much better than it was at Chrysler Corporation a decade earlier. But they at least got bailed out by the federal government. In the case of First Executive Corporation, rather than lending a helping hand, Congress was gunning for them. Fred was called before Congressman Dingell's Subcommittee on Energy and Commerce in June 1990. They wanted to cite his management of the company as an example of the need for more federal regulation of the industry.

To be sure, during their life cycles, most corporations are likely to go through some type of crisis or another. But in 1990 the story at First Executive was a case study in crisis management. I'm not aware of any major corporation going through any tougher period than that experienced by First Executive throughout 1990. During the month of January, there were eighteen separate articles about their woes in the *Wall Street Journal* alone!

Executive Life had no friends either within or outside of the industry. Because of its refusal to support or participate in most industry organizations, Fred's "no information, no response" style with regard to criticism, and his seemingly arrogant attitude about the company's superior performance, the staff were ill-prepared for the crisis. Many companies felt we got exactly what we deserved, and gloated over the turn of events. Later, others became concerned because they saw the possible collapse of a Top 15 company as an industry disaster that could lead to federal regulation. At any rate, they were on their own, just as they always had been.

Somehow, First Executive Corporation needed at least to give the appearance of having a recovery plan, even if no realistic plan was in sight. The regulators were concerned that the company was in a state of liquidation, which it was. It had successfully withstood the incredible run at the bank during the first quarter of 1990, but was clearly weakened. Nearly half of the $5 billion in Single Premium Deferred Annuity business was gone. Because of the reserving quirks explained earlier, when an annuitant lapsed his or her policy, the surrender charges and reserves that were freed up were generally in excess of the surrendered values. The difference went right to the bottom line. This was the main reason why, to the surprise of some, First Executive generated a $45 million GAAP profit for the first quarter and nearly $55 million more over the next two quarters. The regulators and investors understood these issues only too well, and both groups were watching us with great caution, ready to pull the switch at any time if need be. Alan Snyder was the main reason they didn't. The entire turnaround assignment fell on his shoulders. Alan's plan was for a three-pronged attack: stabilize the nervous regulators with a mountain of reassuring data; restructure the holding company, hopefully by finding a partner to infuse capital; and hold on to the sales force by coming up with a viable scheme for writing new business.

Alan is an appealing character, with many qualities I came to admire as well as some dichotomies, which I found very peculiar. For example, he fiercely guarded his Jewishness, which was downplayed both in and outside of the company to the degree that, other than Fred, I was about the only one aware of it. In our company, this made about as much sense as being on the Boston police force and keeping it a secret that your father was an Irishman. Alan also has some irritating habits that frayed the nerves of those of us working with him. He chain-smoked cigars, which of course are offensive enough, but we had a no-smoking policy in our company. So, instead of smoking them, he chewed them down to the butt without lighting them. He would gnaw on a cigar until it became a disgusting glob of tobacco and juice, then snip off the end with a pair of scissors, letting it plop into the wastebasket.

I felt Alan had an arrogant and condescending way about him when dealing with others. He used every popular buzz phrase imaginable and referred to his subordinates by nick-names, often calling me "Big Guy," "Handsome," "Hot Shot," or patronizing me in other ways that made me feel like I was talking to my high school football coach. Perhaps most irritating to me was his almost pathological need to let others know that he knew more than them about any given subject. Even if that subject was our own specialty in the insurance industry, Alan would lecture us on how it was done in the world of Wall Street, where the big boys played. He frequently cut me off in the middle of a sentence by saying something like "Your read on this is all wrong, Slick. Let me explain the facts of life in the big leagues in a way that even you will understand."

I tried to look past his personality quirks and view them mostly as attempts to elevate his own self-esteem. Most high achievers have one tactic, personality trait, or a series of behaviors that are built around their need for self-affirmation. In the world of sales and marketing, one must deal with a lot of rejection, and unless you insulate yourself with some set of defense mechanisms, it can be devastating to the old id. Alan's methods of self-affirmation were, however, different from most. For example, his sensitivity about being qualified for the job he held made him seem very thin-skinned. I think deep down he felt like an imposter. Of course, given the circumstances at the time,

Fred couldn't have convinced any well-known industry figure with recognized credentials even to interview for the job. Furthermore, it certainly wasn't that Alan couldn't have handled the job and grown into it under more normal circumstances. The problem was we didn't have time for on-the-job training of an immature manager, and, in my view, immature was the right word to describe Alan's management style. He seemed to struggle with basic management and people skills that were the symptoms of his inexperience. His Harvard training was probably an impediment in the trench-warfare environment at First Executive Corporation. Even in good times, Executive Life's success was an irritating contradiction to all the training one receives at a good B school. Alan apparently never figured out that Executive Life was the personification of the statistical standard deviation from the norm. Executive Life fit no one's mold.

Still, Alan's shortcomings were acceptable when compared to his considerable strengths, which were intellect and a passion for hard work. Because of these strengths, I eventually came to respect him as an executive as well as like him as a person. In spite of his not being the ideal candidate, Alan made up for any shortfall with pure brainpower and as hard a work effort as I have seen anyone put out. He gave the job 110 percent, and through his efforts, helped keep the company afloat during the first half of 1990. Alan immediately made the critical decisions in a crisis environment between what was pressing and what was crucial. He began growing up as an executive in a hurry. Initially, despite his inexperience, he got the job done about as well as anyone could hope for. He's a good example of the notion that there is no substitute for hard work coupled with a high I.Q.

For the sales force, however, the issue was perception in the marketplace rather than the reality of regulators at the company's doorstep. The ability to assure nervous clients that things were okay and to go out and present Executive Life products on their next sales call were their issues. Alan all but ignored these aspects of the company his first year. Although he had a good excuse for not being more responsive to the field, he never gained the credibility he so wanted with the sales force because of this oversight. What Alan had to deal with were nervous regulators ready to step in and put the company under conservatorship or keep us from doing business in their state, an SEC investigation, stockholders with demands that he and Fred be ousted, politicians seizing an opportunity to use their junk bond backing of pension plans as a political issue to gain votes from the gray-haired constituent, and a host of other things, any one of which could have put the company under. There was a minefield that had to be negotiated. One lapse of concentration could blow the company out of the water at any time. Alan was literally facing these issues his first week on the job. So, when the leading agents, who were accustomed to the accessibility of senior management, called and he did not return their calls, they concluded he was an ivory tower type, not interested in their crisis. I tried to cover for him, but due to my own shell-shocked condition, in hindsight, I did not do as good a job of supporting Alan and Fred as I might have. For this I am sorry, but their refusal to involve senior management in the crisis recovery plan made support difficult.

In a crisis, it is easy to forget that our every move will be evaluated later. No leader ever attained prominence for his or her performance in a calm or routine environment. Alan at least tried to do the big things right. Yet he lost his shot at becoming the company's much-needed new leader by ignoring those little things that are always later remembered. No one beneath the level reporting directly to him appeared to have any meaningful exposure to Alan until late 1990. By then, many agents and employees had already decided he didn't give a damn about them. Actually, he had temporarily staved off certain disaster. Without his around-the-clock efforts, the company would surely have been lost sooner, but he and Fred failed to use this borrowed time to deliver a realistic recovery plan. Alan was right in identifying the critical issues and ignoring the pressing issues, but he shouldn't have ignored them completely. A little attention here and there would have made the difference between a problem solver and a leader. A good lesson can be learned by all managers from this example. One recalls President Bush during the war with Iraq, when he would take time out of his incredible wartime schedule to call the parents of a young soldier struck down in combat. He didn't have the time to do it, but he needed to do so periodically if he wanted to secure the support of the people and the morale of his troops. Furthermore, when he shared their grief, his tears had better be real.

Everyone except Fred and Alan, and the droves of outside consultants they brought in, was completely shut out of the important issues. We did not have a single briefing or meeting of any type among the senior management in either January or February. Eight weeks after the free fall began, senior management was still totally in the dark! We literally knew only what we read in the papers. On the other hand, because we were shut out from the crucial issues, we were able to focus on the pressing issues. While Alan and Fred tried to save the company, we tried to save the relationships of those agents and employees who had helped build the House of Carr. This was probably their intention, and to that extent their silence was effective. The problem was when we held the agent's hand, we had nothing to tell him.

What made the veil of secrecy such an inappropriate strategy was that there was no corporate stated position on anything. Had they let their home office and field people know what was going on, they in turn would have been much more supportive of Fred during this period. The problem, as I later learned, was that not much was going on other than a frenzied effort to respond to nervous regulators and outraged shareholders. Like the rest of us, they were buried with defensive issues and had no resources left with which to launch an offensive (not that Fred would have supported such an initiative even if it were feasible).

Out of frustration, I decided that if Fred and Alan were not going to call a meeting of senior management, I would call such a meeting, and inform them that they were invited if they wished to attend. This got quite a rise out of Alan and was the first time Fred ever hauled me on the carpet for an ass chewing. He said that I was being divisive and not supportitive of their efforts to deal with the critical issues of the moment. Fred was obviously under terrible pressure and did not welcome the internal strife under these circumstances. He had intended to be pretty tough with me. Alan was present as the customary witness Fred always wanted in these situations. I was stressed out, too, and before Fred got going, I unloaded on him and told him that his was an irresponsible approach to managing a crisis. Senior management needed to be involved and needed to understand what the issues we faced were. I also told him that we were scared and uncertain, which was a very difficult place to come from when trying to console and encourage employees and agents that everything was going to be okay. I told him if he wanted me to support him blindly with no understanding of the facts, then he was the one being divisive, and as far as I was concerned he could get himself another boy. I'm sure Alan was shocked at the way I spoke to him. To his credit, that is the kind of leader Fred is. If you want to tell him to go screw himself, you can do so as long as you are right about the issue at hand. That's exactly what I said to close my part of the conversation. All of a sudden, fifteen minutes later, a management council meeting was called.

Fred never apologized to me, nor I to him. From that point on, however, we began having regular management meetings to discuss the crisis in detail. Alan called the meetings and chaired them, although Fred was usually present and sometimes took the lead. Initially, the meetings had some real substance. We discussed the critical issues we faced, and developed plans for dealing with the crisis on most fronts.

Other than the first one, the meetings were not so much the result of my tiff with Fred as they were Alan's resolve to start building a management team. To do so, he had to watch us interact to help decide which, if any of us, would make the cut. Despite Alan's good intentions, the meetings were eventually relegated to a "show and tell" mentality where we dealt with mundane issues rather than the crisis at hand. Noticing that the company had no budget, Alan became alarmed and initiated a zero base budgeting process. We were asked to challenge every expense and bring an expense-saving idea to every meeting. I started out by suggesting we fire the droves of spear carriers Fred and Alan had brought in, namely, the investment bankers who, to that point, had delivered absolutely nothing for the fortune we had paid them, and the law firms that had sucked out over $10 million of the company's cash reserves by mid-1990. In the view of some of us on the management council, the draconian measures needed to save the company could not wait another day.

Alan soon made it clear to me and the rest of the management team that we were not equipped to challenge his judgment in such matters. His idea of cost savings was, as he put it, "in the more symbolic areas like car phones and travel expenses." We then devoted the core of several meetings to subjects that included what type of trade journal subscriptions the company should pay for and what the standard-issue ballpoint pen provided for employees should be. This, in a company that had lost nearly $1 billion in its investment portfolio during the previous year, whose market value had declined 99 percent, from $1.5 billion to $15 million during the same period, and whose net worth on a liquidation basis had sunk from $2 billion to a negative $3 billion. Additionally, we were under an SEC investigation, the California Insurance Department was on the doorstep, and the policy surrenders had us in a state of liquidation!

It was during the discussion about ballpoint pens that I decided to start looking for another job. It was like being in that bunker in Berlin in 1945. We were being bombarded from all directions with little hope of survival and the generals were being asked to design toy weapons out of balsawood that would ostensibly save us, then dutifully report on our progress. It was a sad time.

The Litany of Problems

One of Alan Snyder's strengths is to identify problems and put together an action plan. Executive Life had no Corporate Communications Department, no Advertising Department, no official source of information for either the press or the field. Alan immediately recognized this as a critical need, given our circumstances. He established a Corporate Communications Department his first month on the job, and to run it he brought in a Harvard classmate by the name of Bill Adams, with whom he had worked at Dean Witter. He didn't seem to me the ideal candidate for what we needed. I don't know if my first impression was wrong or if Bill blossomed in the job, but he built a pretty decent department and turned out to be a very good man for the job. We came to respect much of his work and, as he learned the insurance business, he began to grasp the issues and really run with them. More proof that hard work and brainpower can make up for a lot of shortcomings. Unfortunately, like Alan, Bill was brought in too late to have an important effect when the company needed him most during the first half of 1990, and for that matter, all of the previous decade. The Executive Life experience has given me a keen awareness of the importance of communications, perception, and image in the electronic world in which we live today. Once a luxury, like window dressing on corporate facades, the Corporate Communications Department is becoming as important as the Marketing Department to those insurance companies that want to be among the leaders in the year 2000.

Initially, the information to the field and public flowed slowly because it had to pass through two outside law firms, as well as our own Legal Department, before final approval. By that time, most responses to attacks in the press or explanations of what was going on had become seriously watered down and were of relatively little value when they reached their targeted audience.

In hindsight, the swarms of lawyers and investment bankers allowed to invade our embattled company were a big mistake.

They watered down every response and retaliatory effort until it became pablum. We should have taken the advice of Joseph Burke, chairman of Johnson & Johnson, who won great praise in steering his company through the Tylenol poisoning crisis when he said: "Rule One of crisis management is to get rid of the lawyers." Instead, Alan hired the biggest names in the business: Fulbright & Jawarski, Latham & Watkins and Leboeuf, Lamb, Lieby & MacRae. Unbelievably, company expenses for just the outside legal counsel for the year in 1990 topped $20 million! Between the lawyers and the investment bankers, our hands and tongues were tied, while they mounted us for a self-enriching ride that left most of us feeling violated when they finally rolled off and collected their huge fees—which I might add were paid ahead of all creditors and investors. Despite the company rule against smoking, I hope one of them at least offered to light Alan's cigar on their way out the door!

The key to crisis management is, of course, communications. The purpose of communicating is to get through the crisis, and restore the practices and relationships of the corporation to what they were before. If you're really lucky, you can use the crisis as a rallying point, or at least a point of reference for testing the core values of the corporation. The best hope of those managing their organizations through a crisis is to look back someday, arm in arm, and say, "It was pure hell, but now that we're through it, we are a stronger, more viable organization." Then, if you're really lucky, at times like Christmas parties, after a few egg nogs, people will say they're glad it happened. "It was just the kind of test we needed to pull us together and prepare us for the challenges ahead."

Having been through the ordeal of seeing a Fortune 500 company go from leader in its field to a virtual death-watch situation in one year's time, I can tell you there has to be a better way to prepare to meet the challenges ahead. On the other hand, I must say that I feel qualified to talk about the realities of the insurance industry today—problems and opportunities alike. As qualified as anyone I know. I suspect many of those who went through the rise and fall of First Executive would have similar confidence in their readiness for the future, especially if, as many observers seem to feel, our experience was an extreme version of what many other life insurance companies will experience to a lesser degree throughout the balance of the century.

In the spring of 1989, Drexel Burnham Lambert developed the complicated bond offering for First Executive Corporation that essentially became a bank loan by the time it was completed. The deal brought in $275 million. Yasuda Trust & Bank of Japan took $50 million of the deal, then turned around and acted as a sort of subinvestment banker helping them place much of the remaining $225 million with a host of other Japanese banks, for a fee. In total, fifty-two banks were involved in the deal. Surprisingly, the company didn't really find out who these creditors were until it decided it had to restructure the loan. Drexel had done the deal and, of course, by now was long gone. To the company's dismay, there were a total of fifty-two Japanese banks to whom they owed about $200 million. In some instances, they didn't even know where they were located.

When the company approached the lead bank, Yasuda, the Japanese seized the opportunity to gouge them by offering to engage Goldman Sachs to put together the negotiations with the other banks. For their trouble, they wanted a mere $1 million fee just to provide an entree for First Executive Corporation with their own creditors. Unlike the obsequious image many of us have of the Japanese, they can be notoriously ruthless and uncharacteristically rude in situations such as this. The negotiations, almost entirely handled by Alan, were brutal, exhausting, and seemingly endless. Things dragged on throughout 1990 with little progress.

In the last stand, the plan was to play hardball with the Japanese bankers, and get them to restructure the loans or tell them to take the holding company to bankruptcy court. If successful, First Executive could go to the holders of its various Preferred issues and make an offer to swap all of its Preferreds for a new class, common, thus getting it off the hook for the $75 million in cumulative dividends owed to this group. This was Phase II of Alan's plan. Although such an offer required approval by both the commons and the Preferreds, who would be moved down in preference as creditors in the event of liquidation, it was an offer they really couldn't refuse.

Unfortunately, the restructuring wasn't the only life or death issue they were facing. The restructuring was at least something they could negotiate and hammer away on over the next few months. The default/write-down issue was much more frightening, and much less controllable. During the previous nine months, the company had seen its capital base shrink by more than $1 billion on a generally accepted accounting principle (GAAP) basis. On December 31, 1989, the statutory capital surplus and Mandatory Security Valuation Reserves (MSVR) of Executive Life Insurance Company of California were at $850 million. These two figures constitute the net worth of a life insurance company. In October 1990, this critical number was $450 million and sinking at an alarming rate. On this issue, the dye was already cast. Nothing anyone could do would affect what the defaults were going to be over the next few months. All they could do was read about the faltering economy in the papers, knowing that if we slipped into a recession in 1991, it would most certainly cause further write-downs that would spell the end. Furthermore, the underwater issue (bonds which traded at a discount due to doubts about their safety) needed to be addressed by the company's auditors. What the auditors decided would be marked to market could determine whether or not they had a company at the end of the third and fourth quarters, and most likely would ultimately determine its survival.

This was a time when one couldn't help but recall Fred's war cry of "mark to market," with which he taunted the industry back in the mid-1980s when his investment portfolio was half a billion dollars above market, not counting the substantial equity kickers in the form of stock options he had structured into most of his deals. Now he was appealing to his accountants that the market had overreacted to the situation. More importantly, the real problem was that there was no market. Always a thinly traded class of security, junk bonds were so out of favor that the only trades were private placements of blocks with large institutional investors wanting to do some scavenger hunting. As Fred Carr so aptly put it, "Junk bonds have become un-American."

I was reminded of a conversation with Fred and Doug Marcian, our chief investment officer, a year or so earlier, when I asked why we weren't buying some of the high-vacancy commercial real estate in Denver and Houston. I reasoned that a building 60 percent vacant should be a bargain if you price it on a cash flow basis. Fred laughed and asked if I meant we should then pay 40 percent of the book value for such a building. I said, "Yes, because that's what it's worth." Fred laughed again and asked Doug if I was correct. He said, "Nope. What it's worth is what someone is willing to pay for it." Fred added: "And there ain't nobody who wants to pay an acceptable price for that type of asset in this market at this time!" The implicit conclusion was that with bonds you at least always have a market, the pricing of which is a function of interest rates and perceived risk. We couldn't get trapped on the downside the way the holders of commercial mortgages, which were very illiquid in a down market, could. Of course, this was before we learned that in a crisis in confidence, perception becomes reality. This was before we learned about the C-5, or psychomedia risk, that contributed so mightily to putting the company under.

As the crisis in the Persian Gulf worsened, the stock and bond market drifted down, taking recent recoveries in the junk bond market with it. However, the market would only be an issue at year's end, when adjustments were made for this in the audited financials. These were the results signed off on by the outside accounting firm and presented in the annual statement. Everyone figured if the bond portfolio was going to take out the company's capital base, it would happen then, which would be reported upon on May 15, 1991. That might be long enough for Fred to find that rabbit that was so elusive in his hat. However, the 1990 annual statutory statement for the regulators had to be filed with the states by April 1, 1991. The word was that the

California Insurance Department had decided that as long as the company's statutory capital and surplus didn't decline below $250 million by year's end, they would not step in. To this point, the mandatory reserves (MSVR), which are not recognized as an asset in the statutory accounting, were absorbing the brunt of the impact for the losses; but they were now down to dangerously low levels, and when they were gone, all defaults would cut through to the company's capital and surplus account. Thus, there were two ways it could end: bankruptcy on the GAAP (shareholder) side, or insolvency leading to conservatorship on the statutory (policyholder) side.

On a statutory basis, where the regulators reside, the Milliman & Robertson report had pretty much stabilized things for the moment. The NAIC had assigned a special task force to monitor the situation, with whom the company's lawyers were in constant contact. The next big hurdle here would be the fact that California Insurance Commissioner Roxane Gillespie, who was a notoriously hands-off manager, was leaving office in January 1990. John Garamendi, California's first elected Insurance Commissioner, would be taking office as her replacement. A Harvard MBA with his eye on the Governor's Mansion, Garamendi is a serious politician who had made it clear he was going to handle the "Executive Life problem" head on. In the view of many within the company, this meant either nurturing them back to health or putting a bullet in their head, depending upon which approach his advisers felt would be in the best interest of policyholders. A few days before Garamendi took office, the state of New Jersey issued a mandate that Executive Life must either deposit $500 million in an escrow account to protect New Jersey policyholders or the state would issue a cease-and-desist order forbidding the Executive Life companies to do business in New Jersey. The NAIC, which was in session at its annual meeting at the time, was outraged and passed a resolution reprimanding New Jersey for "unnecessary" and "irresponsible" action. In an effort to save face, Executive Life voluntarily agreed to cease doing business in New Jersey. We all held our breath as Mr. Garamendi took his oath of office a couple of days later. The only comfort they had was that they knew Garamendi was smart and thoughtful, and was not likely to do anything before getting a good feel for the situation. Here again, the situation had bought them a few more weeks of time. However, it was during this period, while Fred Carr and John Garamendi were sparring with one another for a few weeks, that Fred finally met his match. Commissioner Garamendi had a Sunday punch that even Fred Carr couldn't slip once it was thrown.

The Emperor's New Clothes

Between struggling with the Japanese banks and the insurance regulators, Alan still found time to immerse himself in the third prong of his recovery plan, restoring the confidence of the sales force through a pet project he called NewCo. NewCo was Alan's code name for an idea of his he hoped would restore some credibility in the company's market, or at least let them poke their head out into new markets without getting it chopped off. The idea was to purchase a corporate shell, that is, a company licensed to do business in most states that has been stripped clean of assets and in-force business, and use it to start a new company. The sizzle would be that this time the company would invest *only* in investment grade securities. No mortgages, no limited partnerships, and above all, no junk bonds! Alan reasoned that with all that was going on in the marketplace, it was ready for a company that offered a safe harbor. To give it credibility, they would do the project as a joint venture, with a well-established financial institution to lend its good name and financial backing to the enterprise. Initially they would fund the company with $50 million of capital—$15 million from Executive Life and $35 million from the partner.

This "halo effect," as Alan dubbed it, was central to the saleability of the idea for the sales force, who would be likely to buy into the idea only if the company could deliver it with a named partner that had good ratings from the rating agencies.

The investment bankers that Alan hired went to a number of financial institutions with the idea, including G. E. Capital and other life companies such as the Lincoln National, with whom Executive Life reinsured all of its business beyond that which they retained. G. E. Capital, which was negotiating the purchase of Columbia Savings and Loan's junk bond portfolio at the time, turned them down. Executive Life had been the Lincoln National's biggest and one of their most profitable reinsurance accounts, but Lincoln National turned them down, too.

One of the problems the management team had with working on the NewCo project was the apparent refusal of both Alan and Fred to be realistic about the situation the company faced. The fact was that without a substantial, credible partner, NewCo would not be a saleable concept. Anyone who bought a less competitive product in exchange for safety would want the company to have the highest ratings from the rating agencies, and NewCo, as a new company, would be unrated. Yet it was an exciting and very marketable idea that most of the management wanted to believe in. They knew that with Executive Life's reputation for innovation and outstanding distribution system, this could, in another time, be the next shock wave sent through the industry. The problem was that Executive Life was now damaged goods. More than damaged goods, it was the very reason for the flight to quality that was taking place and which, in turn, was the reason why the timing was right for NewCo. For Executive Life to sponsor a concept like this was like the Confederate Army sponsoring an underground railroad for the flight of slaves to the North. It was an idea whose time had come; but they were the problem, not the solution, and nothing they did could change the color of their uniforms.

When I confronted Alan with these realities, he resorted to one of his favorite tactics—feigning indifference to the cataclysmic. He instructed everyone to continue with the project as if there would be no partner, because the partner, "although strategically desirable, is not a key factor in the success of the project." He instructed some of us to begin working with First

Boston on a private placement memorandum which, in the absence of a big name partner, would be used to raise the needed capital from individuals and small institutional investors.

Alan is a good salesman, and one of the most strong-willed and positive people I have been associated with. He was determined that if he couldn't bring someone to NewCo, then he could go to the market and find investors. When I shared with him privately the perception most of us had about the feasibility of the NewCo project without a partner, he went into a Churchillesque "We will fight them on the beaches" routine. He said, if necessary, he would sell the private placement himself. If First Boston could not get the job done, then he would get on a plane and go call on the many contacts he had who he felt would be interested.

Although I admired his moxy, I always resented it when Alan insulted my intelligence with this kind of hype. The fact was that no one believed NewCo was a doable deal without a well-known partner. As to the private placement approach, it would be obvious to possible investors that this was a last resort, rather than an original choice as a way of raising capital with a named partner. Instead of looking for one game company with $35 million to invest, they would be looking for thirty-five game individuals with $1 million each to invest. More importantly, the private placement approach brought no credible partner to the project for the "halo effect" everyone felt was needed. The whole world knew that First Executive Corporation was desperately looking for a partner. With no takers, why would agents buy into a concept that would be picked apart by their relentless critics? Dr. Belth alone would have a field day dissecting every aspect of the deal and exposing it as yet another Executive Life ploy. Also, the life insurance industry at the moment was not exactly the most exciting place for anyone to put their money, since the overall industry results were on a steady decline. Clearly, those who had invested their money with First Executive previously weren't too thrilled with the results they

had delivered. Most people knew how Caroline Hunt, beneficial owner of Rosewood Financial, had come out on her investment. I should think they might give her a call and ask her how
she felt about her $100 million investment, which was then
worth less than $5 million, and was ultimately liquidated for
$1.2 million.

When Alan Snyder turned the restructuring and NewCo projects over to First Boston, the staff there had a ton of big restructuring deals they were working on, as they and their peer firms
sifted through the carnage left by the collapse of Drexel. As a
result, they didn't exactly put their first-string team on the job.
They wanted $2.2 million in fees to complete the NewCo deal.
They went to a number of domestic carriers and got the obvious
answer: "Your top MGA is in my lobby waiting to turn over
your sales force to me right now. Why would I want to invest in
your company, when I can have the sales force without bother-
ing to talk to you?" Also, just as was the case with their capital-
raising efforts, no one was interested in doing a deal with First
Executive as long as Fred Carr was still running the show.
Frankly, it seemed like a real waste of time to engage First
Boston to look for partners for NewCo or any other solution to
the problems facing the company.

Investment bankers are both overrated and overpaid, in my
opinion. All they really do is sell deals through their network of
prospects. But in this case, they didn't know the business and
the deal wasn't very saleable anyway. I felt they embarrassed
themselves and Executive Life in the marketplace trying to peddle NewCo domestically and abroad. By mid-September, the
company was at a crossroads on the restructuring and on
NewCo. Both were without a partner—and there were no
prospects. It was clear to most involved that Executive Life was
going to go it alone from here on in. They had gotten where
they were by themselves and were going to get wherever this
thing was going to take them by themselves. In mid-September,
out of frustration, Alan turned back to Kidder. He had some old
acquaintances there that were, in his judgment, "no-bullshit
guys." They were willing to take over the NewCo project on a

completion basis with no up-front fees. They, too, bombed with the idea.

Reality Closes In

For Fred's precious policyholders—those individuals he had always so vigorously pledge to protect—many felt that his staying on proved devastating. As long as they had the Fred Carr issue, the press would use it again and again to drive home the Milken/Boesky/Carr versus unsuspecting consumer issue. These negative perceptions contributed to millions, indeed billions, of surrenders by the public, who paid charges to get out of Executive Life and into policies that were perceived to be safer. Just like those policies they would eventually have had if the Insurance Department stepped in and a firm such as Metropolitan Life had assumed Executive Life's book of business. Only in the latter example, there would have been no surrender charge.

Even worse, there were some cases where investors in municipal bonds backed by Executive Life guaranteed investment contracts (GICs) had losses of principal of as much as 70 percent or more that were at that point unwarranted. On September 24, 1990, a *Business Week* article appeared about Executive Life muni-GICs, which was devastating and is a classic example of this issue. Featured on one side of a two-page spread was Sara Webb, a seventy-three-year-old Tennessee widow, looking up morosely from her rocking chair as she mourns the loss of most of her investment in a municipal bond, which was backed by Executive Life junk investments. On the opposite page was a picture of Fred Carr, the smarmy Beverly Hills Jew, taken at his final appearance at the Drexel Burnham Predator's Ball, held in West Los Angeles in 1988. The caption read: "I'm one of the suckers," implying that Mrs. Webb had been bilked out of her money by Fred Carr. That was not really the case. The problem was that, due to the panic over junk bonds, many people holding muni-GICs backed by junk bond investments wanted to unload them. However, it is a thinly traded market, especially under these conditions, so that one might indeed get 50¢ or less on the dollar for a municipal bond that was otherwise healthy and paying interest as planned.

The issue was exacerbated when the California Insurance Department made it clear that they did not regard GIC holders, or the purchasers of the municipal bonds backed by them, as policyholders. This meant that in the event of a liquidation, they would be viewed as general creditors rather than protected policyholders. That would be a very bad place to be in a company that was $2 or $3 billion under water! This, along with the default rate, caused the price of these securities to collapse. It's hard to say if Mrs. Webb would have been better off hanging in there. The real issue is that she most certainly never knew that when she bought a municipal bond from the city of Memphis, it was a de facto purchase of a junk bond. To this extent, she was wronged; but not by Fred Carr. The municipalities that chose to invest Mrs. Webb's money in an Executive Life GIC were responsible for using her funds in a fashion that was faithful to the premise under which they raised them. If the city of Memphis wants to say, "I'm one of the suckers," that's another matter. It's a large fraternity, to which many of us belong, but not Sara Webb. Everyone associated with First Executive Corporation, from unsuspecting victims like Sara Webb to ill-advised victims like Caroline Hunt, was getting wiped out. Things had to go one way or another pretty soon.

One break came when the company announced a tentative agreement with Yasuda Bank on December 5, 1990, with the hope that pursuant agreements with the other banks would clear the way for a restructuring plan of the company's securities it intended to file with the SEC in February. Still, so many quagmires lay ahead on the road to successful restructuring that few were optimistic. The stock rose briefly with the announcement on December 5, then dropped back to 30¢ a share later in the month. Nothing Fred did was going to change the market's mind. First Executive Corporation was history. Even after Integrated Resources had filed for protection under Chapter 11 in

1989, their stock was two bucks a share! First Executive Corporation's stock price was beyond bankruptcy, it was an expression of contempt.

After the December Executive Life board meeting, Al Handschumacher, our most senior board member on both the Executive Life and holding company boards, and by now a friend and mentor, invited me to lunch. As was customary with my luncheons with Al, while he drank a fine wine and I a light beer, we talked of worldly matters first. He launched into one of his typical anecdotes about spending an afternoon in Leningrad a year earlier, driving around in the back of a limo with Donald and Ivana Trump. He told me Donald treated Ivana like dirt and what a jerk he was. He never explained to me what the three of them were doing in Russia in the first place. Al, who likes most everyone, really disliked Donald Trump. The rest of us weren't any too crazy about him either, since his casino defaults had put us reluctantly into that business. Because of defaults, we now owned major stakes in Resorts International (Merv Griffin) and the Taj Mahal (Donald Trump), and all of us on the Executive Life board had to go through the unbelievably arduous task of getting approval from the New Jersey Gaming Commission to be casino operators. They sent a task force of investigators out to Los Angeles, who literally went over every event of our entire lives, from high school sweethearts to ten-year-old tax returns, with a fine-tooth comb, spending about three days with each of us. It was just one more of the many bizarre experiences of being in business with Fred Carr.

After his third glass of wine, Al opened up to me as he never had before. He was clearly and uncharacteristically down. He complained that his health was starting to fail, and that the stress of the past year was more than he could take. He said that my upbeat attitude in the board meeting was inspirational and he wanted to know how I kept my spirits up. Then he told me he could no longer see a way that the company was going to come out of the mess it was in, and that the reason he wanted to have lunch with me was because he was worried about me and wanted me to be realistic about the situation. He didn't want me to get caught by surprise if things suddenly blew up. I assured Al that my positive attitude was a ruse, and that I had no delusions about what the future held. Al then touched me deeply—and gave me an additional insight—when he told me that he felt the closest to me of anyone in the company. Somewhat taken aback, I asked the obvious question: "Al, you hired Fred Carr seventeen years ago and have been with him ever since. Surely the two of you are much closer than us—not that I don't feel honored?" Al's answer was that no one was close to Fred. They were close business associates, but that was all. A lot of mutual admiration, but none of the affection and intimacy of a strong friendship one might expect in so important and endearing a relationship. I guess I wasn't surprised, just saddened that knowing Fred's great loyalty and respect for Al, and Al's similar feelings toward Fred, they had not nurtured it into a real friendship. Then again, the idea of Fred crying in his beer with an old friend on a depressing Friday afternoon just didn't work. He was too strong, too disciplined, and too dispassionate for such a display of emotion. The only time Fred Carr ever showed his emotions was when he was in complete control of them.

15

The Many Losers

"When I was fourteen years old my father was so ignorant I could hardly stand to have the old man around. But when I got to be twenty-one I was astonished at how much the old man had learned in seven years."

—Mark Twain

Few would argue that the life insurance industry is a lot smarter because of Fred Carr—because of what he taught the industry, and because of what the industry taught him and in the process retaught itself. Less apparent, but perhaps more significant, is the fact that the life insurance industry, like Mark Twain's father, was a lot smarter all along than Fred Carr believed it to be. As it turned out, many of those seemingly stodgy, conservative companies, choosing not to get into the fray of the interest-sensitive "chicken" contest, are the ones that wound up surviving, if not prospering, at least with their integrity in tact. Many companies and home office officials of the era paid dearly for what Fred Carr taught them. The Executive Life agents perhaps paid the biggest personal price of all.

The loyal sales force of Executive Life went through a grieving process similar to that one experiences upon the death of a loved one—first there was shock and disbelief, followed by anger, then sorrow, and finally acceptance. The litany of catastrophes that occurred between January 22, 1990, and April 11, 1991, left the agents reeling.

Vigil

No leader falls harder than those who permit their followers to overvalue their abilities. It is a consequence of the false pride we develop when we begin to believe in our own hype. Of course there were a number of die-hard loyalists who didn't blame Fred and still believed he would pull a rabbit out of his hat and save the day. These individuals still called regularly to berate the press and pump me for information about the big turnaround they were sure Fred was going to spring on us at any moment. Alan Snyder used to say they were looking for us to "sprinkle magic dust on the situation and make it go away." He was right. They were true believers, who could not accept the fact that it was over. They were still in the denial stage, and when I leveled with them about the situation, they usually went to the anger stage with a vengeance. When they did, it got tough. Then, one by one, even the die-hard loyalists faded into the landscape of the life insurance community, picking up a new relationship here and there with a carrier promising Executive Life look-alike products. Eventually the calls stopped altogether. Our sales force was gone.

By Christmas 1990, the Marketing Department of Executive Life, which had been the command center of the interest-sensitive product revolution, was in shambles. The only calls we were receiving had to do with conservation of business or attempts to quietly move nervous clients out of the company. I sat down with Fred and we decided to let 85 percent of the marketing staff go. This left a maintenance crew and, in effect, closed down the New Business and Marketing department of the company. We, too, were now at the acceptance stage of our grieving. Many of the MGAs and their agents had the most financially disastrous year of their careers. Whipsawed by high overhead, which the company had encouraged them to maintain while Fred and Alan got things turned around, and with virtually no new business, many had lost almost everything. Most of the MGAs had managed to align themselves with new carriers, but their agents were leery after the Executive Life experience and reluctant to follow them. Instead, they splintered in various directions trying to strike their own deals with the carriers of their choice.

Executive Life's largest marketing arm, Exceptional Producers Group, was the saddest situation of all. Once the premiere producer group in the industry, and owner of the industry's largest agent owned reinsurance company, this group was hit the hardest. Their agents were in the most upscale, high due diligence markets in America. Their top producers included some of the industry's best-known names, such as Barry Kaye, America's leading estate planning specialist, and past AALU (Association of Advanced Life Underwriters) President David Downey. As one might expect, the client list of such agents reads like a *Who's Who in American Business*. Many had their reputations sullied and considerable egos damaged, at least temporarily, by the disasters of 1990 and 1991. Their agent-owned reinsurance company (AORC), which was still two years from the target ten-year capitalization date, at which time Executive Life was expected to buy it, was rapidly deteriorating as agents bailed out, taking their investment with them. The president of Exceptional Producers Group, Walt Duemer, and chairman/agent Lon Morton worked tirelessly to try to put together a scheme whereby Executive Life would lock in a purchase agreement two years early, in exchange for the agents leaving the business with them. As things continued to deteriorate, more agents left, taking out their money, and in some cases, moving their clients. Eventually Exceptional Producers' agent owned reinsurance company had almost no statutory value, and new production from Exceptional Producers themselves had come to a virtual standstill.

A couple of years earlier, Milliman & Robertson had done a

valuation of their AORC, Exceptional Producers Life Insurance Company (EPLIC), that projected a potential value for the company of between $80 million and $114 million by 1992. Of course there were a lot of disclaimers, conditional assumptions, and caveats, but the number the agents remembered was $114 million. By 1990, the talk of a sales price was between $50 million and $60 million. Then, during the negotiations for locking in a price two years early, in December 1990, Caroline Hunt's Rosewood Financial sold its entire 10 percent stake in First Executive Corporation. The original investment, made some three years earlier, had been $100 million. When Rosewood sold all of it in a private placement to Dallas-based Hicks & Muse, at 14¢ a share, the gross was $1.2 million. This was approximately the amount of money Rosewood officials told me they had spent on due diligence alone, researching the industry and First Executive Corporation during the period over which they made their investment in us. It was a powerful statement to all of us in the company that it was over. First Executive Corporation had essentially no value. The negotiating for the purchase of EPLIC fell apart. Despite Walt Duemer's considerable effort, he had little of real value to sell and Executive Life had nothing with which to buy it. If Ms. Hunt's sales price for 10 percent was $1.2 million, did that mean the entire company was worth $12 million? Exceptional Producers Group was defunct, and the value of their AORC highly questionable.

In six short months, a marketing powerhouse loaded with some of the industry's biggest talent had to close its doors and merge with a brokerage affiliate called First Financial Resources, which represented a consortium of Executive Life's toughest competitors. Some of the agents moved, but many left in disgust. No one was more loyal to Executive Life in good times, bad times, and disastrous times than Walt Duemer. When we had dinner to discuss the closing of Exceptional Producers' doors, he wept openly. It was a horrible time for Walt and the employees of his organization, and especially for those agents who had placed so much faith in the Exceptional Producer concept. As Walt put it, "We aren't going to go down in flames and explosions as the press predicts. Instead, we're just going to bleed to death, but the end result will be the same." Actually, the explosions would eventually occur, too.

A Glimmer of Hope

Things went slightly better for Windsor Insurance Associates, run by Jerry Schwartz, and its associate, Mount Diablo Associates, run by J. Wilcox, which together had done even more business than Exceptional Producers Group. Not ones to wait around for a new corporate strategy, Jerry and his partner J. went to work on the problem by looking for a second carrier into which to move their combined sales force. Just as he did when he had selected Executive Life over a dozen years earlier, Jerry sat down and defined what he wanted: a household name with an A. M. Best A+ rating and a Standard & Poor's AAA claims-paying ability rating, that had no strong distribution system to object to Jerry and his team dominating the company's marketing activities. The answer he came up with was Hartford Life, which because it was part of the Hartford Casualty Insurance Group and ITT Corporation, was perceived to be much bigger than it was.

In reality, Hartford Life had a great balance sheet but was doing little business. Furthermore, since it was owned by giant ITT, known for its commitment to profitability, the company needed to start selling business or face the possibility of being sold off as a dog by tough-minded Chairman Rand V. Araskog, who had recently done just that with a number of other ITT units.

Jerry called on Hartford Life and made a deal within hours to deliver his sales force to them if they would develop Executive Life look-alike products and reinsure them into his AORC, which he and his agents now owned and completely controlled. Jerry is a great salesman, but even those of us who know him were surprised when he pulled this deal off. The Hartford, based of course in the life insurance mecca of Hartford, Connecticut, is about as staid and conservative a company as one could imagine. When it comes to California stereotypes, Jerry and J. are right from central casting—tanned faces, open collar shirts, purses, and just a splash of gold jewelry. Underneath it, of course, they possess the dealmaking skills to bring a Wall Street investment banker to his knees; but still, they and the Hartford people seemed an odd match-up. Yet somehow they won over the confidence of the Hartford, or at least appealed to them as a godsend solution to their dilemma of needing big production gains quickly.

Jerry's deal with the Hartford began to take off while Executive Life was still struggling with the blueprints on Alan Snyder's NewCo project. By mid-1990, most of his and J. Wilcox's agents were selling a Hartford version of Executive Life's Irreplaceable Life℠ products. Even more impressive, Jerry and J. had attracted a large number of other Executive Life MGAs into his organization under the Hartford banner. Then, after a few months of success with the Hartford project, Jerry got the idea that the ITT people might be interested in upping their stake in Executive Life. His idea was for the Hartford to assume all of Executive Life's Irreplaceable Life℠ business, which consisted of all its whole-life policies. This represented some $2.2 billion in assets, which meant they would also be ridding their balance sheet of $2.2 billion of liabilities. An assumption reinsurance agreement was tantamount to selling the block of business. The end result would be that every Executive Life policyholder would have a Hartford life policy, thus mitigating their fears and stabilizing the surrender activity. This, in turn, would eliminate so many problems for Executive Life that they would be willing to give up most of the profits on the business reinsured with Hartford for a few years, since the profits wouldn't be there were it not for the halo effect of their name, which prevented the business from lapsing.

There were, of course, complicated reinsurance, surplus relief, and regulatory issues that needed to be negotiated to make the transaction work; but the essence of the deal was to eliminate all perception among agents and policyholders that their policies were anything other than 100 percent safe. It was a brilliant idea. It would still leave the annuity and GIC policy-holders back at Executive Life, but the transaction required a pro rata removal of the junk in the portfolio so that the quality of assets remaining was not diluted.

One problem was that between his two deals with the Hart-ford, Jerry had eclipsed Alan Snyder's two biggest projects: NewCo, as a place for agents to write new business, and finding a white knight for Executive Life to stem the tide of surrenders. Jerry's new plan solved both problems. To his credit, Alan was gracious and put the value of the concepts above his own con-siderable ego, which must have been very painful for him. It was no secret that Fred had at one time considered Jerry as his successor. Now that it appeared he had scooped Alan on his two most important assignments, it was hard to argue against the idea of Jerry Schwartz taking charge. However, if that was his agenda, he was no longer looking for Fred to anoint him as his heir apparent. Instead, Jerry was going his own way on behalf of his marketing corporation and inviting Executive Life along for the ride. In keeping with the company's tradition, he was gaining power through performance rather than by appointment. The latter had worked poorly for Alan Snyder, and Jerry knew there were none of us in key positions who could seize the opportunity of the moment with the same sense of teleology that he possessed.

Ashes to Phoenix, Phoenix to Ashes

As it turned out, before long there was nothing to take charge of. While Jerry and Al Jacob scrambled to put together the Hart-ford rescue plan, the defaults continued into the first quarter of 1991. It soon became apparent that although the Hartford deal would put some 200,000 of the company's Irreplaceable Life℠ policyholders in safe hands, it would do little to save the com-pany. The transaction would effectively increase the capital base by about $175 million, but this was not nearly enough to offset the avalanche of defaults that was slicing through their MSVR, which by the end of 1990 had shrunk from $550 million to about $40 million.

Fred had one trump card left to play if he could sell the regulators on his idea. The muni-GIC-backed bonds were trading at 20¢–30¢ on the dollar, which, as we have discussed, were probably below their actual value, even if the company went bankrupt. Further, most of the purchasers of the pension GICs were trying to get out at a deep discount. A few securities firms had recognized this as an opportunity and were buying them up on the open market. Fred figured that he could in turn buy the bonds held by these firms for, say, 40¢ on the dollar, giving them a quick profit while he still got them at a deep discount. To get the money, he would simply sell some of his junk bonds. He could easily sell a bond that was 20 percent or even 30 percent under water to liquidate an obligation for 40¢ on the dollar. In other words, he could sell a $100 asset for $80 and pay off a $100 liability for $40, thus pocketing a 40 percent profit to strengthen the company's capital base. It was the ultimate arbitrage.

The scheme could have saved the company, but, as with most of Fred's schemes, there was one problem. Remember Sara Webb, the Tennessee widow who panicked and sold her muni-bond, backed by Executive Life GICs? Now Executive Life would in turn be buying Mrs. Webb's bond at a deep discount from the securities firm she sold it to, or perhaps even buying from people like her on the open market. When that happened, the *Business Week* article implying that Mrs. Webb had been bilked by Fred Carr would be right on the money. Since the California Insurance Department would have to bless such a transaction, it would surprise no one if they balked at being party to profiting by the woes of those who had purchased municipal bonds backed by Executive Life junk bonds. On the other hand, by this time most of the muni-GICS were already in the hands of speculators who had acquired them from the general public. Still, the regulators were not very receptive to the idea, except as a last resort.

When the GIC swap deal stalled, it was clear that without a

white knight the company was down for the count. Obviously there were not many takers at this point, but somehow Fred and Alan convinced a group of investment bankers who were shopping for opportunities that Executive Life still might have what they wanted. The group was headed by Altus Finance, an affiliate of Credit Lyonnais, the large French bank. Their interest in Executive Life was based upon the huge annuity block of business, which to a bank looks a lot like a bunch of CDs. They also were interested in the prospects of reviving the sales force. Fred and Alan kept the negotiations under wraps for weeks. As conditions in the company worsened, it became clear that the interest in purchasing the company might be the only thing that would stave off a move by the California Insurance Department to close it down. Clearly, Commissioner Garamendi would prefer that Executive Life be acquired by a strong institution than have to oversee the largest conservatorship and liquidation in the industry's history. Fred, of course, knew this and arranged for the investment bankers to meet with the commissioner to hype the prospects of Altus Finance taking the Executive Life problem off of his hands. To make the deal fly, however, the commissioner had to reconsider the muni-GIC swap, because without the windfall it would bring to the company's capital base, no one in their right mind would consider assuming the liabilities. Jerry Schwartz's Hartford deal would save the Irreplaceable Life annual premium policyholders, but the French deals would save all the policyholders. In the competition to rescue the policyholders Alan Snyder now had the upper hand over Jerry.

Then, on Monday, April 1, 1991, all hell broke loose for the second time. First, *Barron's* magazine did a blistering cover story on Fred. The front page featured a cartoon of him clinging to the tattered mast of a Chinese junk that was sinking, while drowning people (presumably policyholders) tried to swim to safety. Written by the Los Angeles lawyer/economist Benjamin J. Stein, a long-time critic of the company, the article was the most degrading piece on Fred to date. Stein summarized the situation First Executive Corporation faced with characteristic vehemence: "In a word, the closing acts of a startling drama of fraud, incompetence, and tragedy are being played out in offices on West Olympic Boulevard in Los Angeles, in other offices in lower Manhattan, and, surely not least, in policyholders' bedrooms at three in the morning." The *Barron's* article, which greeted us first thing Monday morning, was the best thing that happened on that April Fool's Day. I kept waiting for someone to shout out that it was all a tasteless joke. No such luck. At 2:00 p.m. (5:00 p.m. EST), which was literally the last possible moment, First Executive Corporation filed its 1990 10-K (annual statement) with the SEC and issued a press release announcing its 1990 results. Some highlights: net losses for 1990 topped $366 million, due to a realized loss on the investment portfolio of $660 million; the market value of the portfolio was $2.6 billion under water; and shareholders' equity fell from $1 billion in 1989 to $378 million. To erase any doubts about what the future held, the auditors, Price Waterhouse, declined to express an opinion on its financial statement (meaning they wouldn't sign it) because of concern about First Executive's ability to remain in business. Of course, all of us spent that day and the next day handling a barrage of hysterical phone calls from agents and policyholders. This time no one was looking for reassurance, they were looking for their money. By now there were no reassurances to give, anyway, and as to those wanting to surrender their policies, we knew that the regulators would be putting a freeze on fund withdrawals long before any new surrender requests made their way through the six-week backlog.

At the end of that awful April Fool's Day, I heard that Duke had beaten Kansas for the NCAA Basketball Championship and was struck by the fact that on that Wednesday Executive Life would be hosting the prestigious John Wooden Award at the Los Angeles Athletic Club. I had been asked by Fred to fill in for him at the press conference where the award was presented and at the awards dinner that evening because he was "unavailable." Fortunately, the 1991 winner was Larry Johnson of UNLV, who is so huge that when he stood up to accept the award, he obscured the Executive Life banner in the background as the cameras clicked away. At the banquet, I sat next to Larry's coach, Jerry Tarkanian, whose loss to Duke earlier that week had cost him his shot at back-to-back national championships. In addition to this setback, he was also in some pretty deep yogurt with the NCAA about alleged recruiting violations. Tark gave me some helpful tips on how to handle defeat and public ignominy. When I got up to make my remarks, I was able to crack a few jokes about our bad publicity and got through without too much trouble. I'm sure that the Los Angeles Athletic Club was relieved that Executive Life's sponsorship of the Wooden Award was expiring in 1991. To top the week off, Executive Life of New York was ordered to cease and desist from doing business, and it was made clear that if it didn't volunteer to do so in the California company, the regulators would soon order it to do so.

Then on Friday, April 5, A. M. Best & Company removed Executive Life from their rating list altogether, while Moody's pushed it down one final notch. I must say, I find it curious how rating agencies are able to sell their services, given their track records. They give ratings based upon the information provided them by the companies they are rating. Then they seemingly take them away based upon the information they read in the press. The downgrades usually lag behind the bad news that everyone has already heard. I can see why they use letters to express their ratings; like a child's report card, they tell only what has happened, not what future performance is likely to be. Perhaps that's all we should expect of them, but in hindsight I believe the prospective policyholder or investor certainly should not rely on the rating agencies for more than just a snapshot of the facts at any given time. Prognosticators they are not. A lot of us who were not financial people relied heavily on the rating agencies and independent studies such as those done by Milliman & Robertson as the source of our comfort about the company. Apparently even the NAIC felt comfortable with these sources as a basis for evaluating the company. In the future, I suspect attitudes will change significantly on this issue and that the rating agencies will have to deal with the strain that has been put on their credibility.

Over the next few days, speculation ran wild throughout the company as to when Commissioner Garamendi would seize Executive Life. They didn't have to wait very long. On April 11, 1991, the commissioner obtained a court order seizing Executive Life of California and putting it under conservatorship. At his press conference, Garamendi said: "Unfortunately, the fallout from the junk bond era continues to rain on innocent American investors. One casualty is the Executive Life Insurance Company. We take this action to save it for the hundreds of thousands of people who entrusted their savings—many their entire life savings—in this company." A few days later, on April 16, New York's Superintendent of Insurance, Salvatore Curiale, took a similar action for Executive Life of New York. Fred Carr resigned as CEO of both companies and the rest of senior management had their duties and responsibilities suspended temporarily. However, most of us were reinstated within a few days, reporting now to the regulators, pending the resolution of the conservatorship. Such resolution would mean either rehabilitation in the hands of a buyer such as the French group, Altus, or the Hartford, or even Metropolitan Life, which had expressed interest; or in the event of no buyers, a liquidation of the company. A few days after they moved in, the regulators told Fred Carr to pack his belongings and get out. He was banned from the company premises on two hours' notice. He even had to hitch a ride home with Alan Snyder, because they demanded the keys to his company car. Shortly thereafter, on May 13, 1991, First Executive Corporation filed for voluntary protection under Chapter 11 of the U.S. Bankruptcy Code. It was over at long last. The Executive Life companies were in the hands of the nation's two largest insurance departments, and Fred Carr was gone, but most assuredly not forgotten.

Valuable Lessons or Just Carnage?

The debate about junk bonds will no doubt continue for some time, although at present the cons clearly outweigh the pros.

Yet, with so much of the "good junk" trading at discounts offering an effective yield to maturity of 20 percent or better, there will surely be those who make fortunes by adhering to J. Paul Getty's explanation for his success: "When no one wants to buy, buy. When everyone wants to buy, sell."

The last week in September 1990, *Barron's* and the *Wall Street Journal* each ran two essays on the Mike Milken scandal within three days of each other. The first, from Los Angeles lawyer/economist Benjamin J. Stein, was a blistering *"Memo to Judge Wood: Why Milken deserves a stiff sentence!"* in which he expressed his outrage at the brazen crimes of Mike Milken, who he maintains stole billions from the public.

> Michael Milken was the maestro of a Ponzi scheme of staggering proportions. Using phony data about his ability to pick junk bonds with value, he built a reputation as a guru of low-rated credits.
>
> With that reputation and a few wonderful pals like Carl Lindner, Stephen Wynn, Meshulam Riklis and Victor Posner, Milken began to create a captive network of buyers of extremely low-value bonds. Passing the bonds among them, he created the illusion of value, exactly the way used car salesmen do by having one after another of their crew tell the hapless buyer what a great car he's getting.
>
> Then he could bring in insurance companies like First Executive, and have them buy junk, and pretty soon, he has a mammoth Ponzi going.

Meanwhile, George Gilder, a fellow at the Hudson Institute, wrote a piece taking a different view and challenging the Ponzi scheme argument. *"The War Against Wealth"* appeared in the September 27 issue of the *Wall Street Journal*. In it, the author portrays Milken as a victim of the contempt the press has for wealth:

> In the perennial war against wealth that afflicts capitalism, envy is always the engine. The prime goal is to discredit the claim that the rich earn the right to reinvest their earnings.
>
> Today in America, the acids of envy are lapping at the foundations of the system, with confiscatory capital gains taxes, new

state surtaxes and an all-out government campaign against so-called junk bonds. Driving the campaign to a climax is the lust for a living sacrifice, to be achieved through the defamation, discrediting and final imprisonment of Michael Milken.

Now as Milken approaches sentence for a series of subtle regulatory infractions, major investment journalists and government officials rush to paint him in lurid colors as a mugger, mobster, or racketeer.

Whether or not Mike Milken is a minor felon, or "stole $6 billion–$8 billion so far," as Mr. Stein asserts, may never be known. What we do know is that he is in jail, serving time for crimes which he has admitted to committing. A compelling argument can be made that the circle of key players who made the Drexel Burnham machine work also were guilty of crimes. Indeed some were and some were not. Given the landmark intensity of the investigations into the subject, those who were guilty presumably were charged and convicted.

If one were to look at the whole situation during this frenzied period as a great big snake oil sales scheme, it is obvious that certain players needed to be in the audience to make the salesman's pitch work. Usually there's a ringer, who steps up and offers to buy the first four or five bottles. If necessary, later in the presentation he proclaims that he'll buy every single bottle of snake oil that the crowd doesn't want. Several journalists have suggested that Fred Carr and Mike Milken schemed to create a false perception of demand for their product. They claim that Carr was the ringer who made Milken's bond offerings a guaranteed sellout. When an issue is perceived to be "hot," it's probably human nature to relax a bit in the area of due diligence. One might assume everyone else has done their due diligence, and that's why they're all so excited about the product, so the issue becomes buying in time to get one's fair share. As we recalled from his earlier days at the Enterprise Fund, this was not the first time that Fred was accused of hyping the price of securities in which he traded. If Fred *was* guilty of this kind of activity, then he used funds entrusted to him by policyholders for safekeeping as recklessly at the worst culprits in the savings and loan crisis. If, in creating a false sense of demand for an inferior product, he ignored the painstaking diligence for which he was so well known, one could argue that he was negligent of his fiduciary responsibility to policyholders.

However, if Fred Carr did deliberately buy into investments he knew were bad ones, one must ask why. One could speculate that it was done for massive kickbacks from the hundreds of millions of dollars in fees paid to Milken for his role in the alleged Ponzi schemes they supposedly put together. If the snake oil salesman made $6 to $8 billion, as Benjamin Stein suggests, then the ringer would have had to get some percentage of that for his role. This scenario was inferred and hinted at in the press, but never actually stated. However, no accusation was ever made because quite simply there was a total lack of evidence of any kind that Fred Carr ever did anything inappropriate. One can rest assured that he was investigated thoroughly by the swarms of SEC and federal investigators and federal prosecutors who took apart every trade Milken made with him throughout the 1980s. One would think that the kind of money involved in such a transaction would leave a pretty visible trail. Despite the unbelievable scrutiny of these probes, they didn't produce a single subpoena, let alone any accusations or indictments. When federal investigators look into a situation as closely as they did this one, had there been any wrongdoing, they would surely have uncovered something, even if they didn't have enough to prosecute.

During the time I worked for him, Fred Carr seldom made absolute statements or any unconditional commitments if he could avoid doing so. Especially if it was in a public forum. As I've stated before, Fred liked to keep his options open. Yet, in 1987, at the height of the Boesky scandal, and on several occasions thereafter, Fred stated from the podium that neither he nor any official of First Executive Corporation would be involved in any way in the criminal proceedings of the Boesky/Drexel/Milken scandals. He also pointed out that in his thirty years of running a public company, he had never traded in his own account for any purpose. These statements were one reason why many of us stuck it out with him to the very end. Only time will tell whether or not we were wise to do so.

Some of his followers choose to believe, with good reason, that Fred Carr was a victim of his own success and nothing more. He got hooked on junk bonds and the extraordinary short-term success they brought him, and he overdosed. Part of Milken's machine was the total loyalty he expected from those whose success he had contributed to so greatly. In a conversation with Exceptional Producers' founder, Erik Watts, Tom Spiegel (ousted chairman of the failed Columbia Savings and Loan, which sank under the weight of its junk bond portfolio) told Erik, "I didn't say `no' to Milken often enough, which is why my company went under. Fred Carr never said `no' to Milken. He bought in on every deal presented to him." Fred may have bought a lot of bonds, more out of his sense of obligation to Milken than because he felt they were sound investments, which was poor reasoning and irresponsible use of his authority as a company CEO. I believe he felt that the financial benefit to the company of being let in big on some of the better deals more than offset the necessity of taking on some of the dogs. Of course, as it turned out, he was wrong; but that doesn't make him a crook. It does, however, say that he exercised very poor judgment and was lax in his responsibilities, for which he probably should have been fired by the board. If there was more to it than that, it hasn't surfaced as of this writing. On the other hand, the proverbial fat lady in the First Executive Opera has yet to sing. Her song could put a different complexion on this aspect of the story.

Those Who Entrusted Their Funds

The policyholders of Executive Life will eventually, I believe, be made whole. But they may be given lower credited interest rates while the company is under conservatorship, during which time, although claims will be paid, their policy values will be frozen. What's more, in order to receive their full values upon surrender, they may have to leave their funds with the company longer than the original contract required. This is at best inconvenient to some and very frightening to many. The life insurance industry and those who regulate it at the state level have done a responsible and conscientious job of seeing to it that policy guarantees hold up. The Executive Life story tested the regulators and the industry-sponsored guaranty funds to the limit. Their sense of responsibility superseded whatever their personal feelings toward the company may have been. The current movement by the Congress to provide an additional regulatory layer over the states is, in my view, an unnecessary and politically motivated action. If nothing else, the way in which the safeguards currently in place skillfully effected the winding down of the Executive Life companies should prove that the industry is adequately regulated, without the further expense to taxpayers that federal regulation would bring. In particular, the performance of California Insurance Commissioner John Garamendi should provide part of his ticket to the Governor's Mansion.

The stockholders, Preferred holders, bond holders, and creditors all lost big. Some investors, such as Caroline Hunt's Rosewood Financial, Bob Shaw's ICH, and Peter Lynch's Magellan Fund, lost between $50 and $200 million. Bob Shaw saw the equity in his ICH Corporation collapse and had to sell off his crown jewels, Philadelphia Life and Massachusetts Casualty, to long-time associate Jack Gardner, who put together an equity-funded buy-out through the Dallas-based buy-out specialists Hicks & Muse and General Electric Capital. After Peter Lynch told off Fred Carr during his ill-fated road show in January 1990, he sold all of his First Executive holdings the next day at a huge loss. A few weeks later, Lynch announced that he would be retiring. Although I'm sure his decision had nothing to do with Fred, I'm equally sure he's glad he won't have to deal with him again.

Another big casualty was the pension GIC holders, those pension fund managers who purchased Executive Life guaranteed investment contracts. They were not regarded as policyholders, and so the company's liabilities to them were negotiated down to half or less by the conservators in an effort to rehabilitate the company. These of course were the big guys, mostly institutional investors. Many of them are active corporations which are making good on the shortfall their retirees received on their Executive Life annuities. The cost to them will likely be in the hundreds of millions. Another potential casualty are the structured settlement annuitants—victims of accidents who accepted Executive Life annuities as settlement for their injuries from the casualty insurers against whom the judgment was made. Should Executive Life default on these annuities, these individuals will have arguable recourse against the original company that owes them the benefit. One would assume the courts will rule in their favor, but not without some consternation, and certainly there are no assurances that this will be the outcome. There were also thousands of individuals who purchased the Preferred issues that were generally regarded as interest-bearing, fixed securities on which the principal was safe. Many lost their entire investment, along with the many investors in the common stock, which was a strong "buy" recommendation of a number of major securities firms throughout most of the 1980s. These people, too, lost virtually their entire investment. Their losses will be in the hundreds of millions.

Of course, along with the agents, most employees of First Executive Corporation were significantly hurt. Many of us had our life savings, IRA accounts, and other investments in First Executive Corporation stock and stock options. Countless agents had invested heavily in the stock, not just personally, but in their individual pension and profit-sharing plans. Not that the officers seek any sympathy; but the notion that there was any profiteering from either the rise or the collapse of the company is a joke. We all had most of our wealth tied up in the stock. We believed in Fred Carr, and many of us lost most of our net worth because of it. I only point this out to quell any notions that there were those who bailed out early because of insider information. I am aware of no such case. Certainly there were no golden parachutes (other than Fred's, which has not, as of this writing been honored). In my own case, due to a misunderstanding with the regulators about this book, they went to court to try to deny paying me the standard five months' severance the insurance department had previously guaranteed me. We all rode the Fred Carr Express to its final destination. And of course Fred himself saw the actual value of his stock drop from about $65 million in June 1986 to peanuts by the end. Interestingly, at the peak in 1986, Fred had to sell about half of his holdings to give to his wife of some twenty-five years, Diane, as part of their divorce settlement. She reportedly unloaded most of her stock shortly after she unloaded Fred, and therefore may be the only member associated closely with the corporation who came out well. The word around the Beverly Hills cocktail circuit is that she has since parlayed her settlement into a centimillion dollar fortune. The rest of us got clobbered.

It's not hard to understand why the industry had so little sympathy for the company—especially when the guarantee fund, sponsored by the industry, was slipped into place in California as a safety net on the eve of Executive Life's final gasps. Still, the employees and agents of the companies were no different from those in other companies. The collapse hurt a lot of honest, hardworking people and put terrible stress on their family lives and financial situations. The collapse of many other segments of the financial services industry has and will continue to hurt a lot of other companies before it is over, including some much more lovable names than Executive Life. Those companies' investors, employees, and agents will all get a taste of the kind of trauma members of our industry have never experienced before. I sincerely hope it goes easier for them than it did for us.

In the go-go 1980s, the life insurance industry didn't exactly lose, but it did fail to win—the agents, the investors, the employees, the policyholders, and the industry. A lot of unnecessary pain was inflicted on a lot of honest people with good intentions. Although Executive Life bashing was a popular pastime among its competitors during its heyday, after the company went into free fall and the adverse press was literally mountainous, the bashing died down somewhat. The attacks slowed as it became apparent the wounds might be mortal. The industry didn't lend a helping hand, but at least it didn't step on Fred Carr's fingers as his company clung to the edge of solvency. Instead, it quietly looked on as the life drained out of First Executive from its self-inflicted wounds. In hindsight, I think the behavior, at that point, was about appropriate. It made no sense to bail out the holding company, especially since the cost of potential defaults and numerous lawsuits was completely unknown, and on a mark to market basis, the company had a negative liquidation value of about $3 billion. There was no way a company or group of companies could justify taking unknown risks like these to their owners or policyholders, even if Executive Life had been part of the fraternity. Not even if the prize would be a company whose policyholders were still among the most upscale in the industry.

The rise and fall of First Executive Corporation paralleled the twelve-year period from 1979 through the end of 1990 during which the life insurance industry was brought from isolated euphoria to a centerstage, spotlighted free-for-all. The experience for First Executive, which did not survive, for other companies whose fates are yet undecided, and for the life insurance industry, which will survive, has been bountiful. Those who will lead the industry to the year 2000 should study the events of the 1980s in detail for what they can teach us. Those of us who experienced the First Executive disaster firsthand should swallow our pride and share our lessons with the rest of the industry.

Glossary

This book contains many technical insurance terms as well as colloquialisms unique to Executive Life. The following list can serve as a quick reference to clarify any unfamiliar or confusing terms the reader may encounter.

AORC: Agent Owned Reinsurance Company. A reinsurance company that is at least partially owned by agents who write life insurance contracts for one or more carriers. Typically, a business arrangement that allows agents to participate in the long term profitability of the business they write by reinsuring a portion of the contracts they produce into the reinsurance company they own.

Capital and Surplus: This is to a stock life insurance company what retained earnings are to a general corporation.

CBO: Collateralized Bond Obligation. A package of individual bonds separated into tranches that represent different levels of risk and interest rate. Each tranche in a CBO can have a different credit rating. Similar to Collateralized Mortgage Obligations assembled from individual mortgages, except that bonds are used instead.

CQRA: Custom Qualified Retirement Annuity. A group annuity product used in plan terminations where the company providing retirement benefits wishes to transfer the retirement funding responsibility to an insurance company. These plans were often used to free excess pension funding dollars for other corporate uses.

Disintermediation: The flow of funds out of an insurance company due to policyholders surrendering or canceling their policies.

Due Diligence: A process by which an interested party investigates the products, investments, overhead, and other characteristics of an insurance company to assess its financial viability and likelihood of meeting product projections.

Eastern Mutuals: Eastern mutual is used in this book to refer to those among the top 50 or so life insurance companies licensed to do business in New York. Although not necessarily domiciled in the state of New York, most reside in the New England area.

FEC: First Executive Corporation. The publicly traded holding company which owned several life insurance company subsidiaries. The largest of these subsidiaries was Executive Life Insurance Company of California (ELIC), which consisted of about 80 percent of the corporation's assets and at its peak was the fifteenth largest life insurance company in the United States. The second largest subsidiary was Executive Life Insurance Company of New York (ELNY), which existed primarily for purposes of doing business in the state of New York. Regulatory restraints in New York are so limiting that it was not possible to do business there through the California company.

GAAP Accounting: Accounting that is guided by Generally Accepted Accounting Principals as opposed to Statutory Accounting principals which are used for regulatory reporting by insurance companies.

GAAP Reserves: Reserves based on generally accepted accounting principles and arrived at by interest rates and other assumptions which the company and its accountants feel they can attain. GAAP assumptions are generally more aggressive than statutory assumptions, so the amount needed to meet future obligations is usually much less.

GAMA: General Agents Management Association. An organization of general agents designed to educate and improve the business performance of the members.

GIC: Guaranteed Investment Contract. A contract between an insurance company and a buyer which performs very much like a certificate of deposit. In essence, a promise to pay a certain amount of interest over a finite period of time with penalties, etc. discouraging early withdrawal of funds. Used frequently by pension plans (401Ks, etc.) to provide a fixed rate of interest over a certain period of time.

Interest Sensitive Products: This is a catch-all term used to reference the *new wave products* introduced throughout the 1980s which passed along competitive interest rates to consumers based upon higher yields companies were then experiencing on new money. Most companies sold *universal life* in this market. Executive Life and a few other companies sold a similar, less flexible, but very competitive product called *interest sensitive whole life (ISWL)*.

LBO: Leveraged Buyout. A buyout of a business entity through the use of borrowed funds financed through the cash flow of the entity being purchased.

LIMRA: Life Insurance Marketing Research Association. An industry-sponsored group that studies trends in demographics, psychographics, products, and other factors that influence the marketing, distribution, and purchase of life insurance.

Market to Market Basis: A process by which investments (assets) are increased or decreased in value based on the current market price. This is opposed to carrying the assets at cost which is the current practice in the life insurance industry.

MGA: Marketing General Agencies. This is a catch-all term referring to those who distributed Executive Life's products in a wholesaler capacity through independent agents. They included both Marketing Groups, which represented the company exclusively, and Brokerage General Agents (BGAs), who carried Executive Life's product line as well that those of several other carriers.

MSVR: Mandatory Securities Valuation Reserve. This is a special reserve or provision required by the NAIC to be set aside by life insurance companies who make certain investments they deem to be riskier than most. It is a cushion, in addition to the regular reserve, to protect against any abnormally high losses the company might experience from such investments.

NAIC: The National Association of Insurance Commissioners. The official association of regulatory bodies which oversees the insurance industry through the Departments of Insurance that operate in all fifty states.

Net Investment Ratio: A ratio calculated from a numerator representing various forms of interest earned, as well as gains and losses on sales of assets, and a denominator representing the average assets held during a calendar year. The result is expressed as a percentage such as 9.5 percent. This ratio is used to compare the investment performance of one company to another.

Persistency: The rate at which insureds continue to pay their premiums as opposed to lapsing their policies.

PPGA: Personal Producing General Agent. An agent who writes business personally and also has agents working for him that write business from which the PPGA earns override commissions.

QRA: Qualified Retirement Annuity. A group annuity product that is used to fund qualified pension plans. A pool of cash is deposited with the company that represents the defined benefits a company believes will be funded in the future.

The pool is used to buy annuities at retirement and receives further contributions if needed or desired.

Reserves: These are funds that a life insurance company puts aside to meet its future obligations to policyholders such as death benefits, annuity payouts, and the cash surrender value to which policyholders are entitled if they want to cancel their policies. The company keeps two sets of books for reserves, statutory and GAAP.

SPDA: Single Premium Deferred Annuity. An annuity product which involves the deposit of a sum of money at a pre-scribed rate of interest for some period of time before payments or withdrawals will be made.

SPIA: Single Premium Immediate Annuity. An annuity which immediately begins paying out periodic benefits. The benefits are purchased with a single sum of money and may continue for the annuitant's lifetime, the annuitant's and spouse's lifetimes, or some other prescribed period of time.

SPWL: Single Premium Whole Life. A life insurance product composed of a death benefit and cash accumulation account that requires only one premium payment.

Statutory Accounting: The accounting practices used by the NAIC in evaluating and reporting on the financial condition of an insurance company. In addition to conservative reserve requirements, statutory accounting measures companies on a cash in, cash out basis, with no allowance for the amortization of expenses or the deferral of acquisition costs for putting business on the books.

Statutory Reserves: Reserves required by insurance regulators, which are calculated at conservative interest rates and therefore require the setting aside of a greater principle to satisfy the future obligation.

Structured Settlements: Settlements in liability cases where the payment to the injured party is structured through the purchase of an annuity from a highly rated insurance company.

Surplus Relief: A form of reinsurance by which liabilities are moved from one insurance company to another, thus relieving the need to contribute increased amounts of capital (surplus) to meet regulatory requirements.

Surplus Strain: The drain on an insurance company's capital created when the reserve requirements of the regulators exceed the premium collected for a new policy. Thus the company must put up the difference from its surplus (retained earnings) until the policy matures, surrenders, or there is a claim, at which time they get it back.

Tranche: A level of interest rate and risk that is "sliced" from a collection of individual bonds and assembled into a Collateralized Bond Obligation.